Always Being Born

SEAGULL
BOOKS
•
CELEBRATING
40 YEARS

THE INDIA LIST

MRINAL SEN

Always Being Born

A MEMOIR

LONDON CALCUTTA NEW YORK

Seagull Books, 2023

First published in 2004 by Stellar Publishers
© Stellar Publishers, 2004
Photographs © Shubash Nandy, Nemai Ghosh, Aranya Sen
and/or their estates wherever applicable.
Published by arrangement with Stellar Publishers, New Delhi

ISBN 978 1 80309 176 1

British Library Cataloguing-in-Publication Data
A catalogue record for this book is available from the British Library

Typeset by Seagull Books, Calcutta, India
Printed and bound by WordsWorth India, New Delhi, India

CONTENTS

Editor's Note to the First Edition (2004)

10 February 2001. The spectacular Kolkata Book Fair was in full swing. I had flown in to the city to launch the English edition of Guy Sorman's French bestseller, *Le génie de l'Inde* (*The Genius of India*). Flanked on my right by the French cultural counsellor, Monsieur Bernard Malauzat, and the phenomenon of cine world, Mrinal Sen on my left, who so graciously had given his consent to do the honours, one was simply bowled over by the august company.

In between the mandatory speeches, commenced a little game of staccato notes, as I passed on the inaugural one-liner to Mrinal-da—

–Dada, you must pen your memoirs for us!

–Could you suffer me if I were to contradict myself in every third line?

–The more you contradict, the messier (merrier) it would be. I love fireworks!

–But to warn you, I do not have the academic discipline.

–Memoirs is a very fascinating exercise, which, like your films, could go backwards and forwards. It only needs motivation. Damn the discipline. That will take care of itself.

–Done. But to warn you again, I am very liberal at making promises and keeping very few, OVER.

–Done.

It continued quietly, as the written words minus the verbal exchange finalized the deal without offending the speakers and the listeners. And we signed right on! Cheers!

Yes, this is one promise Mrinal-da certainly honoured. Over this extensive period, during his occasional sorties to Delhi, which warranted his presence at various film festivals, we followed the ritual of intense discussions over luncheon meetings at the India International Centre. And in the process filtered ideas, argued over the format and vetoed many a title—varying from *Random Recollections, Reflections of a Maestro, Happenings: Discreet Entries of a Nondescript, Reminiscences, A Rambler on Record,* et al. For, there are far too many dimensions to this iconoclast, a witness to the cinematic history as he traversed continents, and documented the inhuman and humane facets on the celluloid.

When Cinema becomes the platform of provocation and creative souls bond with causes, convictions and celebrate life in all its stark reality, sans any blinkers—no wonder, beautiful minds are *Always Being Born* . . .

Jyoti Sabharwal

I wrote and rewrote, and at last I finished writing this book. 1 May 2004. I sent off the epilogue to my publishers. The next day, 2 May, I took the day off. The same day when, 83 years ago, Satyajit Ray was born. From the southern tip of the country came Adoor Gopalakrishnan, making films since 1972, to give the annual memorial talk. He called me, and with his characteristic modesty, said, 'If not for my talk, you must come to watch my *Nizhalkuthu* (*Shadow Kill*) (2002), the least understood of all my films.' I had been dying to watch the film since it had been made two years ago. It was about a professional hangman. But that's not all. There was a beyond, an unreachable beyond. I watched it, I liked it, I loved it. Hidden behind the facade of simplicity were layers of perception, and I was overwhelmed with a feeling of fulfilment.

Tagore came to mind:

Sahaj katha'e likhte ama'e kaho je,
Sahaj katha ja'e na lekha sahaj'e.

(Write simply in the simplest words, what you say,
For simple words there is no simple way.)

In this book, I have told stories of my life, of my times—though not the whole of either, and certainly not chronologically. But throughout I have been intent on writing it 'simply, in the simplest words'.

Three years ago, a writer from Kerala, Madhavan Kutty, met me in Delhi. He gave me one of his books, a lovely volume. Seemingly autobiographical, full of memories, but for reasons of his own he claimed it to be entirely a work of fiction. He called it *The Village Before Time* (2000). In his preface, he mentions a novelist, Uroob (whom, I confess, I have never read). Many years ago, he spoke to Uroob about some of the events narrated in his book. And Uroob advised Kutty to let them lie in his mind, to not write about them 'now'. He told Kutty, 'If you write about them after a long time, chances are they will turn out well.'

My book is no work of fiction. It's about me and my world, about my stories as well as so many others that came my way. Going to and fro, backward and forward, my intention has always been *to connect*. To have a continuous dialogue between the past and the present, and, in the process, to rediscover myself. Always driven by an inner compulsion, and the hope that the stories 'turn out well'.

Now, a short note on how it all began. There was a literary meet in my city. Two books were to be launched—one, a beautifully illustrated edition of Tagore's *Gitanjali*, translated into English by the poet himself, with an introduction by W. B. Yeats; and the other, the English translation of a book from the French. The hall was crowded with book lovers. And it was there, with absolute confidentiality, that an offer came to me, out of the blue, from an editor. Talking between the lines, I thought I'd been delightfully evasive. A few days later, by which time the editor was back in Delhi, I'd had time to give the idea some thought, and finally agreed to write. That was my uncertain beginning.

What I had with me: partly moth-eaten old files, old papers and documents, old letters, and ideas I thought I might pull out later. All clumsily put together: some rejected, some once written for various newspapers and magazines, some notes scribbled to record my reactions to events which at some point in time had shaken me in small or large measure. There were also quite a few articles and plenty of interviews, in which I often repeated myself, or even contradicted myself, that had been published here and there and thus been preserved, though not really with love and care; and a couple of books—collections—one being Seagull Books' *Montage*. But, most importantly, what I had with me were my proud possessions—my memories and anecdotes—a truckload of them, very few of which had been annihilated or withered away. There were also an abundance of trifles and bits of information, even insignificant details, of everyday life that I'd picked up from the entries my wife had been recording, without a day's break, in her diaries. A habit she maintained for over 20 years.

It was all very strange!

But as I began writing and, simultaneously, continued my search for materials, the strangest thing happened: fragments of latent memories came to the surface with effortless grace, as in *Lost Horizon* (1937). Suddenly I had piles of raw material rushing at me every now and then as I wrote. So much so that I ended up having to be rather judicious in my selection. Only one person, my son, living in Chicago, asked me not to blindly trust memory, because 'memories are reconstructive rather than photographic.' We have always been in touch, at least, once a week over the phone, and always on guard through our continuous flow of emails. He was very particular that I take a moral position from which to write my lines.

The editor at that literary meet was Jyoti Sabharwal, now Editorial Director, Stellar Publishers—the one from whom, out of the blue, came the offer. Having read my chapters, and then reading and rereading, she kept telling me about their 'enormous referral value'. Once, in her gusto, she even wrote to me about a 600-page autobiography, *Personal History*, by media baroness Katharine Graham (*The Washington Post*) which received the Pulitzer Prize:

> It's amazing how deeply Graham has gone into the background of the families of both her parents and depicted that era of the 1920s and 30s so splendidly. And the most interesting part is that every character, every name she has mentioned has been characterized so well that you begin to relate to them.

Jyoti pleaded with me to never think that I would make my text unnecessarily 'loaded' with references. On the contrary, she felt, with all the referral value, it would only be richer.

I am not quite sure. But, yes, most of the time she gets what she believes in, always with a bit of gentle persuasion.

We were always in touch. And we are, even now . . .

ONE

My City
Mercilessly Maligned, Dangerously Loved . . .

By accident a maker of films, I am what I am. My city, mercilessly maligned and dangerously loved, is in a way the state of my mind. Good or bad, yes or no, its people know me as an iconoclast. Among them, some are of the opinion that I am always out to attack cherished beliefs and traditional institutions. With no other cause than to sound important and look likewise. I am not quite sure if what they say is true. If it is so, then just a few years ago, when they decided to rename my city, theirs too, why did I oppose it? They say it was a name given by the one-time colonial masters. I say, so what! Is that how you want to fight the colonial legacy?

I realize I belong to a small minority of no-changers. The heads of the state administration changed the name anyway, because they wanted to. They asked for it, and the central government had no problem giving the clearance. They changed the name, and a lot of changes immediately followed across numerous papers and documents. Calcutta Police became Kolkata Police, Calcutta Municipal Corporation became KMC, and so, from then onwards, I have started calling my city Kolkata, like Bombay is now Mumbai, like Madras is now Chennai, Trivandrum is now Thiruvananthapuram,

Calicut is now Kozhikode. So on and so forth. Many more changes are in the offing, I fear, like contagion, one begetting another. And if worse comes to worst, it will neither be shocking nor surprising if the country eventually succumbs to 'the tyranny of the collective mediocrity' and be strictly renamed 'the abode of the Hindus', Hindustan, and never again be what it still is—*Bharat*.

Emotion, history and bigotry apart, I still have one problem with the renaming of my city. Readers tend to read by sight—not by spelling. Call it funny, or plain awkward, but I get an initial jolt, no matter how mild, whenever I bump into the new name of my city which, even now, with an effort, I have to read as 'Kolkata'. And since 'Kolkata', spelling-wise, is partly like 'Kolaghat'—a small town in West Bengal, known to all fish-eating Bengalis for its delicious hilsa fish—I get a bit confused, for a fraction of a second, not more. Interestingly, the moment I run into the age-old 'Calcutta', plenty of associated images appear before me—one after another—even one on top of the other—all in terribly quick succession, and my city becomes incredibly palpable, a city that is mercilessly maligned and dangerously loved. To me at least, 'K-o-l-k-a-t-a' is without that magnetic charm—but 'Calcutta' is not. But, then again, what's in a name! Call it 'Kolkata' or 'Calcutta', after all's said and done, jolts notwithstanding, my city remains mine own—good, bad or indifferent!

I was not born here, but I was made here. I go to the south or the north or to the east or the west, the city, not unlike many other time-worn metropolitan cities, throws me into history at the same time as it pulls me back to my own time—a kind of continuous dialogue between past and present. This is what keeps me young. Even at my age, to quote Arundhati Roy, at my 'dieable' age.

My city, they say, was born in 1690. They say it was one Job Charnock who founded it. In the beginning was heaven and earth and a stinking malarial swamp. One afternoon in August 1690, a big commotion broke out in the busy market at Sutanuti, now on the northern flank of the city. The people panicked at the sight of a fleet of foreign ships approaching the ghat. 'A huge white-skinned man', in tight-fitting trousers and leather shoes, was at the helm. As the ships drew closer, he was recognized as British—and certainly not a pirate. He ended up spending two and a half years at Sutanuti, interacting with the local merchants and natives, but then could not survive the hostile climate any longer. His wife, pretty and young, and allegedly an Indian, died four years later. She was buried in the same tomb where her husband was laid to rest. Soon after, a memorial was built, a mausoleum, now considered one of the oldest surviving monument in the city. All these facts stem from the well-researched compilation of our grand old man Khushwant Singh, untiring columnist and novelist of wide repute who, curiously enough, knows the art of multiplying enemies even at this age. I remember releasing his *Kalighat to Calcutta* (with a foreword by me), in my city in January 1990, during the city's tercentenary celebration.

The city, once the capital of British India, retains practically nothing of its imperial grandeur except a huge memorial named after Queen Victoria, who, advised by her council of ministers, took over the governance of India immediately after what was popularly known as the Sepoy Mutiny and now officially called India's First War of Independence. Also retained are quite a few larger-than-life-size statues of the imperial dignitaries, now looking sad and forlorn. Sad and forlorn, because during one of the radical ruling party's decolonizing drives, these formidable statues were removed from their positions at important street junctions and parks. Uprooted, chained and loaded onto big trucks, they were then driven over and planted unceremoniously all over the sprawling gardens around the memorial of the one-time empress of India. Standing on their regal pedestals, they now give the appearance of excommunicated imperial icons in solitary confinement. The most miserable among them is James Outram, once symbolizing power and glory and arrogance but now abandoned in an obscure corner of the memorial's gardens. Outside this opulent imperial 'estate' spread over several acres, the name of the all-powerful David Ochterlony has long been obliterated from the towering 'cloud-kissing' monument still reigning supreme in the Maidan. It is now called Shaheed Minar (Martyr's Column), the tip of which was once painted red out of atrocious enthusiasm, reminding onlookers of the vermilion applied to the tip of a lingam. Protests were voiced and penned from sober quarters, because the red paint was not in good taste. Much to the chagrin of the concerned minister, the atrocious colour was erased soon after. All these are a sure expression of annoyance and vengeance, which both the elite and the plebeian of the city still harbour, in large or small measure, against our colonial rulers.

The knowledgeable people here still love to remember the unkind words that their colonial masters uttered from time to time about this problem city. They still remember, because of the inconsequentiality of those comments. (Though the highly controversial and, indeed, multifaceted intellectual, Nirad C. Chaudhuri, author of the powerful *Autobiography of an Unknown Indian* [1951], and of a good many other books of high repute, might have altogether contrary views.) To quote from the colonial masters:

Lord Clive, the founder of British India: 'One of the most wicked places in the Universe.'

Sir George Trevelyan: 'The place is so bad by nature that human efforts could do little to make it worse.'

Rudyard Kipling: 'The city of dreadful night.'

Winston Churchill: 'I shall always be glad to have seen it—for the same reason Papa gave for being glad to have seen Lisbon—namely, that it will be unnecessary for me ever to see it again.'

In 1975, a couple of months before the Emergency, Günter Grass, who would go on to win the Nobel Prize in 1999, and who once made a big noise with his mighty *Tin Drum* (1959), and who was, indeed, one of my hot favourites, came to Kolkata for the first time, stayed for a brief period, met a few people including poor me. And such was the extent of his shocks that in his novel about the trip, *The Flounder* (1977), his character Vasco not only misquoted me, but also likened the city to 'God's excrements'. Understandably, I had plenty of reason to be angry.

Before I continue further, I must make it abundantly clear that I am not the person to treat my city as a sacred cow, even though I confess I am not ashamed to call it my El Dorado—of course, not without my tongue firmly in my cheek every now and then. Günter's *Flounder* instantly reminded me of a pamphlet written rather carelessly by one of the greats of world cinema, Pier Paolo Pasolini—poet, novelist and filmmaker, who came to India in 1961 on the occasion of Tagore's centenary as a companion of the famous Italian writer, Alberto Moravia. While Moravia came on official invitation to celebrate the national event, Pasolini made a hurried trip to a couple of metropolitan cities and suburbs, and made an equally hurried exit. He called his little book *The Scent of India* (1974), which, considering the man he became, should not have been written at all—it was written in bad taste and possibly in a dreadful hurry.

It took Günter 12 long years to stage a comeback, with the precise intention to fall vigorously in love with the city. This time he came with his wife and stayed for a longer period. Unfortunately, his *Show Your Tongue* (1987) failed to capture the imagination of the city's opinion builders. May I ask, why not? Maybe I'm right, maybe I'm not.

Even to reject something, one needs to collect a lot of material. And this time Günter did not take any risks. He collected a great deal of material, met a large number of people and formed a small coterie with whom he was continuously interacting. He met me too, quite a few times. One day, as Günter and his wife Ute were spending long hours with me at my tiny flat, I asked why they had decided to stay at Baruipur. It was about 20 km outside his 'subject', and where, even today, after sundown, the mosquitoes far outnumber the villagers. Besides, was he comfortable commuting to and from the city on the terribly overloaded local trains? Didn't he find the travel hellish? Could it be that he wanted to keep his 'subject' at a reasonable distance from the tip of his nose? Perhaps yes, perhaps no. I thought he'd made a mistake, and I said so to both of them. I was afraid, and made no secret of it, that this nightmarish experience might have an adverse effect on his book. I now see that I was right. I am pretty certain that had he and his wife did not manage to survive the first-ever brutal shocks to their system. Living in the thick of the city, a man of his sensibility and compassion could have breathed in the stink and life with wonderful ease. In the process, he would have had no problem in seeing the tip of his nose with utmost clarity and love. Knowing

Günter as I do—a colossus, though not a gentle one—I would have found his *Show Your Tongue* a work close to my heart. The prose was brilliant, but the description of the city and its people was 'selectively' one-sided, with no love and respect for those who, even during the terrible monsoon, when the city is sometimes partly under filthy water, never ask for Noah's Ark to rescue them.

On the other hand, there is the striking quote from distinguished British journalist James Cameron. Twenty-five years after the colonial regime was put to an end, he, a frequent visitor, wrote a passionate account of his sentiments for the city in the *Statesman*, and called it 'My Romantic Association with "Calcutta" '. Here's an excerpt:

> Every time I return to Calcutta, I feel it must be surely impossible that it can continue much longer than this. Yet it always does. An interval of a year makes the visual impact more painful, the squalor more squalid, the poverty more militant, the despair more desperate. Every time I return to Calcutta, I find it an intimidating and even infernal city, unredeemed and probably doomed.

Looking back to the distant past, Mirza Ghalib, the great poet, who stayed in the city for over a year, had said, 'If I were a bachelor, I would have stayed back here for ever. Here, to be a commoner is better than being a ruler.'

Taking everything of mine into consideration, more of failure and much less of achievement, can I call myself the commonest of the commoners? I am what I am, an incorruptible and incorrigible individual, living in a city which has always excited me, provoked me, inspired me and offered me such a bounty of delicious and bitter sentiments. This is my city; it irritates me, makes me laugh and cry, makes me take flight. As much stimulant as it is irritant.

I remember a befitting anecdote, so typical of my city, from my dear friend Gulzar, filmmaker, poet and writer. He lived for a brief period in the city's southern extreme. One day he came out of his house, bag in hand. A neighbour, obviously a Bengali, sitting on the threshold and chewing a daatun (twig brush), asked him casually in Bangla, *Machh kinte jachchen, moshai? Oi goli diye chole jaan, ekhane gooli cholchhe.* (Going to buy fish, sir? Take the lane on that side, there's firing going on this side.)

Hugely amused, Gulzar mused, 'This is Calcutta! A battlefield and yet so cool, so normal.'

Yes, indeed, a battlefield! The lull before and after the storm.

Once again, an anecdote, this one my own. From sometime in 1968, towards the end of the year.

A huge contingent of the metropolitan police. A circuitous barricade across the spacious Esplanade East. Enormous prison vans and hired buses behind the barricade. Further west—the imposing house of the governor, an opulent remnant of the Raj, as if the imperial master's parting gift. At a safe distance, a crowd of curious onlookers. A kind of uneasy calm. That was the scene one afternoon when we got there—my cameraman and I, modestly equipped. I used to do such coverage from time to time, for use in my future films. All to capture the time that my countrymen passed through. All to help characterize the period effectively.

Having patrolled the sensitive area, a police jeep suddenly braked before the barricade. An officer jumped down. Instantly, I recognized him—he was a friend of mine. I walked up to him. He smiled. I asked him if he was in charge of the operation. He gave a broader smile and asked if I had come to do a coverage of the confrontation between the police and the students. Yes, that was the day for a students' rally, when a mob of about 2,00,000 students representing various unions and splinter groups would attempt to break the police cordon. Ostentatiously to build a case for their parent bodies, the left-wing parties, who had gained a government in the state only to be 'unjustly' liquidated by the Central authority.

I asked my friend if he would allow a foreign crew to do the filming along with me. I guessed he would not. I knew his hands were tied by law—foreigners are forbidden to lay their hands on politically sensitive issues.

'Where are they from?' he asked rather casually.

'From France,' I said.

His eyes beamed. 'Filmmakers?' he asked.

'Yes, a three-member team, headed by one Louis Malle.'

'Is Louis Malle here?' he asked with childlike enthusiasm. 'I must meet him. I am a fan. Where is he?'

Malle had landed in the city the night before. He, his cameraman and his recordist. He called me in the morning and said he had come to do a film on the 'fascinating' crowd of the city. I told him that the crowd I'd have an encounter with that afternoon for reasons of my own would be beyond his 'reach'. I told him about the legal constraint. Even then, hoping against hope, he had come along with me in a hired car.

'I must meet him,' reiterated my policeman friend.

I rushed to the car parked a safe distance away and pulled out Malle. 'A fan of yours is waiting for you,' I said.

'Mine? My fan here? In this unearthly place and at this unearthly hour?' he asked, a bit distrustful.

'Yes, very much here, in this battlefield. And your fan is a policeman. Rathin Bhattacharya, a Calcuttan!'

'A p-o-l-i-c-e-m-a-n!'

'That's right,' I said, and presented him before the operation commander. The policeman said he had watched Malle's *Zazie dans le Métro* (Zazie in the Metro) (1960) just a week ago. And, yes, without subtitles. He'd watched the film at the Alliance Française and loved it. Oh yes, he had completed a course in French and also translated Louis Aragon's 'Elsa au miroir' (Elsa at the mirror) (1945).

A speechless Malle gaped at my friend and then at me. Moments later, he took me aside and gushed, 'Amazing, incredible! A policeman ready to beat the students to jelly any moment now is remembering Aragon and his "Elsa at the Mirror"! Mrinal, this can happen only in your city. Nowhere else!'

I was not surprised. From what I knew of him at the time, particularly after the ebullient May 1968 event at the Sorbonne with the students' uprising reaching a peak, as well as his impressive track record right from his entry in cinema, it was but natural that Louis would react the way he did. Incidentally, of all his award-winning and also controversial films, the one I loved the most was *Au revoir les enfants* (Goodbye, children) (1987), inspired by the tragic memory of his childhood and terrifying in its simplicity.

Late in the evening, Louis called me from his hotel. 'Mrinal,' he said, 'this is a day I cannot forget, I won't. When I came here for the first time—that was four months ago, as a member of the film delegation of our government—I rather liked your crazy city and quite liked the unruly crowd. But I never realized that it would be like it was today.' And he repeated, 'Amazing, incredible!'

That was my city in the late 1960s. That is my city, always. And away from its downtown, or in the thick of it, go to a coffee house or to a tea shop, not to the famous one with two wings—Lords and Commons—which once made history and has now lost its lustre—go there, to a moderate backstreet shop or stand at the maddening crossroads where, a little apart from the boisterous crowd, perchance you may capture a young poet with his unkempt beard, busy replacing a line from his yet-to-be-published work with a more suitable phrase.

Calcutta/Kolkata! Buoyant, creative, erratic, even hopelessly disengaged. For reasons of my own, having lived in my El Dorado for ages, I stop a while and look within and ask myself if I have, at any point of time, felt sick of my city. Have I? Ever? Do I? Now? The truth is that I am so much a part of its anatomy. As I write this, I remember a Bob Dylan song—'Love Sick' (1997)—which, not long ago, the actor-singer Anjan Dutt, my friend, made me listen to. *I am sick of love / but I am in the thick of it.* That was it—a kind of love-and-hate relationship with your lover, or mine. Inescapable. Maligned and loved, both in enormous proportions.

But having spent the first 17 years of my life in my hometown, which then had the distinct flavour of the countryside and is now in Bangladesh, how is it that I have not saved a tear for it? Is it because I considered that period of my life to be much less than ordinary? It was neither colourful, which, in all fairness, I would have treasured. Nor dull, which I would have hated to preserve. But was it really so? Less than ordinary? How, then, did my friend Dipankar Mukhopadhyay write a delightful 'story' while writing a sort of biography of me. He titled it *The Maverick Maestro* (1995) and this is how it began:

A strange object was flying across the sky. A toddler, playing in the courtyard of his house, looked at it with curious eyes. It was a bright, sunny day and above him, against the clear blue sky, was the strangest bird he had ever seen. He watched it carefully: it had two silvery wings, which shone in the sunlight, so it must be a bird; but it emitted a peculiar humming sound which utterly confused him.

The boy ran inside to call his brothers and sisters (he was born into a large family). Excited, everyone rushed out to look up at the sky. His father even took out a map to chart the course of the strange object. In the tranquil twenties, an aeroplane was a novelty—more so in a sleepy town of undivided Bengal. In the excitement that followed, the toddler learnt that what they had seen was not a bird but a manmade flying machine. It was an experience he would never forget.

Obviously, the boy was me, though I was a bit older than a toddler, and not exactly as he described. And, obviously, I was the one who told him that story.

As I now see it, it was not a story which should ever have been discarded as inconsequential. Dipankar realized that, and a cursory glance under my bedside lamp at his insistence also made me feel the same. I might as well couple it with a dream I had around the same time I first saw an aeroplane. Perhaps it was even that same night? I dreamt of a midnight adventure: Garuda, the Hindu mythological bird, came to me and offered me his back for a bumpy ride. In my dream, I did as I was asked to and travelled a long way. When I was dropped back to bed, I woke up. Interestingly, the same dream ride came to me once more. Now that I am being pushed by my over-energetic publisher to pen my memoir, I propose to include these two—the sight of the flying machine on a sunny morning and the midnight adventure up in the sky. Much later, in the mid-60s, when I was 43, both the flying machine and the dream appeared before me so very clearly. That was when I was busy writing my script from an Odia story by Kalindi Charan Panigrahi, dating back to the 30s. The sequence I created was not in the text. It was all my own—the same as I've described, coming to me without much effort. Strange! How easily experiences of one kind or other metamorphose into art!

To write more about my distant past: even to make the briefest trip to my old hometown, Faridpur, just six hours by train from the city, I now need a visa. During those 17 years of my life in Faridpur, the whole district was unusually politically charged. The influence of Lal–Bal–Pal—Lala Lajpat Rai, Bal Gangadhar Tilak and Bipin Chandra Pal, the triumvirate of the Indian National Congress—was tremendous. My father, Dinesh Chandra Sen, and the leader of the Bar in the district court, was closely associated with them. But he was not a habitual khadi-wearer and nor did he ever don a Gandhi cap, even for the public meetings. Throughout his legal career, he lent active support to the militant political activists—'terrorists', as they were called then, now 'freedom fighters'—very few of whom, for obvious reasons, could escape death by hanging; the rest were deported to the Andamans. Once he even suffered disbarment. Of course, as punishment.

In the early 30s, Mahatma Gandhi was arrested on his return from a round table conference in England. As a mark of protest, the entire country embarked on a massive hartal. In my hometown, too, everything was paralysed—schools, colleges, offices, shops, markets, everything. My father and his colleagues boycotted the court sessions. The following day, the district magistrate, incidentally, an

Indian, took his pick, singled out my father and 'disbarred' him for a period of six months.

My mother, Saraju Bala Sen, a traditional housewife, loving and affectionate, the likes of whom there were millions in the country, defied the social constraints and did her 'revolutionary' bit by singing a Swadeshi song in a public meeting, presided over by Bipin Chandra Pal. Years later, a dozen friends of mine and I, all primary-school students, chanted 'Vande Mataram' in the face of the law-abiding police and were immediately taken to the nearby police station and thrown into lock-up. We remained confined for a few hours. Then a dirty constable appeared, baton in hand, opened the gate and pushed us out into a big room. Terrified, we stood there, helpless. A police officer walked in, brandished his baton and shouted at us. Without caring to see how the others were reacting, I burst into tears and cried until my father arrived. Much to my surprise and elation, the police officer instantly saluted him. I cared for none of my 'comrades'—I came out free. And I felt so proud of my father, undoubtedly a man to be reckoned with. Then, suddenly, he slapped me hard. This time I did not cry. I accepted the slap in a manner that I thought was right.

Years later, when I was around 15 and waiting for my matriculation results, my hometown began to ready itself to give a rousing reception to the great political leader Dr Syama Prasad Mukherjee, chief architect of the Hindu Mahasabha. There was to be a huge crowd at Central Park. I decided I would go too. Just for the love of the crowd. My mother objected; she sensed there would be quite a few young people wanting to create trouble. One single derogatory remark about Subhas Chandra Bose from the stage and there would be an instant uproar. It was also quite possible that my elder brother would be one of the troublemakers. All the more reason why I thought I should be there—not to take part but to observe. To protect myself from the scorching sun, my mother asked me to carry an umbrella. Or who knows for what! Could it be for my defence in case of a breach of peace or even rioting among the crowd?

Central Park was teeming with people. I tried to locate my elder brother, Mejda, the second of my seven brothers, one of the possible troublemakers. He was quite popular in the area ever since he had played the challenging role of Afzal Khan, army chief of the Nawab of Bijapur, in one of the recent amateur theatrical productions. Instructed by the nawab, Afzal Khan went to meet Chhatrapati Shivaji as friend and benefactor. The purpose, however, was to assassinate him. But renowned as a highly skilled operator, Shivaji outmanoeuvred Afzal Khan and killed him—right on stage. I was annoyed with the man who played Shivaji, because of how ingeniously he had 'killed' my brother!

The crowd listened to Dr Syama Prasad Mukherjee with rapt attention and, true, he was a great speaker. But the moment he said that the friendly understanding between the Muslim League and Subhas Chandra Bose was prejudicial to the interest of the Hindus, there was an uproar. I was standing just behind the shouting brigade. One of them—a sort of opposition leader—was my brother alias Afzal Khan, the villain. Amid the shouting and countershouting, the speaker, a person of exceptional courage, was perhaps trying to arrive at a cool assessment of the situation. A fight broke out. Among those who rushed forward to maintain 'law and order' was my history teacher. I still remember his notes on Chhatrapati Shivaji, they'd been simply superb. Lovingly, he referred to him as 'Shiv-ji'. Now, outside the classroom and in the battlefield, he was a different person altogether. Exuding fire, he leapt on my dear brother. The bald pate of my history teacher appeared huge before my eyes. I saw nothing else, it was like the sky unfolding itself before me—an offering, so to say. I brought down the butt-end of my umbrella on it with a bang.

For obvious reasons, I made myself scarce immediately.

He never found out that I was the culprit. That was in 1938.

To confess, other than that attack—disgraceful, but only out of love for my brother—never in my life have I ever indulged in physical violence.

Two years later, in 1940, my parents sent me to the big city, to the famous Scottish Church College, to acquire a degree. On the eve of my departure, out of sheer fun, I wanted to put my parents in an uncomfortable situation. I asked them if, so far, they had noticed a streak of genius in me. As expected, taken unawares, they were visibly awkward. I immediately asked them not to worry. I remembered Amal-da, one year my senior, who had read a lot outside the classroom texts, and the quote I'd picked up from him: 'We are all geniuses up to the age of ten.' The famous words of Aldous Huxley.

Given that assurance, my parents had no choice but to give me the benefit of the doubt.

TWO

Given the Benefit of the Doubt,
I Walked into the Brave New World—
A Long Way, a Difficult Way . . .

As soon as I came to the big city, I was seized with a kind of fear. I was confronted by a crowd, a vast crowd. I felt lost. I felt I was alone in the crowd—an anonymous, self-absorbed, indifferent swarm, menacing and monstrous. Loved and protected by my parents in my hometown and liked for one reason or other by my teachers at school, including the history teacher as well as my Inter-college physics teacher, I was suddenly reduced to anonymity and began to suffer from an acutely depressing sense of emptiness. Until things changed over the course of time, I remained an out-sider, as though I was living a marginal life.

Amid the incredibly congested bazaars and lanes and houses, most of them century-old residences, some even older, others of recent construction, even a few magnificent palaces, some ravaged by time and weather, in the northern part of the sprawling city stood a three-storey boarding house on Kailash Bose Street. One afternoon, my local guardian, Purna Das, escorted me there. In the stormy 1920s and 30s, in my home district, Das had once trained a large group of intrepid boys and formed a wandering Shanti Sena (Soldiers of Peace). He and his Sena were very close to my parents and our family, and now, at his age, here he was, living a somewhat retired life in the big city. Since he was permanently based here, my parents had asked him to keep a watch over me. And it was he who brought me here, not to a students' home but to a kind of boarding house where most of the boarders were about 30 years old and job holders—clerks, teachers and professionals of diverse kind, all from small-income groups. I shared a room with another student of my age, also from Faridpur. He had come to the big city to study economics; I to study physics. We were the youngest among the boarders. The oldest was about 70, living a retired life, with an entire room at his disposal—a strictly private man. Living under the same roof, the two of us students were a kind of island. Purna Das knew the place very well and assured me that he would be there for me if I had any problems. And, indeed, he had many high connections in the city, mostly with the political bigwigs, and so, for obvious reasons, he was a political suspect, always being shadowed.

Our life at the boarding house was quite different from anything I had known till then.

Day One! The call for dinner was announced. The manager came to my room and lovingly said, 'Treat this as your home. You will get all the facilities, as much as you got at home. The boarders here are all true gentlemen, and no one raises a voice at another. And my boss never entertains unemployed boarders. The gentleman who brought you here is a personal friend of my boss. Come, you will have your dinner at this particular time. But the oldest and the most ancient, lovingly called *dadu* (grandfather), will not join you in the dining room. He will eat in his room. Lunch too. This is a special arrangement offered to him. And you can imagine why!'

The dining room was rather huge, with no dining table nor chairs nor benches. The boarders squatted on the floor in a square, their backs against the walls. There was just one server, one Brahmin cook at the centre and an attendant to pour us water. My roommate and I walked in. Those who had already taken their positions looked at us. I made an effort not to look uncomfortable. Food and water and, of course, salt on the edges of our plates were served rather briskly. Then came rice and dal and a small piece of fried fish—a kind of 'starter'.

'Lemon?' the attendant asked, carrying a plate of lemon wedges.

Yes, please. But then as I squeezed the lemon wedge to flavour my dal—it slipped through my fingers! Everyone stared at the wedge which had flown off and landed on a boarder's plate three seats away. The boarder looked at me and then at the cook. No one made a sound. Quietly, a new plate with rice, dal and fried fish and, of course, salt, not to forget another lemon wedge, was placed before him, and the first plate removed. We continued to eat silently, with no comment made by anyone on my funny slip. I felt miserable. I did not even say 'sorry'. I had no manners then, which was why.

Such a predicament as mine—a provincial boy thrown unaware into an 'alien' world—is not uncommon, unless the victim shows traces of uncommonality in himself. I was an average boy with average intelligence. That is why I was affected so easily.

One day, when I got back from my college, I found Purna Das waiting for me. I was happy he had come, I beamed at him. He asked me if everything was all right. Then he pulled out a booklet from his bag, gave it to me and cautioned me not to misplace it. It was a valuable document, and the only one, and it had been with him all these years.

Amazed, I stared at the cover: it was the speech of the chairman of the Reception Committee of the All-Bengal Ryot (Peasants) Conference, 1923. I had heard about it in Faridpur. Of this pamphlet, there was truly not a single copy left, not even with my father. He had been the chairman who'd given the speech. More importantly, the conference had been presided over by the great Chitta Ranjan Das, popularly known as C. R. Das who, the year before, had been president of the Indian National Congress. Incidentally, that had been Das' last speech. He died soon after in Darjeeling where he had gone for a weeklong respite.

At night, after Purna Das had left and my roommate was away, I read my father's speech. A beautiful speech! Lively and emotional. And informative too. Towards the end, there was a reference to the 'Bolshevik Revolution' that, in 1917, 'brought a new civilization in Russia'. As I finished reading it, I wept. I felt proud of myself, that I was the son of such a father.

Soon after, I lost the pamphlet. I did not know how. I cursed myself for having lost the only remaining copy.

However, it did not take me long to realize that something was fermenting within me. I was beginning to change. Back home, I had made some overtures towards the leftist student movement. I even remembered chanting No pasarán! (They shall not pass!) at an anti-Franco rally. In the big city, I came out of my shell, breathed in a wider world—a world that kept me busy at various levels. But the bigger change was yet to come, slowly but steadily—the change of the interior. Through unceasing interactions of diverse kinds with people within and without my given orbit, through continuous exposure to world events and domestic chaos—war, famine, communal holocaust—I was undergoing a metamorphosis. In

1941, when reckless adventure was unleashed upon the world, Rabindranath Tagore passed away. Around the same time, I read the last manifesto of the great poet, 'Crisis in Civilization'. A gem of an essay and a guide to action! The Great Bengal Famine came soon after, in 1943. Millions of people were forced to starve, drop dead from hunger. In 1945, when the war was over and the death of Fascism was ensured, Hiroshima and Nagasaki went up in flames. And in my city, bigotry, vulgarity and unending violence spread in a mad fury in 1946.

With the tread of the barbarian feet resounding everywhere, it was the worst of times, yet also perhaps the best of times.

And that was the start of my love affair with my city, my El Dorado. Over the years and since then, with this love–hate relationship growing steadily, my city has been both a stimulant and irritant. Till that moment, I had been touched and shaken by its vibrancy and youthfulness, its humour and flippancy, and, indeed, by its tragic dimension, by its greatness and meanness. Once, I remember, I made a witty statement about love and war. Love is to war alike, one never knows when it starts. Now I see it is not exactly that with my El Dorado, even though I have never treated my city as a holy cow.

My first encounters with my city led me to many things but not to cinema. I came to it much later, by accident. And my first step to filmmaking was a bad-bad-bad step. Terrible! But that is a different story, one that even I could not fully comprehend at the outset.

Coming back to my boarding house. A year after my arrival, in 1941, I got a jolt. Dawn was yet to break when I was woken up by a gentle knock at the door. Gentle, but firm. The clock on the table read four. My roommate opened his eyes. Again, a knock, louder this time. Followed by the manager's voice, 'Open the door!'

Outside: two policemen, two officers, the manager and a distinguished neighbour from a couple of houses away. From my experiences back home, it took me hardly any time to realize what they were up to and the reason for the presence of the distinguished neighbour. To raid a house, they needed a respectable witness. They would choose just such a man, even at an unearthly hour, and the chosen would have no choice. Not for my roommate—they had come for me. Why?

The search was a matter of formality. They were quite nice to me, in fact. But they did not answer any of my questions. In a quarter of an hour, everything was over and I was asked to get ready to go with them. Should I carry the daily essentials with me? Kurta, dhoti, towel and most important of all—toothpaste and brush? No, not required.

I felt relieved.

Seven of us—the other six were also students, though older than me—had been picked up from different parts of the city and put under police custody for seven days, at Lalbazar Police Station, the police headquarters. Over the next seven days, we were driven to another part of the city, the office of the Special Branch. Over the next seven days, we were questioned, threatened, tempted— all in separate rooms. Not allowed a bath or a change of clothes, not even allowed to comb our hair. On the eighth day, we were taken to court where, strangely, we found that there were advocates present to defend us. They argued for bail, and bail was granted. Different dates were given for each of our reappearance before the judge. And that, finally, was the end of our seven-day 'ordeal'.

As I came out, I found my roommate and, yes, my father waiting for me. My father had come all the way to the city to organize my defence. I went close to them and forced a smile. This time my father did not slap me; he simply patted me on the back. I realized I had come of age.

There was no serious charge against me. But they had 'definite' information that I was the person organizing secret meetings between an underground student leader, Biswanath Mukherjee, and an important faction of the activists. However, the police inquiries, the Special Branch investigations and the threats failed to lead them anywhere.

Two court appearances followed by an unconditional release ended the matter. But I was not quite sure if the matter had truly ended. I had a hunch for some time afterwards that I was being shadowed. My elders advised me to be on my guard.

17 January 1941—a couple of months before that little game was over. A big day in India's freedom struggle against the Raj. That desperate day, very early in the morning, a man who made history got into his car and was never seen again. He was on parole when he outsmarted the powerful British administration with perfect ease and made a smooth escape. *The Forgotten Hero,* as Shyam Benegal calls his 2005 film on Subhas Chandra Bose, kept the secret of his journey all to himself until he crossed the borders of the North-West Frontier Province and Afghanistan.

News started filtering in, and rumours and wild conjectures flew all over the city. In the thick of that charged atmosphere, I was drawn to a distant past through a kind of sharp flashback: back to my hometown, to my father and Bose jotting down points for a massive all-Bengal conference to take place soon. Since the conference would take place in my hometown, Bose depended on my father and half a dozen other congressmen to deal with the local hazards. My father being more independent-minded than the others, it is possible that Bose felt more comfortable with him. In my flashback, however, neither Bose nor my father occupied centrestage. It was I, suffering from acute toothache in the next room.

The pain was unbearable. At a neighbour's suggestion, my mother applied an indigenous paint to the aching tooth. Immediately, my mouth began to burn. I burst into tears. My father rushed in. Bose thought something serious had happened. He appeared at the door, watched me, then prescribed an analgesic—even wrote the name down for us. The tablet was brought from the chemist. I took it and the pain vanished. Bose said it would ensure temporary relief, and only removal of the tooth would give me total relief. Until that was possible, Bose promised that on his next trip he would bring along a good painkiller with hardly any side effects. He left by the night train and returned two days later. Despite being so busy at the time, he did not forget to bring the medicine for me. Later, my mother told Bose that it had worked like a miracle. I was terribly proud that Subhas Chandra Bose had been my first dentist. It took me much longer to realize that for him, it was no more than a trivial detail in his daily life. Even then . . .

7 August 1941. Classes had just begun. The teacher took up thermodynamics. Suddenly, in the other building, the principal rushed out of his office. Reverend Allen Cameron, barefoot, standing before us, gasping and distraught. 'The great poet is no more!' he said. His voice was choked. Without a word, without waiting for the teacher's permission, all of us streamed out. In less than a quarter of an hour, all the students—girls and boys—and the teachers—of Indian nationality and of Scottish origin, all barefoot, set off on our way to Jorasanko, the house of the Tagores, in the north of the city, where he had been born in 1861 and where he had passed away that morning. When we reached the huge residential complex, a century and a half old, the large courtyard was swarming with crowds, all making futile attempts to rush towards the room on the first floor, where his body had been laid out. Outside, amid the surging waves of people, I could not make out how far I was from Tagore or how close. When at last I glimpsed some sky above, a few tree branches swaying and bowing, and felt a gentle breeze, I discovered I was on the terrace. I had no idea how I climbed up to the terrace—I could not remember taking a single step upward. Down below were people, swarms of people. Even at the risk of a possible collapse, I pushed my way to the weather-beaten parapet and leant over it. A bird's-eye view of a mass of people, men and women, young and old, a huge spectacle. Amid that pandemonium, there was a sudden silence, a sharp cut, so to say, when not a voice made a sound and none moved an inch. Slowly, quietly, majestically appeared the poet from inside the age-old palace, carried by pallbearers. Who were the pallbearers? All the city's intellectual giants! The poet floated over the sea of heads. Bedecked with flowers, as he receded from my view, I recalled his lines:

Thou hast made me endless,
such is thy pleasure.
The frail vessel thou emptiest
again and again, and fillest it
ever with fresh life.

The whole city went mad, it throbbed and wept, it was at once empty and fulfilled. At some point in time, I allowed the procession to pass by. Then I walked on quickly so that I could reach the crematorium well in time and take up a vantage position.

Nimtola Ghat, along the Ganges, had been under strict official protection for about a week to ensure that the cremation could be performed with grace and dignity. A police cordon around the entrance kept me at a distance. Many others who, like me, had reached well in advance had no choice but to wait patiently. But inside the large cordon I saw something that made me shudder. A tall handsome young man in his mid-twenties, clad in milk-white dhoti and kurta, stood there, bewildered. He stood there with a child in his arms, wrapped in a milk-white towel. Perhaps he had come to cremate his child and was now trapped in a cruel situation. Why did he not go to another crematorium? How far was the other one? Had he come alone? Could it be for sentimental reasons that he had asked his people, if there were any, to go away and was bent upon cremating the child at Nimtola?

All of a sudden, the crowd moved in. From different directions. As if to attack the crematorium. More than half a million, walking along a long circuitous route, accompanying the mortal remains of Tagore. The protective measures were swept away, the cordon smashed. Everything was out of control. Confusion all around! A stampede? Any casualties? Anyone's guess! And the child? The child was lost, drowned in the crowd. So was the man, possibly the father.

An unforgettable experience! An unforgettable day! 7 August. According to the Bengali calendar, 'baishey shravana', 22 Shravana. The day that Tagore died.

Nineteen years later, in 1960, when film producers had accepted me as a full-fledged film director, and a reasonably dependable one, I made my third film, one that made me feel great for the first time. I called it *Baishey Shravana*—the day that Tagore died. And the day that, in all probability, a dead child was crushed before he could be cremated. In my film, a middle-aged villager hawking his merchandise on the local trains, and by Indian standards certainly not a presentable groom, was married to a sweet girl much too younger than him. The man was no villain, the woman was all grace, and the couple lived through good times, bad times and cruel times.

The title raised an objection from the censors. One member, an eminent educationist, Professor Apurva Kumar Chanda, found the title pointless; he felt I had somehow obliquely shown some disrespect to the great poet. He was very loud about his point of view. Another member in total agreement with Professor Chanda was the deeply involved social activist, Mrs Ashoka Gupta. The others were noncommittal. I was called for a conference. I had a huge argument with the two members. I said that my film had nothing to do with Tagore. In fact, it had been the incident of the man with the dead child in his arms, probably crushed in a stampede, that had been at the back of my mind. True, Tagore's death had been a headline for the world media, and very rightly so, but as an eyewitness, I had every right to save a tear for the man and his child. 'You, young man, are very adamant,' said the veteran educationist. 'Couldn't you have any other date, a day earlier or a day later?' he asked.

'You could as well have *Teishey Shravana* (23 Shravana), couldn't you?' said the lady, a bit impatiently.

'No, I couldn't—because they got married on Baishey,' I said.

The two members stuck to their point and I stuck to mine. So the case was referred to Delhi (not Bombay, in those days). The ministry in Delhi was kind to me, and *Baishey Shravana* got its clearance. But, as has been my fate throughout my career, the film was a failure at the box office.

If not the lady, then the veteran educationist, groomed at Oxford and close to Tagore, and I became friends. He liked me, and I adored him. Once, years later, I remembered taking up the *Baishey Shravana* case to tease him. I told him about one of Aldous Huxley's novels, which started with the loaded line, 'It was the day of Gandhi's assassination.' But the text had absolutely nothing to do with Gandhi or his philosophy of nonviolence. The novel was *Ape and Essence* (1948).

'Forget it,' Apurva-da said, and patted me on the back.

Apurva-da did not want to raise the subject ever again. But he did not forget the film. He liked the film for 'its interior strength'. He liked the way I had captured the famine. It was *elliptical*, he said.

'You know what I mean?' he asked me like a schoolmaster.

I nodded like an obedient pupil.

I was happy with his words. Coming home, I did something in my infantile enthusiasm: I pulled out the *Oxford English Dictionary* from the shelf and found out that the word *ellipsis* means 'the omission from a sentence of words needed to complete the construction or sense.'

Yes, in *Baishey Shravana*, I did not show the famine except for one very long shot: villagers heading to the city in search of food.

The physical anatomy of the famine was actually omitted from the sequence of famine.

While making *Baishey Shravana*, I made sure that mine would not be a journalistic approach, that I would not count the number of people who starved and died, that I would not show vultures and jackals fighting over carcasses, that I would not create a scene where an emaciated baby fiercely sucks at the breast of its mother who has just died. I had seen enough of such dreadful scenes at very close range in my city and in its outskirts. Forced to be familiar with the famished millions forfeiting their right to die a natural death, I was sick of death.

The famine of 1943 came later in the film. Slowly but inexorably, it walked into the second part, the part where the film grew more ugly. Inside the house, all was quiet and oppressive. Till the end, it was the story of the two—a bitter husband and a bitter wife. Both of whom, unable to endure the ruthless reality of the famine, hurled against each other in impotent fury and hatred. They breathed in not air but the stench of death. There was nothing to salvage them, to pull them out of the filth, and that was what the film tried to focus on. Not the statistics of a lacerated society, but a vigorous suggestion about the slow but inevitable liquidation of the last vestiges of human decency. I kept my camera indoors, glued to the couple. And, hell, there was no exit, no escape route for either of the two.

Yet the man was no villain, the woman all grace.

When I completed the film, I proposed to my producer that we take a chance and pack off a subtitled print (I called it *The Wedding Day*) to Venice for the festival in August. The producer thought it a risky proposition; even if it was accepted, it would involve expenditure beyond his means—a new print, subtitles, publicity material (stills for distribution among the journalists), etc. He said he could strike out a new print, and that's all.

I was disappointed.

But I was desperate.

I rushed a short synopsis of the film to Venice, along with a personal statement and half a dozen stills. Instantly, on receipt of the material, the festival director sent me a telegram, asking for a print, subtitled in French if not in Italian. As promised, the producer gave me a new print. And that's all. I lost no time in spending my own money, whatever I had, to prepare, reel-wise, a dialogue text in English with accurate lengthwise spotting in frames. Within a week, the consignment was sent off to Venice, though I knew very well that a print with no subtitles, with only dialogue text, that too in English, would be rejected straightaway.

The next week, I got another telegram, regretting that a print without subtitles could not qualify for the competition. But as a very special case, they were ready to accept the film in the non-competitive section. That in itself was recognition for me. I was thrilled! In addition, I got an invitation to visit the festival for three days. I quickly prepared sequence-wise synopses, from beginning to end, 10 pages or so, got 50 copies printed and packed them off to Venice with the request that they be selectively distributed.

Though an orphaned entry, with not a single soul to present it at the festival, the response to the film was positive. Later, through unknown channels, it even received a number of reviews, among which I still remember two in particular: one by Georges Sadoul in a French journal, *Les Lettres françaises*; and another by Gene Moskowitz in *Variety*. Both made me happy and confident. And that is how, in 1960, I made a quiet entry onto the global cinema scene. At the request of the festival's directorate, I presented the print in its original to the Venice archive.

Soon after Venice, I came to know from the Ministry of Information and Broadcasting, Government of India, that the National Film Theatre in London would like to present *Baishey Shravana* at the London Film Festival in November. One of the selectors had seen the film at Venice and made the selection. So they needed my consent as well as a print with English subtitles. I had no problem organizing consent from my producer. But instead of preparing a subtitled print, which would cost money, I planted a reel-wise voice-over on the original soundtrack, a bit like a running commentary. Again, out of sheer desperation! In the middle of that flurry of activity, there was a stupid suggestion from a Delhi official. It was obligatory, he wrote in his letter, that a particular sequence be removed—the sequence of the hungry man obnoxiously licking his fingers as he eats some rice. I called the officer concerned and asked why. His answer was forthright: one of his colleagues in the ministry had seen the film in a Calcutta theatre with a friend who'd been living in England for a long time. He thought the sight of the man licking his fingers would be considered nauseating by international audiences. I was so disgusted with this that I disconnected the line right away and called the person concerned at the National Film Theatre. Not to my surprise, he informed me that a subtitled print would be a bigger draw at the festival.

'I'll try,' I said, 'but . . . '

'Don't worry,' he said.

At the London Film Festival too, *Baishey Shravana* was shown with a voice-over, not subtitles. Of course, the licking-fingers scene remained uncut. But there was no one to present the film. Not even a representative from the Indian High Commission.

After London, the same print went to two small festivals in two Scandinavian countries. Always with an English voice-over and always a lone journey, with no one to represent it.

For *Baishey Shravana,* which I made in 1960, materials were collected from the period around the Bengal famine of 1943. Taken unawares, in the same year, the year of the famine, I discovered cinema. Let me tell you how.

To be absolutely honest, I originally had no interest in cinema. True, I had encounters—once or twice, I'd watched a movie 'wide-eyed' and 'open-mouthed', just for the wonder of talking pictures. Later, along with friends or family, I watched another half a dozen films or more. I never kept count—for reasons I never cared to analyse, the viewings never left a lasting impression. Even when I came to the big city, I failed to become an addict; I was not a regular filmgoer. In the city, I had various other things to get involved in. One such thing was reading. Reading what? What not? I say. Nothing in particular! All that I could catch hold of *minus* any particular direction, *minus* any specialization—history, philosophy, sociology, politics, religion, literature, plays, poetry, art, etc. Reading a couple of essays by Karl Marx one week, and Friedrich Nietzsche's *Thus Spake Zarathustra* the next. Which was why, perhaps, I barely had any academic discipline, or any direction, for that matter.

Everything I read was at the Imperial Library, now called National Library. One day, by accident, I bumped into a book on cinema and its aesthetics titled *Film as Art* by Rudolf Arnheim, a gem of a text. Part of it I understood, part of it left me confused. Over the next three or four months, I read the library's entire stock on the aesthetics and sociology of cinema. Only then did I feel I had been adequately educated. Then I started haunting the city theatres, watching films of different genres, even though I was uncertain if all of them were worth viewing. Gradually, with my exposure to world cinema through several foreign consulates, and later through the Calcutta Film Society, I became a full-time film activist. Then I turned my hand to writing on the aesthetics of cinema, on its philosophy, its social relevance and the need to evolve a new language. *New Cinema*!

The first film I made was *Raat Bhore* (The dawn) (1955). It was based on an ordinary story: a village boy, poor and neglected, made to meet his destiny in the big city where he was brought by the head of a well-to-do family. The film was a disaster, the biggest of all big disasters. Because everything I had thought earlier was wrong, because I realized I was not educated enough, because the point was not just to decide what to say—I did not know how to say it. And that turned out to be my biggest problem, my biggest weakness. Having made such a lousy film, I reckoned I had humiliated myself.

And that was when, in 1955, a great film was made—*Pather Panchali* (*Song of the Little Road*). The film that shook the world. Ray's all-time best. As world opinion declared, a classic for all times! But for me, the most living, the most complex, the most con-temporary of all of Ray's films, and so the most important, is the second of the Apu Trilogy—*Aparajito* (*The Unvanquished*) made a year later, in 1956. Through a study of *Aparajito*, I could realize that *contemporaneity* is determined not by the period but by the attitude. Which is why I consider Carl Dreyer's *The Passion of Joan of Arc*, made in 1928, to be strikingly contemporaneous.

I went into hiding until I made my second film—*Neel Akasher Neechey* (*Under the Blue Sky*) (1958)—which, despite my reservations on several counts, was received on the whole with a certain grace. Even Nehru liked the film, and remembered it for quite some time. Most possibly, he liked it for its content which unequivocally espoused that our struggle against colonial rule was inseparably linked to the democratic world's fight against fascism. More so, because the story was set in the mid-30s, when a militant Japan attacked China. Singer-producer Hemanta Mukherjee was immensely happy when the audience gave its verdict—they liked the film very much.

Funnily enough, since the government files, particularly in this part of the world, move at snail's pace, the concerned officials of the Ministry of Information and Broadcasting sat up three long years after the film's fairly successful run, played havoc with the files, made them move from one ministry to the other and then finally banned *Neel Akasher Neechey*. This was in the mid-50s, when the growing tension over border issues between India and China turned violent.

Fortunately, there was someone to take up this ridiculous issue on the floor of the Indian parliament. Hiren Mukherjee, Communist MP, made an appropriate speech in the presence of Prime Minister Nehru and Defence Minister V. K. Krishna Menon. They too were terribly annoyed with the official order, and the ban was withdrawn immediately. The ban, therefore, lasted only three months, perhaps the shortest ban, just like my father's six-month disbarment in the early 30s. My father had appealed the matter in Calcutta High Court, and Sarat Chandra Bose, elder brother of Subhas Chandra Bose, had defended him. When his case finally came to court after three months, it was immediately dismissed.

Coming back to filmmaking. I could not be happy with my friend Ritwik Ghatak's first film, *Nagarik* (The citizen) (completed in 1952). His second, *Ajantrik* (*Pathetic Fallacy / The Mechanical Man*) (1958)—strong depictions, very strong and very original, the best in his rather short career—is an incomparable achievement. On the surface, it is the story of a ramshackle automobile and its love–hate relationship with its crazy driver, located in a rugged terrain, punctuated by tribal pockets. Against such a mighty backdrop are the passengers, carrying along their different stories. While Ghatak's camera captures it all—and extremely beautifully too—beneath this facade he builds a story of his own, of the tribals and their rituals. They all looked very powerful, though in my opinion they are not without their unevenness and irritating excesses. All, I think, because of Ghatak's innate recklessness! However, discerning spectators hailed the film as a great achievement, and a section even rated it better than Ray's.

Anyway, I survived, I grew and I made *Baishey Shravana* at the very onset of the 60s—taking me back to the 40s—war, famine, riots, Partition. And in the Far East—Hiroshima and Nagasaki going up in flames. A cannibal time!

THREE

Hiroshima and the Cannibal Time . . .

Since 1965, my trips abroad had been too many, too frequent and always to the West. Understandably, all of them were to film festivals or seminars on allied subjects. So I hardly had any touristic priorities when I travelled abroad until, in 1979, I was invited by the Government of Japan for a fortnight-long stay. The invitation came from the External Affairs Ministry, and I was told that if I so desired I would be free to plan my own timetable. I was thrilled. My list was much too long, and, for obvious reasons, Hiroshima was at the very top. Kabuki, the traditional dramatic form, came next. I left the rest to my hosts which, of course, would include interactions with their filmmakers, particularly with Noriaki Tsuchimoto, for his single film, a brilliant film, which, years ago, I'd seen in Switzerland. Officially, he was less than acceptable. The little I had come to know of him through that one film, I was not surprised that he was not in the good books of the establishment.

Along with an External Affairs Ministry official to receive me at the airport was my good friend, Akira Iwasaki, whom I had first met at Finnish Film Archive. Or at the Moscow International Film Festival, or maybe at Tbilisi. At Narita Airport, that was our second meeting. Apart from his expertise in the history of Japanese and Russian cinema, his admiration for Tagore, Gandhi and Nehru drew us close. On our way to the hotel, I was told that Akira would accompany me as long as his health permitted it. He was not keeping well and, true, he looked rather pale though, presumably, he was the same age as I.

Sunday, 18 March 1979. Akira and I reached Hiroshima via Kyoto, and then Nara, the ancient capital of Japan. Then we prepared to get to the heart of the city, to the open museum where the ruins had been preserved with meticulous care. The sky was clear and cloudless. As we came to the museum gate, Akira led me to a particular spot and stopped. What a sight! In silence, I stood there, my eyes riveted on the gruesome past of Hiroshima–Nagasaki, staring at the face of a boy, larger than life, silent and static, his eyes filled with an awesome vacuity, and horror everywhere. The boy with a rice ball in his hand, now turned into an image. The photograph had been shot at Nagasaki on 10 August 1945, the day after the city was devastated by an atom bomb, a little before noon. The photographer was Yamahata Yasuke, caught unawares and now presented before the world. That was all the information Akira had, nothing more. He was just one among the large nameless body of humanity that witnessed hell. He too, perhaps, succumbed to the radiation, maybe not that day, maybe a couple of days later, maybe many days later. Who knows—Akira did not—perhaps he was one of the survivors, put in strict quarantine in a special hospital in Hiroshima, doomed to carry the grisly memory of that day. That day, looking into the boy's eyes, I saw history embodied—a history that I could follow through to the moment when all of humanity witnessed that reckless terror unleashed upon the world.

I looked around. Akira did not have to explain anything to me. He collected an audiocassette, paid for it and gave it to me. Handy recorders with earphones were supplied free, to be returned after use. The cassette said it all—the story of the devastation, followed by instructions, which way to go, how many steps to walk, when to turn and what to see. Thus, over that two-hour-long journey through history, walking back and forward at will, I grew wiser and through wisdom I gained understanding. Terrible, terrific. A cannibal time.

Akira, who had been silent all along, asked me if we should rest a bit. I looked at him and could see that he was tired. We sat on a threshold in the ruins, broken walls and decayed arches behind us, all threatening to collapse. But thanks to the Japanese passion for the preservation of history, they would never fall. Akira asked me to look up. I did so and saw a heavy wooden plate hanging above me. On it was written just three words, shining brightly: NO MORE HIROSHIMAS

After that terrible journey's end, there could not be a better expression—simple and profound.

'You like it?' Akira asked.

'Great!' I said, and added, 'It is so Japanese.'

'What do you mean?' he asked, a bit unsure about my reaction.

'Because of the minimalism. It's typically Japanese. Like a Japanese painting. Like a haiku,' I tried to explain.

'Haiku, you say!' Akira said, admiringly.

'Yes, haiku. Your poetic form, ancient,' I said, a bit hesitantly. Then, gathering up courage, I recited a three-line haiku, the only one I'd came across in my language, translated by Tagore in his *Japan Jatri* (A visitor to Japan) (1919):

Purono pukur.
Byang-er laph.
Jal-er shabdo.

(An old pond.
The leap of a frog.
The splash of water.)

Tagore called it 'heart's frugality'—a perfect description of the Japanese mindset.

Akira pressed my hand and said, 'Tagore was great. I've read his letters to our great national poet, Yono Noguchi. He did not spare Noguchi when he defended Japanese militarism and the aggression of China.'

'You know all this!' I said, quite elated.

'Yes, I do.' He was proud of Tagore's censure of Noguchi, 'Even today, I can memorize the concluding line of his last letter: "I wish your countrymen whom I love so much not success but remorse." '

I was overwhelmed. I mentioned Nehru's tribute to Tagore on his seventieth birthday: 'He has given to our nationalism the outlook of internationalism.'

Akira smiled.

On our way back to the hotel, Akira told me a story about Marshal Zhukov. I knew the story already, but I let him tell it, and I let myself listen to it as I returned from the ruins of Hiroshima:

30 April 1945. In the middle of the night, Kremlin received a call from the Berlin gate. Zhukov wanted a word with Stalin. Sorry, he had gone off to his Black Sea dacha to rest. At Sochi. According to Stalin's calculations, the war had virtually come to an end.

Zhukov called him at his dacha. Stalin was woken up.

'The war is over,' said Zhukov.

Stalin quipped, 'So, the little game is done!'

Zhukov: 'It's rumoured that Hitler's committed suicide.'

'You couldn't catch the man alive?' The voice came from the other side, unperturbed.

Then followed a conversation, very short. Stalin quickly dismissed Zhukov and asked him to think of tomorrow—the 1st of May . . . May Day . . . Red Square . . .

I felt amused. The story sounded delightfully Chaplinesque. Just a bit. The last sequence of Chaplin's *Shoulder Arms* (1918) flashed before my eyes. Charlie arrests 'the Kaiser' by employing a typical Chaplinesque trick, and there appears on the screen a simple line: *And peace to the world*. And soon the film ends.

One can add to it another of Chaplin's films, *The Great Dictator*, which premiered in 1940. And yet another, *City Lights* (1931)—Chaplin's midnight advice to a heartbroken millionaire— *Tomorrow, the birds will sing*. Years later, in the middle of the night. 30 April 1945. Zhukov heard Stalin saying, '*Think of tomorrow*—the 1st of May . . . May Day . . . Red Square!'

Alone in my room, I remembered what I'd heard on the tape at the Hiroshima memorial:

None of the Allied partners was taken into confidence about the horror that was going to be perpetrated over the next few days. As a matter of fact, perhaps to camouflage the entire operation, the US Air Force dropped anti-war leaflets over Hiroshima and a few neighbouring cities for some days at a stretch before the three bomber aeroplanes appeared in the sky in the early morning of 6 August; and then, without any warning, one of them zoomed down on the city. In an instant, it swooped up again and disappeared into the western sky. That was 6 August 1945, at 0835 hrs, Hiroshima time.

It had taken just a moment—yet the sky erupted into flames, followed by a terrible blast, and in a mere ten minutes a fire raged through the city, the heat rising, red-hot, with temperatures ranging 2,000–7,000°C, reducing the whole area to a burnt-out wilderness. Tongues of flame, a sheet of blazing heat and an unbearably forceful wind rushed through the city, tearing it down, shattering it to shards, burning it to the skies, wiping it away from the face of the earth—all in just a moment. Then came the rains, a ceaseless downpour, black rain, dark and sinister. The river burst its banks, throwing up piles of fish. A magic wand seemed to have silenced forever the barest throb of life.

Yet there were a few who survived. They survived, only to die a few days later. Some clung to life dismally, some fell victim to leukaemia, or cancer, or incurable intestinal diseases. Some lost all their hair, some others found their hair turned totally white, some went blind, some were disfigured, their skin scarred and discoloured. Something that had never happened in the world happened in Hiroshima that day, the handiwork of a single American bomb barely three metres in length, weighing four tons. And three days later, on 9 August, Nagasaki fell in the same manner . . .

There was a gentle knock at the door. I opened it. Akira was standing outside, smiling. He had a book in his hand, a thick volume.

'Are you tired?' he asked, somewhat awkwardly.

'No, not at all. Come!' I said, and let him in.

We had a fairly long session, Akira and I. We talked life, politics, cinema and a great lot on Hiroshima. He handed over the book he'd brought—a pictorial publication on the holocaust, accompanied by text, well researched and well produced, edited by Akira Iwasaki. Title: *Hiroshima*. A gift for me. I looked at him and nodded in appreciation. He told me rather apologetically that politics had to be left out of the book. Apparently, the publishers had a problem with that aspect. I had no problem understanding either him or the publishers. As I leafed through the pages, Akira raised the issue. Soft-spoken by nature, he made his point sharply and powerfully: When the war was virtually over, what was the need for such a mass-killing operation? Why, of all conventional weaponry, the nuclear bomb? War or no war, had anybody heard of dropping an atom bomb? Ever?

Those were the basic questions fermenting within Akira. He did not expect an answer from me, he did not need it. He had the answer: American hegemony! What else?

I did not speak a word, I did not have to. I kept looking deep into his eyes.

He relaxed. He smiled and said, 'Sorry.'

The session came to an end soon after. He said we would have to catch the first flight the next morning. To Tokyo. Then he left.

I was alone in my room. I switched off the light but could not sleep. Suddenly I remembered one of the many adda sessions at home with my son and his university friends, sessions that covered so many topics, a kind of free-for-all. One day, they were discussing the story of the nuclear bomb; they were sharing some exciting revelations, including many apocryphal bits. I was a silent listener that day. Today, on 12 May 2003, as I am writing this chapter on Hiroshima and Akira, I think of Dipankar Home who'd done most of the talking that day. He is now an accomplished research physicist at Bose Institute, and author and co-author of several books. I called him and asked if he could quickly do a write-up of the story of the nuclear bomb for my use. From his office he sent me an e-mail, which I reproduce below:

> Here is the write-up you wanted. I am also faxing it. I wanted to double-check its authenticity against relevant sources. Hence the delay.
>
> In 1939, the discovery of nuclear fission (splitting the uranium nucleus by bombarding it with neutrons and releasing huge energy) in Germany, and the consequent possibility of developing a nuclear bomb, gave rise to the strong fear that the Germans might develop the bomb during the war. This suspicion was compounded by the fact that one of the most leading experts in this area, Werner Heisenberg, had chosen to stay back in Germany during the war and been appointed the head of the German nuclear-energy programme. A large number of eminent physicists subsequently gathered in the US, and the Manhattan Project was launched to develop the nuclear bomb.
>
> This project intensified after Heisenberg visited the German-occupied Denmark and met with eminent Danish physicist Niels Bohr (ironically, Heisenberg's research guide in his early years). The actual content of that meeting still remains shrouded in mystery. But the essential

upshot was Bohr's suspicion that the Germans perhaps knew enough to build a nuclear bomb. He was deeply shaken and soon escaped from Denmark, then met with the Allied scientists and informed them that Heisenberg was actively leading the German effort.

Further, in order to accelerate their own project and get final approval for the bomb from the US President, Einstein was persuaded to write a letter to Roosevelt suggesting that a nuclear bomb was a technically feasible proposition and, therefore, also an effective weapon in the war. In his letter, Einstein recorded his suspicion about nuclear research in Germany and laid stress on the need for the US also developing such a bomb. However, after the bombing of Hiroshima, Einstein admitted that writing such a letter had been 'one great mistake' in his life. If he had not written it, and if the fateful meeting between Heisenberg and Bohr had not taken place, one wonders whether history would have been different.

Evidence gathered after the war indicated that the Germans did not really make any substantial progress in making the bomb, and that Bohr had perhaps received the wrong impression from Heisenberg. Historical studies on this much-debated issue suggest that Heisenberg himself was not too sure whether the Germans would be able to make the bomb. His intention of talking to Bohr at that stage could have possibly been to try to convince the Allied scientists that such a project should not be pursued.

It is hard to know the exact 'truth'. Had the group of Allied scientists not been so apprehensive about a possible German bomb, the Hiroshima–Nagasaki tragedies could have perhaps been avoided.

True, it is hard to know the exact *truth*.

When the war was virtually over, how was it that secret plans were afoot in the US? And why were the major partners of the Allied Forces kept in the dark? Why were secret tests conducted somewhere in New Mexico just 11 days before the bomb fell on Hiroshima? Secrecy was so absolute that news of the Hiroshima attack was a bombshell even for the partners of the Allied Forces. Why all this drama?

Akira Iwasaki's line comes to mind: American hegemony! What else!

Next day, early morning. Our Tokyo-bound plane took off on time. As we were passing over the city, Akira asked me to look out. From above, Hiroshima looked magnificent. A new Hiroshima! A new history! A modern city comparing favourably with any of the cleanest of clean cities in Japan. Gleaming in the sunshine. Incredible!

Akira was not available the next day. He had an appointment with his doctor. A young girl, a reliable interpreter, accompanied me to the largest national theatre to watch the finest Kabuki group in action.

Kabuki is a form of popular traditional Japanese drama with highly stylized songs, dialogues and gestures, performed only by males. Sergei Eisenstein, the great Soviet filmmaker and aesthetician, had been deeply impressed by the form and written several seminal essays on the connection between the language of cinema and Kabuki and coupled the two with the Chinese hieroglyph. I had done my homework on the form even before my plane touched down at Narita Airport. Kabuki had been my agenda number two.

My interpreter and I walked into the huge auditorium, all wooden, opulent in its simplicity. The audience was, however, depressingly thin and composed mostly of elderly folk. The interpreter told me that this entertainment was not meant for the young. What about her, then? She said she had come three times already, but always with the foreign tourists, always on duty. Just as she had come with me.

For the next two hours, I struggled hard to make a connection, but failed. Failed miserably. I could see I was nowhere near Eisenstein. So, during the 15-minute interval, I made a decision: to get out. I did a bit of play-acting; I told my interpreter I had not expected the play to be so long. I had another appointment with a friend to which I needed to go.

She called a taxi, dropped me off at my hotel and directed the driver to take her to the nearest railway station. It was all very swift. I was pretty certain she was quite relieved.

Akira showed up the next morning. He looked much better.

'How did you enjoy the play?' he asked.

I told him the truth. Despite my vigorous homework, I had ultimately, and sadly, failed to connect.

I could see that Akira was neither surprised nor shocked. 'How long did you suffer?' he asked, softly.

Suffer!

I was taken aback. Was this the indulgence of a taskmaster? A touch of irony? I stuck to the truth. I said I'd stayed for two hours only—and he heaved a sigh of relief. He shared another experience, that of a much bigger man, Jean-Luc Godard, who came last year but managed to endure it for only half an hour. Not only that, as he walked out, he had unashamedly broken into a yawn. I cannot vouch for Godard, but I do know that I felt terribly awkward about my exit before the play was over.

Irrespective of either Godard or I being unable to appreciate or understand Kabuki, Eisenstein's enormous volumes on cinema, but also on art, literature, sociology, philosophy, history, politics, even circus—everything he came across—remain unparalleled in the history of aesthetics. That giant of a man is still considered the most innovative aesthetic thinker of the twentieth century. Born in 1898, he died prematurely in 1948, in the middle of the night, sitting in his chair in the reading room, with a yet-to-be-completed thesis on colour film lying in front of him.

On one of my visits to Moscow, to render a silent tribute, I spent a good length of time in his reading room, surrounded by heaps of his books, his wonderful sketches, and my dear friend, Naum Kleiman, the director of the archive, standing beside me.

Madame Kashiko Kawakita, renowned for introducing Japanese cinema to an international audience, invited me to her office. I spent several hours in her archive—Japan Film Library Council— watching films made in Japan as well as elsewhere in the world. Madame Kawakita was such a wonderful lady, and never missed a film festival worth talking about. She was sorry she could not organize a meeting with Akira Kurosawa—he was busy making a film. My wife Gita and I met him later in Moscow and then again at a seminar at Repino on the Baltic Sea, the beautiful health resort of the Soviet filmmakers.

Apart from meeting half a dozen old friends among the filmmakers and film-society activists, and making some new contacts, I watched a few films and visited a few exhibitions, the most fascinating being at the Hakone Open-Air Museum. There were several eating houses in that large complex, and of course Japanese delicacies were an intrinsic part of each menu. Since eating and relishing are two different experiences, I ate many varieties of raw fish—but relished none. Sightseeing simply for the sake of it was not my cup of tea, but people-watching proved to be an eye-opener. I saw people always on the move, busy all the time.

On my last day there, I met that wonderful man, documentary filmmaker Noriaki Tsuchimoto, who had also been on my agenda. I had seen only one non-feature film by Tsuchimoto, just one—but never met him. I'd seen his film in 1972, at a small festival in Nyon, near Geneva. I had been in delightful company: Basil Wright, the doyen of the British documentary, was there. There were six of us on the jury, of which, to my discomfiture, I was made president. We knew nothing about the director; we could collect only a little information about the film. Moritz de Hadeln, then director of Nyon Film Festival, and later of the Berlin Film Festival for many years, laboured hard to organize a good print along with some information about it. He organized the print, but could not present the director.

A mysteriously incurable and fatal disease broke out along the river. The young director rushed there to meet and question a cross-section of fisherfolk. In the film, we saw that he had interviewed the entire community—men and women, young and old—without exception. Continuous interviews, often two hours long, revealed the hidden truth: that behind the dreadful disease was the systematic crime committed by a huge chemical factory on the riverbank. Toxic by-products were thrown into the river, and the matter was criminally downplayed by the management. A number of cameras and crew moved among the fishermen—day in, day out—even followed them to the cities. Finally, when it blew up into a national issue, there was no way but to have an open confrontation between the victims and the management—absolutely spontaneous and therefore absolutely great. Without any kind of script at hand, Tsuchimoto told me when I met him in Tokyo. The last bit—a kind of epilogue, so to say—struck us the most: the quiet dignity of an old fisherman fishing alone in the tranquil midstream, muttering to himself about life in the waters, about the lovely fish, about cooking. All spoken without any malice against anybody. So tender! And so profoundly touching!

The name of the river is Minamata, the name of the disease was Minamata. Tsuchimoto's film was thus also called *Minamata* (1971).

The interpreter who escorted me to my Kabuki viewing—she was requisitioned to me for the last few days of my visit because, again, Akira was not available. He had to be admitted to hospital. He was not keeping well, the young woman told me.

The External Affairs Ministry official called me on the day of my departure. A matter of formality. I thanked him profusely for the warm hospitality and wonderful arrangements. I asked about Akira. He was still in hospital and not likely to be discharged soon, he said. He was suffering from cancer. I had thought as much. I had no way to reach him, alas. When I heard about him much later, Akira Iwasaki was dead. Dead! So I was told. But I could never get the tragic news reconfirmed.

FOUR

Long Years Ago, We Made a Tryst with Destiny,
and Now . . .

Back home. A journey backward, in a time machine, as it were.
From 1979 back to 1947, via Hiroshima–Nagasaki, 6 and 9
August 1945. Now to the historic occasion on Indian soil, 14–15
August 1947. From Delhi, Jawaharlal Nehru's midnight speech to
the people of the country:

> Long years ago we made a tryst with destiny, and now the
> time comes when we shall redeem our pledge, not wholly
> or in full measure, but very substantially. At the stroke of
> the midnight hour, when the world sleeps, India will
> awake to life and freedom.

That was the moment when a new era of history unfolded. To the
accompaniment of dazzling fanfare, a national celebration. Much
against the will of the dissidents—the birth of a nation. On that
historic occasion in Delhi, there was just one notable absentee—
Mahatma Gandhi.

The Mahatma came away to my big city, that same day, that
same night, and stayed for a few days—not out of disgust, not in
self-willed exile, but to fight communalism and to bring the warring

fanatics of the city to their senses. The great killings in 1946 were over but the frenzy resurfaced. The blood did not dry. Neither in East Bengal nor in the West. The Mahatma rushed from one place to the other in search of sanity.

14–15 August 1947. The country celebrated Independence at the same time as it mourned the Partition. On the one hand, people were in a state of tumultuous joy; on the other, filled with anger and despair, shattered to pieces—the homeless from East Bengal and West Punjab crossing the frontiers in successive waves—each and every one in search of a place under the sun. The joy was maddening, but it did not last long, in either of the two neighbouring countries. In the west, the news of communal troubles cast a long shadow, especially in the Indian capital and also of course in Pakistan. Movement of refugees from both sides of the border continued unabated. News of cruelty, murder and destruction compounded with loot and arson spread like wildfire.

The Mahatma, now in Delhi, felt terribly distressed. He sent for the leaders frequently, all of them top administrators, and kept asking for updates. The situation came to such a pass, beyond any control, that once, with his characteristic calm and simplicity, he said, 'I am not in China now, I am in Delhi. Nor have I lost my eyes and ears. If you ask me to disbelieve the testimony of my own eyes and ears . . . I surely cannot convince you nor can you convince me . . . '

The Mahatma felt that he had no choice then but to use his strongest weapon—fasting. He said with tremendous confidence, 'I must expiate through my own sufferings and I hope that my fast will open their eyes to real facts.'

A few days later, everybody believed that a miracle had occurred. The wind shifted—and the result was electrifying. The Mahatma, even though he could not recover from his weakness, continued to have his prayer meetings at his usual evening hour, with the accompaniment of verses read out from the Gita, Quran and Bible.

On 30 January 1948, he was shot dead.

Once again, Nehru's voice on the air, five months after Independence. Grief-stricken, he spoke to the nation:

The light has gone out of our lives and there is darkness everywhere. I do not know what to tell you and how to say it. Our beloved leader, Bapu as we called him, the Father of the Nation, is no more.

Yet, life and governance went on, and still is—people living, loving and desiring, and also, at every turn, fighting and eventually perishing or reliving.

My parents, still in Faridpur, never thought of leaving the home they had so lovingly built and nurtured. Months passed, a year rolled by. The problems kept coming, day after day, and things continued to take a turn for the worse. Finally, forced by circumstances, my parents decided to sell whatever properties they had and leave the country. Everything was sold at a throwaway price, and finally, one day, they arrived at the big city as refugees. Before leaving the house he had built and cared for, my father made a small request to its new occupants: 'I do not want you to promise, but do try, if possible, to preserve the little memorial over there, by the water's edge.'

It was a memorial for our youngest sister, Reba. She had died at the tender age of five. She slipped and fell into our pond. She drowned.

Reba was the dearest of all my sisters and brothers. We grew up in a large family—seven brothers and five sisters. I was the sixth among the brothers, and Reba the youngest among the sisters. And she was the most lovable one—everyone in the neighbourhood was so fond of her. On the fateful day—it was a holiday, as far as I remember—we were having lunch together. Reba left us in the dining room before we'd finished eating and quietly walked down to the ghat. I distinctly remember, the ghat was such a lovely construction—steps leading down to our pond, and a projection, just inches above the water, reaching up to almost a quarter of the pond's breadth—all made out of bamboo poles. We loved walking along the projection, sitting on it and dangling our feet over its edge and into the water. Reba was no exception. She loved to sit right at the front, so as to be able to sway with ease as she hummed to herself. Nobody knew exactly what happened that day, because nobody was there. All we could conjecture was that she walked up to the head of the projection, sat down, dangled her feet into the water and then, without realizing, somehow slipped and slid into the water. When, much later, we began to look for her, she was nowhere—not in the neighbours' houses, no trace of her anywhere. At last, Mejda, my swimmer brother, jumped into the pond and, in a moment, brought out her body—but not her life. She had died under water.

The news of Reba's death spread through the locality. Everyone rushed to us, because everyone loved her. My eldest brother, Sailesh (Dada to us all), then in the big city, sped back home. With him came Jasimuddin, his dear friend, because Reba had been precious to him too. Soon after his arrival, Jasim-da heard bits of the story from some of us and then, without wasting a minute, walked out straight to the killer-ghat. He spent the whole day there. He was offered a cup of tea but he refused. At noon, he was served food—he ate a little. Very little. Late in the afternoon, he called for my mother. She dragged herself to the ghat. Jasim-da embraced her and cried like a child. Then, after some moments of silence, Jasim-da told my mother one of Reba's secrets. Reba had plenty of secrets, some of which only Jasim-da had known. The one he narrated to my mother was from about a month ago. Reba had wanted Jasim-da to promise that one day he would let her stay awake through the night with him, so she could see how and when the flowers, the water hyacinth, bloom at night.

Much later, my mother told me this and many more stories about Reba.

Jasim-da had a poetic streak since the time he was in primary school. When he came of age, he became an eminent poet; even Tagore took loving notice of our dear Jasimuddin. In fact, one of his classic ballads, *Nakshi Kanthar Math* (The field of the embroidered quilt) (1928), a brilliant musical drama was recently staged in Calcutta. All his poems and songs are embedded in the rural soil.

That day, after sundown, Jasim-da came away from the ghat and spent some time with us. Before he left for his home in Gobindapur, four–five miles away from our village, where his father lived, he handed over to my mother a long poem he'd written at the ghat. He cautioned my mother not to let it be published, ever. It was exclusively hers.

It was a poem about Reba.

My mother kept the poem to herself until her death in September 1973. In an envelope. Even when she had left home with my father, she did not forget to carry that precious envelope. When she was cremated, the envelope too was consigned to the flames.

After an interminably long time, in 1990, 47 years after I had left my hometown, my wife and I stood before the same house in the same town, now in Bangladesh, a sovereign state. The house where I spent my childhood and adolescence. In those 47 years, its occupants had changed only once. The man who had purchased the house and other properties from my father passed them on to the new occupants, together with the 'promise' he'd made to my father—to look after the memorial by the water's edge—and then apparently left for Karachi. In those 47 years, strangely, not once had I looked back to my distant past. Could it be because during all those years my mind did not suffer even the tiniest pangs of Partition? If that was so, why now? Why not during the last 15 years, when I had visited Dhaka on several invitations? Why had I turned down requests from my hometown about half a dozen times during those years? At long last, after 47 years, why now?

Honestly, I had no answer.

In my childhood, the trip between Dhaka and Faridpur, though lovely, used to take a full day, always by river transport, a two-tiered ship from Narayangunge, the *Emu* or *Ostrich*. A cruise on the turbulent Padma and then a midstream changeover to a tiny ferry, *Dumdim*, onto a narrow canal, and then, leaving behind the jute and paddy fields on either side, finally to Faridpur. Now, with the incredible growth of the transport system—first, an automobile; then the automobile, complete with its passengers, onto

55

the ferry across the Padma; and then finally, the automobile on the road again. All in four hours.

This time, in 1990, the moment my wife and I reached Dhaka, we decided we would go to Faridpur, even if for only a few hours. For no specific reason. We were in Dhaka for three days to attend an international film festival, and we planned to go off on the fourth day. With us was my young cameraman, Shashi Anand, whose parents had come to India from Rawalpindi during Partition. When they came, they had been refugees, but Shashi was not. He was born in India, born in my big city, and, like me, was made here. As he grew up, his parents had told him many stories about their hometown. Now, he wanted to see for himself what my hometown was like.

That was an unforgettable journey. We, the foreigners from India. And our guide, Abul Khayer, my friend.

As we approached the town, I was visibly tense.

'What's the matter?' our guide asked.

'The canal is up ahead,' I said confidently, and then, to give him a shock, 'And a wooden bridge!'

'The wooden bridge was dismantled just before it could collapse,' said Abul Khayer, 'Now you will see a concrete bridge, a little away, 15 years old.'

Our car crossed the bridge, continued straight on and turned into a lane—all very tidy, civilized and respectable; in my time, this had been the red-light area.

The car stopped in front of a house. We got down.

After the welcome and the pampering and eating were over, we had a bit of a rest. Then we set off in search of the past. On foot.

The memories crowded upon me, spontaneously, one after another. About a hundred local inhabitants or more recognized me, followed us, in twos and threes, their number increasing as we made our way closer to rediscovering the house. I was excited because, with every onward step, I was confronting a host of uncertainties. Uncovering bits of memories. Like Ronald Colman in *Lost Horizon* (1933). And I wanted the locals to allow me to go my own way and not speak a word, even if I got confused and lost my way. That was an experience I will never forget. And I did it—I found it, all by myself. After 47 years!

I stood in front of the house. No one in the crowd around me spoke a word—neither to themselves nor to us. A silence that was truly eloquent!

Gita whispered, 'Can you recognize anything? And them?'

I turned my head. Gita touched me, gently. I wanted to cry but did not.

Someone came forward. He said that the people in front of me were the new occupants of the house. A middle-aged woman, dressed as an ordinary housewife, walked a few steps closer, handed over a bunch of flowers to my wife and said, smiling, 'You are in the house of your father-in-law.'

Gita was visibly touched.

The lady then told me, 'Come, you will see the memorial at the water's edge.'

I was startled. So was Gita, who had heard from me everything about my sister.

'The memorial for Reba, your sister,' the mistress of the house said, softly, with an stress on 'Reba'.

We looked at each other, Gita and I. I felt a lump in my throat.

'Come!' she said once again.

Suddenly, I remembered the Father of the Nation, the Mahatma. I remembered the agonies he had suffered before he was assassinated. If only the Mahatma were here now!

If only I could proudly tell my father that the memorial for his little Reba had been lovingly protected by those who had purchased his house and property. Still preserved by the new owners. Right where it had been built, by the water's edge!

If only I could tell my mother that the soft-spoken daughter of hers was still beside the killer-ghat, where Jasim-da had spent the whole day alone and written that special poem!

Suddenly, there appeared before my eyes the picture of a long-lost son in his mother's embrace—the last meeting between my mother and Jasim-da. Three years before she died. Most probably that was when Jasim-da had just retired as the head of the Bengali department at the University of Dhaka.

That was a memorable occasion, when Jasim-da was conferred a DLitt (*honoris causa*) by Rabindra Bharati University, in appreciation of his creative work. The event over, he stayed back for a few days in my city. He called me a number of times. I was out of town. On my arrival, I called him back. He asked me to come at once to his friend's house and take him to 'Ma'. Ma meant my mother. She was staying with my brother, the third of the brothers, Ganesh, in Naktala, a southern suburb of the city. Our mother was very ill, bed-ridden, suffering acutely from cardiac problems. I told them about Jasim-da, and in half an hour we arrived at the door. The moment the engine 'roared' and the car stopped in front of the house, we heard Ma calling out, 'J-a-s-i-m!'

'M-a-a!' Jasim-da called back. He lost not a moment; rushing out of the car, he made a dash for my mother. I saw them in the middle of the inner courtyard. They were in embrace, the mother and the son. Crying like children.

Quietly walking in and sitting on the porch, I watched them from a distance—watched reverentially.

A face appeared before me, the face of Ritwik—Ritwik Ghatak—the one who cared so much about the facts of Partition! All his life! In his talks, in his films, in his inflamed passions.

'Times have changed and so have I,' said my father, one day in the big city, in 1948, a year after Partition.

My father said it to me and my friends—Salil (Chowdhury), Ritwik (Ghatak), Tapas (Sen), Kalim (Sarafi) and the closest of all my friends, Nripen (Ganguly). They used to come to our Park Circus apartment regularly. Even in the smallest of the four small rooms marked for me, we made ourselves perfectly comfortable. My mother was a constant supplier of tea, and my father used to walk in, unannounced, and listen to us. At that time, we were bubbling over with youthful enthusiasm and wanted to be a *somebody* in one or other aspect of show business—theatre, cinema, et al. My father loved the adda but in his presence, more often than not, we were a little uncomfortable.

'Do not identify me as a refugee, I am an insider, one of you,' my father used to say all the time. 'Neither my wife nor I are so regretful, as you boys might think. No, we are not refugees.'

Yes, indeed, my father was a brave man and never worried about dying an ordinary death. He died in 1954. Bibekananda Mukhopadhyay, distinguished editor of the important daily *Jugantar*, wrote the lead story in his editorial. That was how my father's life ended.

Ours was not a gang of five but more—seven, eight, nine, even ten—all aspiring to be not less than eminent in our respective arena. Unmistakably, our most unrestrained meeting place was a small teashop, Paradise Café, where the owner cared more for the races and much less for the shop. So, realizing that we were well-meaning people, he left his teashop to us, for our use. The use was less for consuming tea because each cup cost money; it was mostly for adda, which cost nothing. One way or other, Paradise Café was our own and was treated as the seat of discourse, so to say. More often than not, such addas used to run for five–six hours at a stretch. Except for one—Hrishikesh Mukherjee, who was on the payroll of New Theatres—we were all practically unemployed, not doing much in particular, except nurturing dreams, and so time was no factor. We were planning to be 'big' and that was our only source of sustenance—*our tryst with destiny*.

One day, I located a much sought-after American periodical, a rare copy, rare in this part of the subcontinent, the American Communist Party's cultural organ, *Masses and Mainstream*. The one I located was the latest edition. Apart from the essays and reports, each of which was supposed to be great reading for all of us, the particular edition carried a long poem by Pablo Neruda, 'The Fugitive' (1948), written from somewhere in the Americas. From 'somewhere in the Americas', because, to outsmart the police, it was obligatory on the part of the publishers to be extremely cautious about the whereabouts of the great Latin American poet who, of late, had fallen from official grace and so deserved to be given adequate cover. For obvious reasons, I did not waste a moment and rushed to Paradise Café. The house was full, as if the entire gang had come to know about the periodical, and particularly about Pablo Neruda.

Everybody knew I was not very good at reciting poetry. But because I had made the exciting discovery, I could not resist the temptation to read the poem out myself. Drinking a glass of water, coughing a little to clear my throat, slowly and perhaps gracefully, I started reading.

It was a very long poem, covering eight to ten pages. As I continued reading, everybody was enraptured. Halfway to the end, I came to a particular line when, one afternoon, hot and humid, 'the fugitive', having had an aimless walk for a long time, went to a nearby drugstore and, to quench his thirst, bought a bottle of Coca-Cola.

Coca-Cola!

Each of my listeners yelled. Yelled in a fit of disbelief.

In those days, when the McCarthy witch-hunts were at their peak in the United States, and when even Chaplin was treated in a manner unacceptable to any civilized society, a hate campaign against the Federal Bureau of Investigation had spread spontaneously all over the world. Reportedly, there have been extensive files on Chaplin by the FBI, covering a period of 50 years and running into more than 1,900 pages.

Since the fanatics always go to extremes, the extremists among the hardcore Marxists in India would surely give a mandate to boycott the popular American beverage. Expecting such a mandate very soon, many of our people had already begun to say no to Coca-Cola. So, when Neruda said that 'the fugitive' bought Coca-Cola from an American drugstore, and said it to all his readers, our whole gang yelled in instant disbelief. I also lent my voice to the collective yell, even though I was not a card-carrying member of the Communist Party. But a moment later, all of us realized that

Neruda, after all, was Neruda! As a result, while we continued to despise McCarthy and his despicable witch-hunts, at Paradise Café we decreed that the ban (!) on Coca-Cola be withdrawn forthwith. A great relief, indeed! Not that any of us had money enough to buy a Coca-Cola to quench our thirst.

This and so many other stories from our time at Paradise Café are still preserved in my memory. The endless hours we spent there. Learning, unlearning and growing. Where, through unceasing dialogue and continuous brain-warming, we became more careful, if not more wise—in life and art.

Gita knew all these stories and many more. I told her everything. She understood what the stories were all about. Gita was also beginning to go deeper. One day I bought a book from my favourite book stall, a little volume, and presented it to her—my first gift, 'with love and admiration'. It was a book by Julius Fucik, Czechoslovakia's political activist, arrested by the Nazis. Arrested, tortured and thrown into a concentration camp. Once, after he was beaten to jelly and left unconscious, the doctor came to examine him. For the dying and the dead, it was just a formality. Strangely enough, instead of issuing the customary death certificate, the doctor wrote a quick note and left the cell in disgust. The note read: 'He has the constitution of a horse.'

Fucik survived and was once again able to write. The diary he wrote clandestinely was smuggled out by a Nazi sentry and handed over to those who eventually published it. Immediately on its publication in the original Czech, the book was translated into numerous languages and circulated the world over.

My gift to Gita was that same book, *Notes from the Gallows*, in Bengali translation, titled *Phnashi-r Mancho Thekey*.

Gita was a girl from the suburb of Uttarpara, 20 km away from my city. When I saw her for the first time amid a group of people, I was impressed by her looks. Extraordinarily ordinary, shy and graceful. The like of hers I found later in Smita Patil, one of the most powerful actors of Indian cinema. We always met in a group, but after several meetings, we discovered that, despite the people around us, we would possibly fall in love very soon. We got married seven years later. Remembering Billy Wilder's lovely film, a friend of mine called our affair *The Seven Year Itch*.

I vividly remember one incident, because it is worth remembering, when, one evening, we realized that in the course of time we would be destined to build our future, all by ourselves.

Those were the days when we started avoiding the larger group. One day, Gita and I were supposed to meet. She was coming to the city to stay with her aunt for two weeks. To rehearse with a theatre group for a major role she was playing. We decided that I would take a local train from Howrah station, collect her from her home and drop her to her aunt's. Everything went smoothly; I got to the station on time. I browsed at the bookstall, scanned the shelves, took my pick and then broke into a run to catch the train—which had set off by then. The book I purchased was the Penguin edition of *A Case for Communism* (1949). I heard about this gem by William Gallacher, member of the Communist Party of Great Britain and the sole Communist member in the House of Commons. Right from the first page, the book was a great read, stranger than fiction. I looked at my watch, looked out and immediately realized that the train was running by the loop line— not by the main line. I got down quickly at the next station, hurriedly took another train to put myself on the right track. When I reached Gita's home, I was already late. The sun was setting.

On our way back, we took a shorter route to the city by crossing the Ganges. We decided we would walk along the bridge over the river and take a bus from the other end of the bridge. But neither of us could resist the temptation of watching the sunset.

As we got to the middle of the bridge, stopped and stood close to the parapet. We looked beyond, we looked down. The river was flowing below us, and the ripples dashed against the pillars, the lively sound rising and falling. The wind blew gently but there was not a whisper to be heard. All was quiet on all fronts. Irresistible!

Moments passed, and then the inevitable happened. I clasped her hand for the first time in my life and drew her close. Instantly, *A Case for Communism* slipped from my hand and dropped into the darkness below, the water gurgling on and on.

Never after did I buy another copy, or read the rest of it. I don't know why!

My father had a wonderful rapport with Gita. He liked her for some very sound reasons. He liked her for her arguments, for her story telling, for her ability to recite poetry, for being a good listener. He gave her a name of his own choice—Kalyani. All this much before we got married.

One day, my father called Gita, took her aside and told her a secret of his life. About his affair with his young aunt, younger than him, sweet and serene, widowed at a very early age. But there were social constraints. He still remembered her, he confessed. My father said it all to her and then requested Gita to keep the story to herself. To not tell me, to never let me know.

Then, after a few moments of silence, he asked Gita, 'Do you know whom I have quoted just now?'

Gita did not.

'A variation of a line from *Enoch Arden*,' my father said, 'Alfred Tennyson's masterpiece.'

He then narrated to Gita the sad story of Enoch, and told her how much he loved Tennyson and his *Enoch Arden* (1864) and especially the line he'd just quoted: *Not to tell her, never to let her know.*

This was a year before we got married. Gita kept it a secret. Only after my father's demise did she tell me the story of his clandestine affair.

My father wanted to see Gita on the stage. He never had the chance.

FIVE

We Make Things Spectacular,
but Not by Their Exceptional Qualities . . .

Jotting idly, scribbling aimlessly, crumpling up my half-informed thoughts and tossing them away and finally leafing through my clumsy diary, I began to take my pick from my randomly written entries—trivial, personal, some about important events in India, some about significant moments elsewhere in the world, all jumbled up, all dating back to the early 50s.

In 1950, great Soviet filmmaker Vsevolod Pudovkin and one of the greatest of actors, Nikolay Konstantinovich Cherkasov, came to my big city and spent a busy week. In 1951, a Bengali book of mine, on the life and art of Charlie Chaplin, had been published. It was called just that, *Charlie Chaplin*, not really an ambitiously attempted title. In the same year, Jean Renoir came with his cameraman and nephew, Claude Renoir, to make his film, *Le fleuve* (*The River*). On 10 March 1953, Gita and I got married, with absolutely no fanfare nor any money—not even a bank account to either of our names. On 24 September 1954, my father died a quiet death. The same year, on 21 October, our first and only son Kunal was born.

In-between, in 1952, a great event took place in Calcutta and three other cities, on a massive scale, and for the first time in the country—the International Film Festival of India. After a weeklong session in New Delhi, the festival came to my city; then it would go to Bombay and finally to Madras. The Directorate of Film Festivals did not exist at that time. The festival was entirely conceived and organized by the Ministry of Information and Broadcasting. A stupendous feat! When it came to my big city, it took just one day for all of us to realize that it was an outstanding festival. All-time international greats had been selected and screened in a number of theatres scattered all over the city. The selection had been meticulous, and the programme was curated with professional finesse. Whether a film was one or three years old, or even older, was not taken into consideration. The best of films was all that mattered, the best and never before seen in this part of the continent. It was a non-competitive, non-exclusive festival, entirely unrestricted. It was an event that truly shook my city!

The films that had the greatest impact on my friends and me were the Italian ones. We'd read a lot about postwar neorealism but had not so far seen any films of that genre. We'd read about Roberto Rossellini and Vittorio De Sica, but not heard much about Cesare Zavattini. And it was Zavattini who summed up neorealism in a few pithy words: we make things spectacular 'not through [their] exceptional, but through [their] normal qualities'.

Allegedly, the American producer cited an example:

This is how *we* would imagine a scene with an aeroplane. The plane passes by . . . a machine gun fires . . . the plane crashes. And this is how *you* would imagine it. The plane passes by . . . the plane passes by again . . . the plane passes by once more . . .

67

Zavattini concurred:

> But we have still not gone far enough. It is not enough to
> make the aeroplane pass by three times; we must make it
> pass by twenty times.

According to Zavattini, the fact of an aeroplane crashing is also a reality, but only in exceptional cases. It's normal quality is to fly, and fly, and fly. Thank god neorealists do not invent.

Simplicity and austerity inextricably entwined. The quintessence of neorealism! And, true, this was neorealism made easy. Of course, there were other films of extraordinary power, such as those by Akira Kurosawa and Jacques Tati, the latter reminding me constantly of Chaplin. In the post-Chaplin period, Tati stands out foremost. Tati's original inspiration was Max Linder, who made his screen debut in 1905 and killed himself in a suicide pact with his wife in 1925. Linder was largely responsible for the creation of the classic style of slapstick comedy. So Tati's first intellectual teacher was Linder; Chaplin came next. Tremendous. Tati's best film, to my mind, is *Jour de fête* (*The Big Day*) (1949).

Since its inception in 1948, four years before the festival, the Calcutta Film Society, founded by Satyajit Ray and Chidananda Dasgupta, had been consistent in its efforts to present its members and guests with various examples of world cinema. Its attempt to build an awareness of cinema was, indeed, commendable. But, all said and done, a film society anywhere in the world tends to be restricted to its members who eventually earn the distinguished status of 'individual activist'. Status symbols, as such, fail to lead a movement to its desired end.

So a festival of the kind that came to the city was exactly what we had been looking for, not just once every few years but as an annual occurrence—we wanted continuity, we wanted the involvement of a large number of people and, in fact, to keep multiplying that number and, in the process, spread film literacy all over the country.

Nevertheless, the movement generated by film societies cannot and should not be undermined, and it will continue to function as it has done since the beginning. The festival of the kind that we witnessed in 1952, with similar festivals to follow, was the logical extension of the film-society movement. The film-society screenings would carry on through the year, and an international festival was held just once a year. The festival did go on to become a regular national feature much later, from 1965 onwards.

The festival was over, but the mood of festivity did not wane. So much so that even the insiders in the studios carried on discussions about films they had seen and loved.

Outside the studios, the noise was more intense. Surpassing all, the story that went down in world history was the one made by an intrepid band of young outsiders, headed by their leader, Satyajit Ray—a man of profound integrity—ably assisted by his cameraman and his art designer, Subrata Mitra and Bansi Chandragupta, respectively. They made an aggressive infiltration from outside, and it worked. An event of unusual measure—*Pather Panchali*. With the film's release, Ray embarked on an extraordinary journey, one that made a spectacular beginning and seemed to know no end. The country was proud of Ray, and so was the world.

At home, we were three—Gita and I and our lovely child. But it was a rather dreary life that we were living. At one point of time, I lost my cool and even thought of setting aside cinema and going back to what I once used to do, during my Paradise Café days.

Pressed by financial constraints, I removed myself from our marathon adda sessions for five months. During that time, I took up a job as a medical representative in the Bombay-based pharmaceutical firm Cipla. In a week, I was packed off to Uttar Pradesh in North India, with my base in Kanpur, an ideal place for marketing. I travelled through the neighbouring towns and did my job as assigned.

For two months, my bosses scrutinized my performance and felt I was ideal for the job. I became their blue-eyed boy. They were delighted that eminent consultants were prescribing their medicines; that I was getting them good business. Did that mean I was a good 'retailer' of the company's products? Did that prove that I could explain the chemistry of the medicines fairly well? Honestly, I did not know as much about the products as I did about the stories of the Sepoy Mutiny. And who did not know that it had all started in Barrackpore in Bengal in 1857 and erupted violently in Cawnpore (Kanpur)? All I did was meet the doctors, speak a few words about the Cipla products and then switch over to the history that I loved to talk about.

I left the job after five months. It was insufferable!

Anyway, after the great debacle on my film front, I did not repeat my performance and somehow survived the personal humiliation. After hibernating for two years, I made my second film *Neel Akasher Neechey* in 1958, produced by famous singer-composer Hemanta Mukherjee, and then my third film in 1960, *Baishey Shravana*, which made me feel proud of myself. Since then, I did not have to look back, even though most of my films were failures at the box office. I collapsed, I survived, I kept going my own way. All through my career. It sounds incredible now, but that was my reality. Success, material and aesthetic, came at intervals and even in a big way. But I never ceased to be a controversial film-maker. I took it all in the spirit that it deserved—*The truth is always controversial.*

A short flashback here. While my bosses at the pharmaceutical firm treated me very well, internally I was suffering. I had once gone to Jhansi on a business tour. That was where I watched the wonder that was history at the same time as I continued to sell medical products. Meeting the doctors, most particularly the consultants, talking less about the medicines (about which I did not know much), and trying to talk more about the history of nineteenth-century Jhansi, I slowly grew bored. Then one day, on a hired bicycle, I rode along a lonely avenue and arrived at a lovely spot. There were boulders everywhere, big and small, all standing immobile for ages, with practically no vegetation around them. The time was almost evening, the western horizon was changing colour. Everything except the sky seemed dead, desolate. I could almost hear my own heart beating. It was terrible, it was inhuman, it was so absolutely indifferent. At least to me, and to my mind. Only an hour ago, I had grown sick of people because they seemed to me so anonymous, so self-absorbed and physical, and, now, having come to a place where I thought I would enjoy solitude, I hated it.

Suddenly, from behind a boulder on which I had sat down, a boy appeared, hardly ten, looking like a beggar. He stood before me, his eyes shining bright. I smiled and he smiled back. I pulled out a ten-rupee note, a large sum in those days, and gave it to him. He could not believe it. I drew him close, patted him on the shoulder and gave him a gentle push. The boy ran away with the money, turned back once from a distance, his eyes gleaming, and then disappeared. Instantly, I felt I was a different man altogether. I sprang to my feet and shouted at the top of my voice into the emptiness: *Dyakh-re shala-ra, kemon aami nirbaashan-e aachhi!* (See bastards, how I'm stuck in exile!) There wasn't a soul around. It was the first time I'd spoken Bengali in the last three days—it was Greek in Jhansi. Could there be a streak of madness in me? Or, to quote Jacques Tati, was it *inspired nonsense?*

I returned to my hotel, shut myself up in my small room and stood before the tall mirror. I could see myself from top to toe. As I looked deep into the eyes of my 'double', I wanted to see more of 'it'—all of 'it'. Without a care in the world, I threw off all my clothes. There stood my 'double', stark naked, face to face with me. Was the look menacing? The double's? Or mine? I do not remember. I remembered the 'talk' I had with 'him', though:

> There you are, Mr Mrinal Sen, you who've read so much on cinema, written substantially on its aesthetics, made frantic efforts to impress others! Now, here you are, Mr Sen, a dawai-walla [medicine seller], who once wanted to be a filmmaker! Didn't you, Mr Sen, manage to hook a funder but then backed out, afraid to make a lousy film? Oh no! Serve your bosses well, rot here and try to get an increment. To feel bored is not your business, you cannot afford it, can you?

I made faces at myself, muttered words in all the languages I knew, giggled and laughed and made all kinds of absurd gestures and finally, unable to control myself, began to cry. I cried like a child. All alone in a hotel room in Jhansi!

After three days, I sent a long telegram to the management in Bombay and resigned.

Once again, back to my big city! Once again, to Paradise Café! Once again, to our marathon addas!

Following *Baishey Shravana* in 1960, I seized my courage in both hands and continued to make films one after another. But in one case I was compelled to make a rather weak compromise—I tried to go commercial with *Abasheshe* (And at last) (1963), a stupid comedy on divorce. It was sad and very foolish of me; in an unguarded moment, I surrendered to the silly dictates of my producers. It happened only once—never again. I went back to being on my guard again. I did face controversies. I confronted them all, I fought, I survived and, realizing that I needed to expand my area of operations, also corrected my own conclusions. That, after all, is a positive sign of growth.

In 1965, a big controversy was raised over *Akash Kusum* (Up in the clouds), where the protagonist, a modern young man with a less-than-modest lifestyle, wanted to cross the wealth barrier in a desperate bid to change his life. He put up an innocent bluff before a young girl he happened to meet. Frequent meetings thereafter forced him to pile up the bluffs. His friend, well placed in life, cautioned him about his actions, but he turned a deaf ear. Then the inevitable happened—he reached a dead end. Finally, the young man emerged wiser but not without paying heavily for his bluffs. I presumed it would be great fun watching the film, but I framed it in a manner that caused it to end in despair.

This is how the controversy began. A review appeared in the city's leading daily, the *Statesman*. It was not very positive but not entirely negative either. Ashish Burman, author of the story on which the film was based, wrote a sharp rejoinder. Then Ray called me and said he was going to write a short piece without hurting me. And that set the ball rolling. In his inimitable style, Ray made

73

a sarcastic comment about the author of the story and was obliquely critical about the film too. Though a long-time friend of Ray, Burman hit back. And I too joined the fray. It all began as a sort of wordplay, one dropping names, one dropping a bombshell, another dropping three or four, even launching a missile or two. The battle continued for about two months. By the end of it, there were about a hundred people writing! Ashish, Ray and I were crossing swords; the others were commenting, for or against. All in the columns of 'Letters to the Editor', all in the *Statesman*! Four or five or six in a column, sometimes five or six more in an additional column. It was a wordy battle, but not signifying very much. Finally, it was nobody's gain and nobody's loss.

The edited version of the controversy involving only Ashis, Ray and I featured in a book titled *Les visiteurs de Cannes* (The visitors at Cannes), published in 1992, for the 45th anniversary of the festival. It was a beautiful book about Cannes, about the filmmakers who were regulars, written primarily by themselves—by Kurosawa, Fellini, Antonioni and plenty of others—their thoughts, their sketches, their diaries, their sentiments. A very lovely publication!

Around the same time, or even earlier, from 1960, my Paradise Café friends had been growing steadily, going from strength to strength.

Ritwik Ghatak—the tallest, the thinnest and the most daring of us all—was always on the eternal quest for a greater truth. He used to say, 'I look for a language which will talk less, which will mostly suggest, which will not be loaded with "references" and which will lead me to *archetypal images*.' People loved his films, and had their problems too. As did I.

Tapas Sen grew into a lighting wizard, experimenting with light and shade, 'dividing the light from darkness', playing with umbra and penumbra, with diverse shades in-between and with inducing particular moods through each variant. He was very much in demand, by all the theatre groups especially, whether big or small.

Salil Chowdhury got an opportunity and was already one of the finest composers in Indian cinema, combining Western styles with Eastern. A stupendous leap from the folk variety was his forte. As a lyricist of different moods, he was unparalleled.

Hrishikesh Mukherjee, the single earning member in our group at one point of time, migrated to Bombay and very effectively struck a balance between art and commerce, earning the Bombay film industry's love and respect.

And despite a struggling career at the beginning—just like the rest of us—Bansi Chandragupta, born and bred in Kashmir, migrated to my city out of love and then became one of the most creative art designers in Indian cinema.

I remember, during one of my trips to the United States, possibly in 1975, at a lecture theatre in Chicago where one of my films was to be screened and I was to deliver a lecture, I met an Indian man who said, admiringly, 'I am proud of you and your friends at Paradise Café.' Who was the man? I wondered. Then he told me, quite proudly, that during our days at Paradise Café, he had been one of its employees, serving tea to the customers.

'What do you do now?' I asked.

He replied as if he had committed a crime: 'I am now teaching English at a private college in Chicago.'

It was now my turn to say how proud I was of him, a teacher of English but once a tea boy in a backstreet of my city.

On the theatre front, I was overwhelmed by what I saw on stage—
stark reality presented with extraordinary skill. Way back in the
40s, I'd watch every show, be it in the city or outside it—in the
theatres but also on temporarily erected stages inside parks and
even in fields. In addition, there were various other events—ballets,
ballads, musicals, etc. All these went into wide circulation during
the war years, and the year of the Bengal famine. They were all
about a society ruled by the colonial masters and their native
lackeys.

I never missed any. One play in particular, Bijon Bhattacharya's
Nabanna (Harvest) (1944), and two events: the Ramleela (a
traditional musical, now modernized, redefined and restructured),
and *Gandhi–Jinnah Meeting Again* (a ballet projecting the demand
of the common people) were the biggest draw among all classes of
people. I was an outsider, but like many others, I got terribly
involved, both thematically and artistically. The group that
presented all these events was a pan-Indian organization called the
Indian Peoples' Theatre Association. The motto it coined was most
befitting: People's Theatre Stars the People.

I wondered how, despite remaining an outsider, I became an
inseparable part of the movement. There was magic in their
events—that's why. There was magic in their commune living—
that's why. I was never a participant, neither in their events nor in
their commune life. But I was one with them, one of them, in spirit.
Was that why I decided at that time itself that I should be in show
business? Perhaps yes!

However, a big change came with Independence. Along with
the infighting in the like-minded political parties, there was
infighting on the aesthetic front. As a result, the stability of the
group was weakened. Soon after, it disintegrated. It was a big blow

to IPTA! Though it was unavoidable in an independent sovereign state. The split, as I understood, was partly due to a clash of personalities but more because of conflicting views among the mentors. The group broke up; some of them carried on with the courage of conviction, the rest sank below the mark. The most powerful fragment, and professionally the most equipped, was the one led by actor-producer Sombhu Mitra, solid as a rock, setting a glowing trend and creating a legacy entirely his own.

At that point of time, the one who stood most alone was Bijon Bhattacharya. Incredibly creative, right from the birth of IPTA in Bengal, Bijon did not know how to organize a robust team. So unlike Sombhu Mitra!

Around the same time, and time and again, there have been trends and trendsetters appearing as new men in a new theatre. Groups formed, and individuals came up, each in different form and with different content; some of them even crossed the frontiers of proscenium theatre—their shows were 'on the go'. And as a theatre lover, I was very drawn to them because, in a highly conformist society like ours, anything that is offbeat deserves attention.

Controversy notwithstanding, Utpal Dutt and Badal Sircar, operating at extremes, brought a fresh breath of air to Bengali theatre.

One instance from Utpal Dutt's play *Kallol* (1965), a play on India's naval mutiny, can be safely presented in this context. Utpal and his technicians built a narrow extension in the theatre—a kind of appendix, projecting from the middle of the proscenium down almost to the centre of the auditorium. Several times during the play, Dutt made his players walk down that long platform and move stealthily upward; he even made them stay on it for a while and play their part. It was very much a new experience in Indian theatre, and Dutt's audience did not fail to make note of it. This and some more oddities gave the play an altogether different look—the audience following the actors, as they moved back and forth and diagonally upward, and listening even in total darkness.

About Badal Sircar, I will say that he did a courageous act by grounding his theatre in the city's public parks and allowing his actors to interact with their audience. His actors, without any make-up, spoke their lines and made mathematically precise movements. A fascinating experience, rejecting both stage and proscenium.

Apart from acting in plays, such as in Bijon Bhattacharya's, Gita performed in a number of Utpal Dutt's plays, *Kallol* in particular, and loved acting with his group. She loved acting on the whole. In the 50s, she had gone to the villages and acted in the open fields, both in summer and winter. Even the unlettered villagers loved those plays, because the themes were about the contemporary reality of rural life, their sufferings and struggles. Once, even when she was pregnant, she could not avoid a 'call show', because the play was part of a conference of landless farmers. The leaders said it was important; there was no way for her to say no.

The new men and women of the new theatre were all dedicated workers.

Those were the days, a long time ago—from the 1950s to the mid-60s.

FIGURE 1. Kali Banerjee in
Neel Akasher Neechey (1958).
A ridiculous ban was imposed on
the film for three months.

FIGURE 2. Gnanesh Mukherjee
with Madhabi Mukherjee in
Baishey Shravan (1960). With
this film, I made a quite entry
into the global scene.

FIGURE 3. *Akash Kusum* (1965). It generated a 'delicious', unending controversy that had the intellectual fraternity in knots.

FIGURE 4. Banumati Devi in *Matira Manisha* (1966). The rule of the patriarch.

FIGURE 5. Utpal Dutt and Suhasini Mulay in *Bhuvan Shome* (1969).
'Big Bad Bureaucrat Reformed by Rustic Belle'.

FIGURE 6. Satya Bannerjee in *Calcutta 71* (1972).
A history of the exploited, of the oppressed . . .

FIGURE 7. Simi Garewal and Dhritiman Chatterjee in *Padatik* (1973).

FIGURE 8. The line between self-criticism and slander is slender but unbreakable.

FIGURE 9. Filming *Chorus* (1974).
A satirical fantasy that coincided with the promulgation of the Emergency.

FIGURE 10. Directing *Mrigayaa* (1976).
A big game is a big game, a prey a prey.

FIGURE 11. Vasudeva Rao (*above*) in *Oka Oori Katha* (1977).

FIGURE 12. A devastating story of poverty and strange idiosyncrasies.

FIGURE 13. Sreela Majumdar and Arun Mukherjee (*above*) in *Parashuram* (1979).

FIGURE 14. On the plight of pavement dwellers.

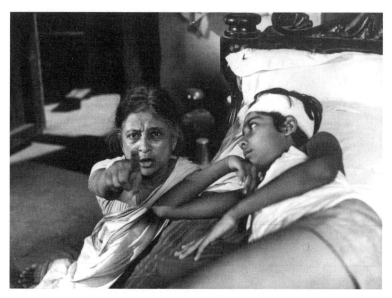

FIGURE 15. Gita Sen and Kausik in *Ek Din Pratidin* (1979).

FIGURE 16. Exploring connivance in a patriarchal and conformist society.

FIGURE 17. Smita Patil and Nilkantha (*above*) in *Akaler Sandhane* (1980).

FIGURE 18. Rooted in the ineluctable connection between past and present.

FIGURE 19. Filming *Chaalchitra* (1981).

FIGURE 20. Indranil and Debapratim in *Kharij* (1982).
A slap on the class I belong to.

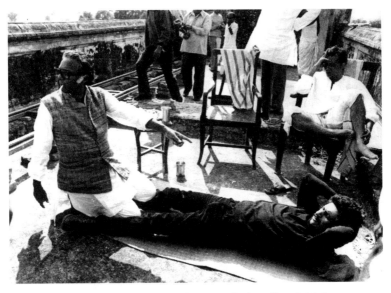

FIGURES 21 and 22. On the sets of *Khandhar* (1984)
with Naseeruddin Shah (*above*) and Shabana Azmi (*below*).

FIGURE 23. Om Puri, Shabana Azmi and Naseeruddin Shah in *Genesis* (1986).

FIGURE 24. A world built or gained is but the world lost.

FIGURE 25. *Ek Din Achanak* (1989).
The crisis deepends—we cannot correct our conclusions.

FIGURE 26. Soumitra Chatterjee in *Mahaprithibi* (1991).
Conflicts unresolved.

FIGURES 27 and 28. Dimple Kapadia (*above*) in *Antareen* (1993).
A woman confined by circumstances.

FIGURE 29. Nandita Das in *Aamar Bhuvan* (2002).

FIGURE 30. Celebrating life and death at its rhythmic beat.

FIGURE 31.

SIX

I Live in the Instant Present.
I Invest the Past with Contemporary Sensibilities . . .

All my life, I have lived in the present. As everybody does, I too encounter the past, distant and not so distant, or visit museums or go on trips to historical sites. But my spontaneous reactions have always been to look at the relics not as museum pieces but as contemporary phenomena. In other words, I invest the past with contemporary sensibilities. This is a statement which, I believe, is abundantly illustrated by what I have written so far—by *connecting* the past with the present, by having a continuous dialogue between the past and the present.

To connect is the thing. An example comes to mind. An incident of no apparent consequence. But deep within me, it caught me unawares and suddenly opened the door between past and present.

It happened at Sarnath—that great Buddhist centre near Varanasi where the Buddha, having attained Enlightenment under the Bodhi tree in Gaya, delivered his first sermon and turned the Wheel of Law. January 1951, my first visit to Sarnath. I was then working a medical representative elsewhere in Uttar Pradesh. I'd taken a day off and gone to Sarnath. That was before I had come to cinema.

I was all alone there, pacing up and down, looking at the columns and the famous Lion Capital. Aided by a guide, I then made my way down the steps, to the rooms arrayed in a line. Those were the rooms, I was told, where the Buddhist monks—the chosen few—used to live. Walking down the corridor, I stood before a door, a small door, more a frame with a small opening. Since I was taller than the door, I had to stoop to enter. And that was precisely when I was caught by some mysterious force. The moment I stooped, some magic worked upon me—and I turned into a monk. Just for a moment. As I stood up straight again inside the room, I returned to my own self again, a medicine seller, taking a day off and being a tourist.

It was amazing; it was a *rite* that I performed, a *rite* that I enacted, the very simple *rite* of stooping to enter, with absolutely no religious compulsion—yet the magic worked. Just that act of stooping or bending, which the monks at the time of the Buddha used to do, as many times as they required to come and go from their rooms. I had done a kind of re-enactment, and instantly a mysterious door opened before me—a door between the distant past and the instant present. And, without my knowing it, I attained—should I say—*Enlightenment*!

Here is another story, about my trip to Dhauli, near Bhubaneswar, capital of ancient Odisha or Kalinga as it was known then.

In 1965, I went to Dhauli on a professional mission: I was assigned by the Government of India to make an hour-long documentary on 5,000 years of Indian history with an emphasis on the officially approved concept of Unity in Diversity. When the film was completed, I titled it *Moving Perspectives* (1967). To make the film, I decided to travel all over the country and capture all that I felt I could use—museum exhibits, bits of historical relics, historical documents and so on. Dhauli was very much on my agenda—the capital of Kalinga, where Emperor Ashoka fought a battle, a sanguinary battle, his last battle, before he turned a devout Buddhist.

It was all quiet in Dhauli when we arrived—my crew and I, and two 'extras'—my son and Gita. They had not been there before, so I combined my professional schedule with a bit of domestic entertainment. It turned out to be lovely trip. In the mid-60s, it was almost barren, with just one temple somewhere on the site. An undulating plain, with cattle grazing and the river Daya flowing silently. In the middle of the site, on a mound, stood the historic figure of a white elephant—the Buddha motif and, most importantly, Emperor Ashoka's edict inscribed on a rock. There were plenty of such edicts inscribed on rocks and pillars, all done under the direct supervision of Emperor Ashoka. They were scattered right through the pan-Ashokan empire, stretching all the way to Afghanistan. The one at Dhauli was Edict Number 13. Such edicts bore evidence of the great metamorphosis which the emperor went through after the cruel battle of Kalinga. The text here, as in the other edicts, was a kind of atonement for what the emperor considered his misdeeds, and also his pledge: 'I, Priyadarshi, Beloved of the Gods . . . ' That was how the text began; what followed was the claim that the king looked upon his 'subjects' as his dear 'children', and that anyone who did any offence to his 'children'—officer or whosoever he might be—would be punished. These and many more assuring words formed the text. All of them were messages aimed at restoring peace among his 'subjects'.

I sat before the holy rock and tried to find a vantage position for the movie camera. The sun was blazing, a hot and sultry day; we were extremely uncomfortable. There was no vegetation around, no tree to offer any shade. Suddenly, I spotted a woman, very old, her skin wrinkled and her body bent over with infirmity, sitting a few yards away. What business could she have here, at such an awkward place and at such an awkward time? Perhaps she was keeping an eye on the cattle grazing in the distance.

I looked at her and smiled. She smiled back.

Instantly, there was a mysterious connection. I neither remembered nor realized how the chemistry worked, but it did. And a door opened, a door between the past and the present. And I found myself back in the past, more than 200 years before the birth of Christ. Thus, turning into an ancient, I looked at the old woman who had lived in Ashoka's time. I was irresistibly drawn to the strange world of Ashoka. The woman, now transformed, looked oppressed, wronged and humiliated. She had lived to see that monstrous battle, a battle that left her drained of all hope for survival. All she had now were the ruins, and the blood flowing down the river Daya. The river had no water then—only blood, the blood of the people of Kalinga.

Then, again, travelling a long way into the future, leaving behind the Ashokan past, it was she, that same woman, now looking at me. It was she with her cattle in the field, it was she sitting at the foot of history—Edict Number 13, which carried not a word about the battle (it might have acted as provocation to the survivors). But in a number of texts elsewhere, or perhaps on most of the others, there are inscribed words about the deplorable slaughter and/or deportation of thousands. Thanks to the Archaeological Survey of India, those texts still survive.

I was already back to my own world, to my own self—one assigned with the production of a documentary which would include a glowing sequence on Ashoka's conversion to Buddhism.

Having made my journey to the past and back to the present, I was convinced that the mention of the Kalinga carnage had been deliberate. And to be honest, I did not have to make any conscious effort to arrive at such a confrontational conclusion. A door opened, and what followed was the interaction between my own time and the time of those who lived long, long ago in Kalinga, between past and present. All that I did was to invest the past with a contemporary sensibility.

I am no historian, I am no keeper of records, nor do I have any flair for archival research. But ever since I arrived at this unacademic conclusion, I had been dying to share it with some knowledgeable people. I did speak to such a few, but it seemed that none of them shared my interest. Only one, a professor of history at Kalinga University, appeared to take me seriously. I remember going to meet the vice chancellor. There in his office, I was introduced to this professor. I told him about my perception of Ashoka and Kalinga, and he seemed to be deeply impressed. That was all. We never met again. I thought I had made a fool of myself, but I did not close the chapter.

Moving Perspectives was yet to be completed when a man from Gujarat, then living in Odisha, came to me one day, ready with money and a story. My friend Kironmoy Raha, an official of the Government of India, acted as liaison. Raha and the man from Gujarat wanted me to make a feature film based on a famous Odia novel. I thought it was a delicious idea—'delicious' indeed, for a man from Bengal to make a film in Odia with money from a man who'd come from Gujarat many years ago. I agreed. Setting aside the documentary, I quickly made the film and named it after the award-winning novel on which it was based—*Matira Manisha* (Man of the soil) (1966).

The documentary was taken up a year later and completed in due course. A shorter version was edited from it by the Films Division.

To return to *Matira Manisha*. A film capturing the rural scene in Odisha with an emphasis on its socioeconomic factors. A study in depth, through the eyes of a so-called outsider, me.

The year was 1966, the locale was an interior village in an agricultural belt. The story dated back to the late 30s, and was set in the heart of a traditional joint family. After the death of the old patriarch, the story focused on the two brothers, the elder having three children—two girls and a boy. The void created by the death of the father had to be filled, and it was the elder son who became the new patriarch—a good brother, a good husband, a good father. So far so good. But when I scanned the logic of events in the story, I discovered *the rule of the patriarch* hidden beneath the facade of a happy home.

'The rule of the patriarch, you say?' challenged a scholar. 'The author hasn't said so in his text.'

True, it was not in the text, but I assured him that I had not 'invented' it either. I thought, as one transplanting a story from a medium to another, it was obligatory on my part to recreate, to redefine and to reinterpret the subject. Of course, with adequate attention and respect to the text and to the people on whom the text was based.

'What do you mean?' asked the inflamed researcher.

I kept my cool. I merely said that it was my privilege to serve three mistresses whenever I made a film—the text (the subject), the medium (the language of cinema) and my time. My time was the most exacting mistress. Then I told him my story of Dhauli and the old woman, and added that without being irreverent to the socioeconomic and cultural values of the 30s, on which Kalindi Charan Panigrahi had based his novel, all I had done was to invest the story with contemporary sensibilities.

We reached a point when neither of us could be silenced.

In the meantime, lunch hour was over and shooting was to resume. We fixed a time late in the evening to continue our debate.

I sum up our after-dinner session—

Both of us agreed that it was a two-unit joint family—one consisting of the elder brother, his wife and three children; and the other, with just two, the younger brother and his newly married young wife. In my opinion, the elder brother was the patriarch. Obviously, the researcher did not like the term. But it was true— being the eldest, he was the head of the family.

'And the rest were his dependents,' I quipped.

'Precisely!' he said.

'Would you agree that the wife of the younger brother was treated with indifference, and that she was sadly underprivileged within the family?'

'She was in a new environment, a new set-up, and so . . . '

'So, she was an outsider. Right?'

He violently differed.

But we left it at that.

I did not meet the man ever again, and I forgot to make note of his whereabouts. Even though in our attitudes to life and society we were poles apart, I would unhesitatingly admit that he was a learned man, and that he knew how to ask questions. We met in the village, on location. I worked and he watched. I had my lunch, I invited him to join me, and then we had our evening session. That was all between him and me, he becoming entirely unknown to me ever after.

The producer organized a special screening in Bhubaneswar. Some liked it very much and some, a smaller group of hardcore academics, had mixed reactions. In small or large measure, they felt I had taken undue liberties with the text. It was sacrilege. But to my satisfaction, this point was fiercely debated in Odisha. Thus, a lovely controversy, which lasted long, was, both for others and me, a sign of health.

I loved the film, I loved it more with every viewing. Every time I watched it, I found a 'double' of my childhood in the younger brother—in his sighting of an aeroplane and my midnight dream-flight. Every time I watched the intimate scenes between the newly married couple, which Chidananda Dasgupta, friend and renowned critic, had once sarcastically branded as puritanical, of the look-but-don't-touch variety—I wondered if those funny sparks were obliquely related to my own conjugal life. All these moments had walked out of my autobiography!

The film flopped. The producer came to me and asked me to do him a favour—change the beginning, make a change in the middle and make a big change at the end. I asked him to remove my name from the film, and pulled out the stumps right away.

Nevertheless, the film, now titled *Two Brothers*, went to a couple of festivals abroad and was shown unofficially at Berlin and Frankfurt. As usual, there was no one to present it at any of these occasions. Strangely, years later, a dear friend of mine, Ulrich Gregor, a Berliner and a fantastic archivist and an incorruptible activist of unconventional cinema, discovered a perfectly useable copy, with perfect English subtitles, in the projection room of a theatre, the cans scattered on the floor, abandoned. He made inquiries—but no one claimed ownership. No one, in all these years.

Much later, Gregor told me about it how he felt about his discovery:

> Suddenly, Chaplin's *The Kid* came to my mind. The woman leaving the charity hospital, a child in her arms. A title: *The Woman*—whose sin was motherhood. She leaves the child in the back of a fashionable car, with a note written on a card asking a finder to protect and care for him. Two crooks of murderous look steal the car. Finding the child in the back, they roughly dump him in an alley— the child who, some years later, would grow into Jackie Coogan of the film—Jackie Coogan, the kid.

Unlike *The Kid*'s villainous crooks, Ulrich lovingly collected all the cans, took them to his archive, treated them with care and affection, and entered '*Two Brothers* by Mrinal Sen' into the archive records. Since then, it has been circulated in the film-society circuit all over the country. Ulrich even gave me photocopies of some of the reviews. One was a rather longish and good analytical piece, published in *Frankfurter Allgemeine*, written by reputed critic Dr Wilfred Wigand.

Amazing!

One dreary day during the war years, Julius Fucik was lying in a concentration-camp cell. The doctor came to issue the death certificate. He examined the prisoner, then walked out. The report, written hurriedly, was a one-liner: 'He has the constitution of a horse.'

Throughout my career, whenever any of my films suffered a setback, I felt like collapsing. Collapsing and assuming it was my funeral film. I would go into hibernation for a short time, then sit up and begin again. Every time. Every time refuelling myself, looking deeper. So, taking a cue from the concentration-camp doctor, I could say that I too had the constitution of a horse.

Matira Manisha gave me a jolt, as always. For obvious reason, I became poorer and did not have enough money to make ends meet. Our family was visibly and keenly affected. Even to keep the kitchen running became somewhat of a problem. But all that was part of the game. I could not escape it, nor could some of my colleagues and fellow travellers. Gita, for one, well realized that there was no way out—we had to endure it, we had to. Her cousin, Anup, a popular actor, both on stage and in film, stood by us. Most importantly, he saw to it that our son's well-being remained undisturbed. They were deeply attached to each other.

Life went on.

As always, without indulging in fragile optimism, I could see a glimmer of hope somewhere, everywhere, all around. I smelt a certain freshness in the air. I smelt it, really; I am not given to empty rhetoric. The wind had begun to shift. My colleagues and I felt an irresistible urge for change. Not compromise, for sure, but *change*. Personally, I thought it was a good enough moment for me to launch a breakthrough—tear away from existing convention and try my hand at creating a new one. In the face of crisis, I became desperate. Come what may, I must break the rules and build anew!

Like a godsend, a long-time friend of mine re-appeared in my life. I was on my way to Pune, to conduct a weeklong workshop with the students at the film institute. I arrived in Bombay by the morning flight and was to board the Deccan Queen train late in the afternoon. I thought of spending the morning with my friend Arun Kaul, originally from Kashmir and now settled in Bombay. He was a good planner but always drew a blank. He had something up his sleeve now, a new plan. Without wasting a moment, he took me to his two-roomed office and threw me into a chair. On the table before me was a typewriter and a heap of paper.

Then he came out with his new plan. I was to write a script based on a story I'd told him a long time ago.

'Script? Now? But I have to catch the train.'

'You will. You've got four hours to type it out.'

'Four hours to write a script!'

'An outline will do. Eight to ten pages. Maybe twelve.'

Since I had mentally chalked out a concept of the script which I'd once narrated to him, he was pretty certain that working out a sensitive outline would not take much time. But it must be decently dressed in order to be presented before a committee of decision makers.

Who were these decision makers, I asked. He said he had already spoken to the chairman of a Government of India undertaking, the Film Finance Corporation (FFC). The chairman had asked Kaul to go ahead because the idea of a low-budget film was perfect for the corporation.

Tea was brought in for both of us. He assured me that more would be supplied every hour and a half, lunch too when it was time. Then he picked up his teacup and walked out, shut the door from outside and quite literally locked me in. Hilarious!

I knew the chairman of FFC. His name was Himmat Singh, a gem of a man. A close friend of Krishna Menon from when they'd both been in London, studying law at Lincoln's Inn. I'd met him once, a highly civilized man and one who sadly could not complete his studies in London.

I finished typing in three hours. It wasn't the outline that Kaul had in mind, but as a document it was much better for the decision makers, focusing primarily on the principal characters and their interactions that formed the building blocks of the plot.

Kaul was happy and asked me about the cast. Then he said that it would have to be in Hindi.

'Hindi?'

'Don't forget that your last film was in Odia!'

So, if we did receive the grant, we would make the film in Hindi and, ideally, cast Utpal Dutt and Shekhar Chatterjee, both theatre activists and my close friends. The actor to play the village girl could be finalized later.

In the meantime, someone rushed to Victoria Terminus to cancel my ticket and buy a new one for the morning train the next day. On his way back, the man collected the application form for a loan from the FFC.

Till midnight, Kaul and I discussed various details, worked out a budget and calculated the loan amount we had to apply for. Kaul filled in the application form and I signed wherever required. And, of course, we included a covering letter, duly typed and signed.

Kaul saw me off the next morning, reminding me to finalize the technicians and locate a sweet girl to play the village belle.

Incredible, everything that happened in one day!

Himmat Singh did not take long with our request. Much later, an officer of the Government of India told me that Indira Gandhi herself had taken an interest in the project and recommended we not be asked for any collateral security or even a guarantor to ensure repayment. It could be treated as a test case, she felt. The agreement was signed in FFC's Bombay office, and a cheque amounting to two-thirds of the loan was handed over to me on 21 October 1968. Incidentally, that was the date when, 14 years earlier, our son was born. While signing, I was not aware of it. Gita reminded me about it over the phone when I called her that evening. Kunal, our son, was very proud. He wished the film every success. That was how *Bhuvan Shome* began, based on a novella by Banaphool.

In many ways, *Bhuvan Shome* (1969) was new to us. It was my first film in Hindi, Utpal Dutt's first role in Hindi and Suhasini Mulay's first role anywhere, whether it be on screen or on stage. She had not acted even in school plays! Vijay Raghava Rao composed music for the first time for a feature film, and K. K. Mahajan made his debut as a feature-film cinematographer. And interestingly, Amitabh Bachchan made his first earning in cinema by doing the voiceover, for just a minute and a half, two at most. He was most reluctant, but I persuaded him to accept a cheque for the princely sum of 300 rupees. The total cost of production was unbelievably low, lower than the unbelievably lowest—2,00,000 rupees! Two lakhs—only two! After all, what we were planning to make was a low-budget film and set a record! And a trend!

Bhuvan Shome was all about Bhuvan Shome, a widower, a top railway official now approaching retirement. Suffering from Victorian morality, he was a strict disciplinarian, sparing none for negligence of duty, not even his only son who committed a petty offence. He had no friends, no one to build a rapport with. His world consisted of his office chamber, its door swinging open and shut as a flurry of files came and went, and phones that rang every five minutes or so. Perhaps out of sheer boredom, he once took a short leave and left his world to visit into an entirely alien one, a world of fresh air and open spaces and birds and sand dunes. There, he had a sweet and mysterious encounter with a village girl; that encounter formed the bulk of the film. After which Shome-sahib came back to his own world!

Given a 'blank cheque', answerable to no one, not even to any of the official agencies, the entire team of workers was bubbling with 'infantile' enthusiasm, as though a group of children had been given a box of building blocks to play with. In a highly conformist set-up as ours, it was sheer delight on our part to rush into a world of madness. Madness, true, but we saw to it that there was method in our madness—method implemented through skill and inherent discipline.

An instance. We came to a sequence—the tough bureaucrat *back to his own world!* Frankly, I had not quite managed to come to grips with the scene. Back in his own world, he would be an unhappy figure of ridicule—not a figure of fun. Yet it was not as simple as it sounds here. There was not much to explain, but there was a lot to feel. I looked at Utpal, I went up to him and took him aside. Then, recalling my own medical-representative past, I recounted that episode of mine, the one from the Jhansi hotel in 1951—how I shut myself inside my room, how I stood before the mirror, stripped myself, stood naked, made faces at my reflection, shouted madly and how finally I broke down, cried with convulsive sobs and then, three days later, I resigned.

Dutt did not speak a word. He looked deep into my eyes and squeezed my hand.

'Give me just ten minutes,' he said, and left the room.

Then, juxtaposing images and sound, all that happened to Bhuvan Shome in the film was his tragic realization—that he would remain the same as he had been all these years, a tough, duty-bound bureaucrat, a lonely prisoner trapped within the four walls of his office with heaps of files around him and his telephone ringing unceasingly. What we did at the end, Dutt and I, was to grant the man a touch of insanity and allow him to temporarily escape into a kind of burlesque and 'inspired nonsense'.

A truckload of improvisations created no problem for us during the editing. In the end, the script was not the same as the eight-page 'outline' we had submitted. I was relieved that nobody at FFC raised any questions. But a legal problem crept in. The final clearance was to come from the new chief—B. K. Karanjia. He loved the film immensely, but his secretary pointed out a slip: a particular clause in the 40-page agreement categorically specified the minimum length for a feature film. But *Bhuvan Shome* was shorter, even shorter than the average Indian film which is always on the longer side. It was a violation of the agreement between *the President of India and a citizen called Mrinal Sen, son of . . .* ! So, seeking an amendment, Karanjia packed off his secretary to Delhi, to meet the related authority in the ministry. He carried a note from Karanjia which, allegedly, carried a few lines only, which may be summed up as: What are we looking for? A good film or a long film?

A few private screenings were received extremely well. As a result, to find a good theatre in my city for commercial release was not difficult. However, the attendance at the first show was much less than adequate and the manager, one Daruwala, was sceptical about the fate of the film. We felt frustrated. Hoping against hope, we were waiting outside the theatre doors. When the show was over, the crowd rushed into the foyer, recognized me and then mobbed me with a storm of praise. The crush was unmanageable. I was bewildered. Our distributor, Ashim Dutt, felt I should be rescued immediately. So he whisked me off to the famous Coffee House, roughly a kilometre away. Sitting in the hubbub of the Coffee House, a series of images flashed across my mind—all that mattered during the last two years—Arun Kaul's office, where I was put under lock and key for a few hours with an ancient type-writer before me. And all that happened, till that moment, when Ashim Dutta saved me from the violence of affection. All that now seemed a dream!

Widely circulated, the film was discussed at various levels in most of the metropolitan cities, but the interpretations differed from person to person. They baffled me at times but also helped me dis-cover myself. The dominant view was that the film was about tam-ing a bad bureaucrat. Another view, held by a particular group of my European friends, was that *Bhuvan Shome* was a lovely erotic film. An eminent critic and historian in India, Dnyaneshwar Nadkarni, had an identical view, and even pointed out some erotic motifs of the film in his long essay in the *Times of India*. The press, by and large, branded the film as belonging to the New Wave, though that was not my opinion, for sure. Not my opinion, I repeat. As far as we were concerned, in a desperate drive, we ran wild and made a film. De-emphasizing plot and incident, we told a human story within the framework of a simple storyline. All done on location, made on a throwaway budget. And that was all!

This time, in Venice, *Bhuvan Shome* was not a lone traveller—I kept it delightful company.

Back home, one afternoon, two persons appeared at my door: one, a friend of mine, an avant-garde writer, Lokenath Bhattacharya, who spent long years in France and translated *Pather Panchali* into French, in collaboration with his French wife France Bhattacharya and another woman called Nathalie Sarraute.

Nathalie Sarraute! That trailblazer French playwright and novelist, one of the architects of the nouveau roman! Yes, it was she! She had come to the big city with her lawyer husband, and my friend had taken them to watch *Bhuvan Shome*. As soon as the show was over, she dropped her husband back to their hotel and came straight to my home with my friend. She spoke to me continuously for two–three minutes in French, then realized she was not communicating. So she apologized and quickly switched to English. She had liked the film very much and, as usual, she had her own interpretation which indeed impressed me: A sweet, simple, serene village belle outsmarts an 'incorruptible' bureaucrat with no malice against anyone. A charming comedy and profoundly human!

Interestingly, the one who reacted in a rather unwholesome manner was Ray who, when a big noise was made about the film, first published a long essay in some important periodical or daily which was later also included in the anthology *Our Films, Their Films* (1976). It was all about the New Wave, brilliantly written and superbly analysed. For the anthology version, he added a small paragraph—a kind of appendix—on *Bhuvan Shome*, not mentioned earlier in his meaningful essay. I reproduce an excerpt:

Among recent films, *Bhuvan Shome* is cited widely as an off-beat film which has succeeded with a minority audience. My own opinion is that whatever success it has had has not been because of, but in spite of its new aspects. It worked because it used some of the most popular conventions of cinema which helped soften the edges of its occasional spiky syntax. These conventions are: a delectable heroine, an ear-filling background score, and a simple, wholesome, wish-fulfilling screen story. Summary in seven words: Big Bad Bureaucrat Reformed by Rustic Belle.

I refrain from writing a long rejoinder because it is rather inconsequential. I simply comment on his *summary in seven words* (Hollywood's one-time criterion for a good screen story): *Big Bad Bureaucrat Reformed by Rustic Belle.*

My business, in plain and simple language, was not to *reform* the bureaucrat—because he belonged to an incorrigible tribe. Bhuvan Shome, as I saw him on screen, was an arrogant man, lonely and sad, who, behind the facade of burlesque and *inspired nonsense*, finally came to a tragic realization.

Who, then, had it wrong? Ray? Or me?

Either of the two—it could not be both.

Or it could just be that, following the usual content on view, the audience had developed a propensity to see a bad man turn good at the end. Responding to stock responses! *Wish-fulfilling screen story!*

Once, I was on a long taxi ride in Bombay, for 50 kilometres or more, along a traffic-ridden road. The driver, a never-ending chatterbox, talked about everything under the sun, and did not spare even the chief minister and his dealings with the mafia. He was driving me to downtown, during the peak rush hour. Finally, I got to ask him a question. Had he seen a film called *Bhuvan Shome*? About birds and a girl? Yes, he had seen it. A 'class' film! And suddenly, he braked to a halt, turned and looked at me.

'Are you Mrinal Sen, sir?' he asked, wonderstruck.

I nodded.

He stretched out his hand. We shook hands, a warm shake. The taxi stood still. All in a split second. Behind us hundreds of cars began to honk in impatience. The taxi began to move again. Another ten minutes or so and I would reach my destination. But no further speech, not a single word, emanated from the driver . . .

Finally, the taxi stopped.

But the driver refused to let me pay for the long drive.

SEVEN

I Am Twenty

For One Thousand Years, I Remain Twenty . . .

Gita was very happy. Her maiden name was Shome, she began to say that two Shomes had rescued me from disaster. Kunal, our son, warned me against forgetting that the deal with Film Finance Corporation had been signed and sealed on his birthday. Ungrudgingly, I shared my success story with both of them. Taking a cursory glance at a couple of national trade bulletins, my well-wishers in the industry assured me that, by now, I had become a commercially viable proposition. I, for one, was not quite sure. But proposals came to me from regular producers, mostly from Bombay. Two among those were so enthusiastic that they rushed over to my city; and the third, the owner of two collieries, was the first on the waiting list. All three offered me lucrative terms. And two conditions—one, that the trend we set for ourselves—making low-budget films—must not be departed from. And two, that like *Bhuvan Shome*, the films would have to be made in Hindi. Their conditions arose from a simple truth: *Nothing succeeds like commercial success.* As a result, I could see that my position had changed neither for the better nor for the worse. I remained where I was. The struggle, therefore, continued.

The struggle! On the political front, the struggle of the extremist faction had already assumed immense proportions. Starting with a peasant uprising in 1967 at Naxalbari, an area in North Bengal, it soon spread like wildfire through several other peasant belts of the country. A quote from Mao Tse-tung, 'A single spark can start a prairie fire', assumed great popularity among the extremists, or the 'Naxalites', and was even painted onto the walls as a slogan of the times, both in the city and the suburbs. Rightly or wrongly, the peasant, and thus rural, movement eventually grew into an urban one. The students erupted—not only in my city but also, to an extent in Andhra Pradesh, Kerala, Punjab, Odisha and Bihar. Around the same time, the movement also assumed shape elsewhere in the world. The most significant was the Latin American one, where, to combat the so-called *peace* of the neocolonial system, the people learnt to *hate*. As the explosive feature-length documentary, *La hora de los hornos* (The hour of the furnaces) (1968), by Octavio Getino and Fernando Solanas of Argentina, said it: 'We fear peace more than war.'

That was a decade of violent protest. In contrast, the European movement was short-lived and largely romantic. The one that got wide publicity was in Frankfurt and then, on a comparatively bigger scale, at Sorbonne. But even more quick to grab international attention was the scene in West Bengal. Protests and violence carried and were met with shocking levels of police brutality, almost a mad fury of repression. A large section of the Bengali youth was caught in the maelstrom. The most advanced and, naturally, the most dedicated among them were the university and college students. Kunal was still in school; one day, he brought home a secret pamphlet and hid it away. In his absence, I pulled it out, read it and gently put it back. I felt a little disturbed. Being more practical, Gita asked me not to create a scene.

Amid the Naxalite maelstrom, yet another spark, another slogan rent the air. New posters flooded the city. Outside the border, in the suburbs, and deeper, in the heart of the countryside: *Sattor-er dashak mukti'r dashak*! (The decade of the 70s is the decade of liberation!)

The Bangladesh counterparts of the Indian militants had a different slogan, a catchy one: *Bhaat de, haramjada* (give us our daily bread, you swine). Though that came later, because at that time they were fighting a bitter battle to wrest themselves from the clutches of Pakistan and become an independent sovereign state. India, of course, lent their efforts a big hand.

In my tiny kingdom, my crew was waiting at the door, waiting for my command. Funds or no funds—which in other words meant a lean fund—they wanted to start a new production. To strike another surprise! Led by K. K. Mahajan, who did a marvellous job in the world of birds and sand dunes, the entire group was bubbling over with excitement and anticipation. Mahajan wrote a letter from Bombay, a quick note, asking when, how soon, I would call him again. So sweet of them all. For him and for everybody, my answer was: Soon!

'How soon?' asked Kunal.

'Don't be in a hurry—make sure that you have a full script this time,' said Gita.

Neither Mahajan nor I cared for a perfectly laid-out script. So far we had not encountered any problems that prevented me from improvising during a shoot, nor had he in ungrudgingly capturing it all. I used to ask him to do so many things on location, do this and do that, and quietly he did it all, this and that. The proverbial cold war between a filmmaker and his cameraman never showed up between us except on a few occasions which could not be avoided. While filming *Bhuvan Shome*—and that was his first film—we did the running about almost all the time, and he accepted everything with wonderful ease. From then onwards, till the last film he did with me, in 1989, we enjoyed ourselves thoroughly. On location, going from one spot to another, I walked faster. Faster than everyone else in the team, I was always on the move. Once he said, and they all agreed, that I was the youngest in the team. Walking and working like a 20-year-old boy!

Later, Mahajan developed a problem with his vocal cords. But he never stopped smoking. In 2001, he finally lost his voice.

Anyway, turning a deaf ear to the noise outside, I picked up a thin storyline from my friend Ashis Burman, re-dressed it and started working on a quick script. The screenplay, as I called it, was stuffed with bits of empty space, such as, a fish-market, barber shop, trams and buses, a police station and a multinational company's conference room. Such spaces would have to be filled in by the real people—commoners, policemen and big bosses. They would be doing more of 'behaving' and much less of acting and speaking their lines. The protagonist would walk onto the scene all the time. All these would be more than adequately punctuated by newsreel coverage of political manifestations, which I had been filming from time to time without any precise intention. Tying them together would certainly not be a comprehensive text unless all of it could be given a definitive twist at the editing table. The story in three lines: a young man of modest earning in search of a lucrative job appears before the board of a multinational company; although, he had been assured, that the interview, would be a mere formality. In the end, as a kind of epilogue, the protagonist, aged 25, is interviewed against a dark background by an unseen interviewer who calls himself *a viewer* and who chases the young man from dawn to dusk. Following such an interview—an attack! Fact, fiction, fantasy—all mixed up, leading to blind fury! Quixotic? Anybody's guess.

In-between, at the insistence of the minister concerned, a film for Children's Film Society was quickly made in three weeks, of approximately 50 minutes' duration, something to be seen and forgotten. It was made a long time ago, and now it's time to call a spade a spade. The idea was very good, the story by Tagore was excellent: *Ichhapurana* (Wish fulfilment) (1970). A domineering father and a son, wild and untamed. Disgusted with their whole-time familial occupations—that of the father and the son—both were dying to change their identities. The grace of the goddess fell on both. The son turned into the father—and the father into his child. A chain of hilarious incidents follow, until finally, good sense prevails upon them, and the father reverts to his parenthood and the son to his childhood. To cut a long story short, the film version was much less than expected. Was it because the disgrace of the goddess fell on the filmmaker? Not unlikely.

The truth, as I could clearly see, was that given all that was continuously fermenting within me, I was bubbling over with enthusiasm all the time. How soon we could start the film on the interview—at the time, that was my real preoccupation!

We took two and a half months to start and finish the city film, all in the big city, and we called it *Interview* (1970). Most of the performers, including the protagonist, appeared before the camera for the first time. It was summer when we shot the film; it was sheer delight when we worked in the editing room, and the final mixing was done in a mad hurry because the film was booked for a swift release in the biggest city theatre downtown.

Incidentally, a short note about how it all began. It was barely a month before shooting was to start. Funding remained an uncertain factor, though the most vital factor, even after everything else was ready for a 'go'. Unannounced, the owner of two collieries came to see me one day. Casually, he asked me about my plans, if any. I said I had just completed a new script. What was it about, he asked. Since discretion is the better part of valour, I narrated a particular sequence instead of telling him the whole story:

> The 'hero', played by Ranjit Mullick, manages to get onto a running tram. The tram is filled to capacity. A girl is leafing through a film magazine. Ranjit is standing beside her. The girl stops at a particular photograph. He looks at it. It is his own, under the headline: 'Mrinal Sen's New Find, Ranjit Mullick'. The girl looks at Ranjit standing beside her. She tries to compare the two faces. Every time she looks at the man standing beside her, he tries to hide his face. This juvenile game continues between the two. An old passenger, one seat apart, gets irritated. Before a scene is unnecessarily created, Ranjit steps forward and looks directly at the audience. And explains the situation: 'Look, it is all my fault. Let me confess that, yes, it is my photo. But I am no actor, no star. My name is Ranjit Mullick, I live in Bhabanipur and work for a weekly journal. I go to the press, correct the proofs and do odd jobs. Mine is an uneventful life. But that somehow attracted Mrinal Sen. You know, Mrinal Sen . . . the film director. He told me he would chase me from dawn to dusk. He asked me to permit him to cover "one day of mine". He and his cameraman, K. K. Mahajan . . . Look, he is there . . . there . . . Mahajan, with the camera. Tell me, does it make any sense?'

Wonderstruck, the passengers look at one another and at Ranjit Mullick. The photograph, 'Mrinal Sen's New Find', prominently displayed, is in the crowd. Ranjit Mullick continues: 'Mrinal Sen assured me that I do not have to do anything special, to just be as I am. I told him I have to appear before an interview board. You know, it is such an important event that I could not suppress it. As I told him about my interview, Mrinal Sen exclaimed, "Fine! That will be really dramatic." '

The tram arrives at a short stop. Mahajan, holding the movie camera, gets down. Two more passengers follow.

Ranjit continues, 'Just see, how they are chasing me. But I tell you, whatever you have seen so far is not all true. I am real, you are real, this magazine is real, this young lady is also real. And my interview this afternoon is also very real. But the lady who has been playing my mother is not my real mother. She is an actress.'

On screen, an excerpt from *Pather Panchali* pops up— Karuna Banerjee, playing Sabojaya, breaks down as she can no longer suppress the news of Durga's death. The excerpt lingers for a few moments. Then, back to the running tram. Ranjit continues: 'She plays my mother, but in a similar situation, my real mother in her real life would have done the same.' He looks at his wristwatch, then excuses himself and gets off the running tram. He is already late, so he hurries off to the press.

I narrated just this much and then looked at the colliery owner. That look of mine was enough for me to conclude that he had no way to turn away.

'I'll give you money,' he said, 'all of the money.'

Then he looked at his watch, said he had an appointment. That evening, he had to take his family to Rajasthan, to his village, to attend a wedding and would return only the week after. But since he realized that my unit and I were already on the job, he brought out from his handbag 1,50,000 rupees—yes, a lakh and a half in cash—and handed it over to me. The balance, whatever I would require, would be paid immediately on his return. And then he rushed off.

Incredible! Every bit of what he did, unbelievable! Carrying so much cash in his handbag, making no mention of any business matters, not asking for any receipt against the money, not making note of how much more remained to be paid or who would produce the film or in which language! Not a word.

Gita was in the kitchen. She came to my room and asked what had happened. Kunal was not at home. I handed over the big bundle of cash to Gita and told her the whole story.

Sultania, the colliery owner, returned after a week and the additional money was provided, no problem. It was mutually agreed upon that I would remain the producer and he, the distributor. Yes, indeed, *Interview* was a low-budget production, financed and distributed by Dayashankar Sultania.

Blending fact and fiction was not a problem at all. To start with, we used a simple ploy to lend credibility to the story: we named all the characters after their real names. As simple as that. Next step, and a surer step, was to create a favourable condition in the running tram when Ranjit Mullick, the protagonist, introduces himself and, in the process, also presents the story in a nutshell. When he refers to his 'mother', he does not hesitate to disclose her real identity. To evidence the fact, we had a sharp cut to a short extract from *Pather Panchali* only to return to him in the running tram. From the beginning to the end, all these and many more, even those seemingly extraneous, all coming and going in quick succession, were juxtaposed with utmost precision. Extreme care was taken to ensure that the rhythm in cutting was never disturbed. While editing, we found ourselves caught in that perfect rhythm. Besides, we were flexible enough to break the lines spoken by the characters, to remove and change them as and when we found it necessary. We even took the liberty to borrow lines from the actors and, going to an extreme, even from the crew as well as the crowd who collected to watch our shoots.

This is how it happened. As organized, on a certain day, my crew and I went to the multinational company, IBM, to film the interview sequence. Of course, Ranjit Mullick, the candidate, was with us. Clad in the traditional white dhoti and kurta, he looked a perfect Bengali. He had no option but to be so dressed; all his formal Western clothes were at a city laundry, and all the laundries were on strike. He had organized a suit-and-boot outfit from one of his friends, in truth of much better quality than his own. On his way home with the package, he got into a brawl with a pickpocket on the bus. Ranjit managed to catch him, and so his presence in the police station became obligatory. In the confusion, he left the package on the bus. By the time it occurred to him, the bus was far gone.

Back at IBM, the big officers, headed by a foreigner, interviewed the Bengali babu. In fact, during the company's short stint in the city, all that the IBM officers used to do was to interview young aspirants. The lines they spoke were their own, merely edited by me. It was all done on the spot. Ranjit's lines were sharp, also edited by me. He looked smart and answered well enough. In the meantime, the one who took me aside to tell me something special was Nemai Ghose, Satyajit Ray's Boswell (writing with camera instead of pen). He told me he had been with Ray the previous week when, in the studios, he too had been shooting an interview sequence for his film *Pratidwandi* (*The Adversary*) (1970). Nemai said it had been a fascinating scene; he'd particularly loved a rather difficult question and its courageous answer. In his enthusiasm, Nemai quoted the lines to me:

EMPLOYER: What was the biggest event of the decade?
CANDIDATE: The war in Vietnam.

Nemai said, 'Isn't it great?'

I was grateful to him for giving me that piece of information. Safely, without being accused of plagiarism, I thought up the last question and answer then and there.

Q [from the foreigner]: What is the biggest event of the day?
A: My interview, sir.

The sequence ended with loud laughter and a warm handshake.

Ranjit was happy and almost certain that he would get the job.

But, no, he did not.

We were wondering whether our target audience would have any problem in drawing the line between fact and fiction, whether it would realize where and how fact ended and fiction took over. In either of the cases, we would stand to gain. To us, it was a kind of creative game, both aesthetic and technical.

At a private screening before its release, quite a number of people were intrigued. I told them not to ask me; it would be better if they took up the matter with the actors who played the roles and created such confusion. To Ranjit Mullick, in particular, acting for the first time. A friend of mine, an African American, the same age as I and teaching cinema at the University of California, Berkeley, came to my home one evening. He was on a short trip to India under the aegis of the US government. A junior officer from the US Consulate accompanied him as an escort. He'd watched the film in a matinee show. Our evening session was brief, but I could imagine he had a number of questions. At around midnight, he came again, alone, without his escort. The first thing he asked me was if Ranjit Mullick was a member of a militant group in West Bengal. No, never, and the family he came from was miles away from anything of that kind, moderate or extremist. That and some more issues were raised, all mostly arising out of our continuous play with fact and fiction. I enjoyed his confusion. He loved it. Loved it all the more because he could freely relate fact and fiction to contemporary life and reality.

'That was a novel way of understanding the times and history,' he said, sounding like himself, an academician. His name—Albert Johnson.

The 'first day first show' was outstanding. The response from the young viewers was tremendous. Never before and never after have I seen a cameraman being chased by an admiring crowd. Mahajan was mobbed—and then rescued soon after. Rescued, because he begged for 'help'! (By temperament, Mahajan always preferred a low profile.) For two consecutive weeks, the film ran very well. In the third week, the excitement diminished and, soon after, when the ticket sales fell below a mark, the film was withdrawn from Globe, the theatre in the heart of central Calcutta. In other theatres, the run was moderate. In suburbs and smaller towns, no better. All in all, it was a popular failure. However, Sultania got his money back along with a reasonable overflow from the foreign market and, later, from the rest of the domestic circuit. So much so that he was ready for my next film, and for that he wanted to act the producer.

The heat was yet to subside. An evening show, in the third week of its run at Globe. I was in the brasserie upstairs; a friend of mine had just left. The show would end at any moment. Then yes, it was over, and people began to walk out; it was not really a big crowd. I heard a harsh comment from behind me, the voice a bit finicky and presumably of a knowledgeable woman. I turned and saw a small group of men and women, all immaculately dressed, looking for a comfortable table. They had just come out of the theatre but did not seem to be in a mood to discuss the film. But the voice I'd heard was still at it, repeating the same harsh comment over and over again, 'Won't you agree that it's an anti-social film?' Quietly, I left, because my presence might have embarrassed them. Did they see me? Could they identify the filmmaker?

On my way home, I wondered if that group was cut out for watching a film like *Interview*. Questioning myself, I was almost convinced they'd come to see another film by the maker of *Bhuvan Shome*—'a simple, wholesome, wish-fulfilling screen story'. Instead, at the end of the film, they watched a young job seeker, now in the realm of fantasy, engaged in a midnight adventure, breaking the show window of a departmental store in his quixotic fury and stripping naked the suited mannequin.

Arun Kaul, my friend, called me from Bombay and told me that the vice-president of the festival committee at Karlovy Vary, on his search for films from South Asian countries, had arrived at the city on his way back to Prague. Could Arun organize a screening of *Interview* for him? Arun had a copy with him for English subtitling. I asked him to go ahead. The selector watched the film, and without waiting for the Festival Directorate in Delhi to take necessary measures, packed it off to Prague via the diplomatic bag. Arun gave him the English dialogue text for subtitles in Czech. Soon after, they sent me an invitation to the festival and asked me to request my actor also for a quick trip. Neither my actor nor I could make it but, later, the entire team was gratified to know that Ranjit Mullick had bagged the Best Actor award.

Interestingly, while making *Interview,* I never knew it would have a follow-up. It just happened. And it was called *Calcutta 71* (1972). In it, the protagonist of *Interview* was charged with the criminal offence of breaking the show window of a metropolitan departmental store and stripping an elegantly suited mannequin. The film was a kind of collage, a collection of apparently unrelated events and objects. Again, fact, fiction, fantasy, all mixed up but not in the same manner or order. Then, as I completed *Calcutta 71,* it occurred to me that I must make yet another. Eventually, a third one was made, called *Padatik* (The guerilla fighter) (1973). Structurally, unlike the first two non-linear films, *Padatik* had a linear framework, a complete narrative in a pattern that suited the film.

Interview began with an independent sequence, a kind of starter that presented the decolonizing drive in the city that was uprooting the imperial icons from its streets and parks. *Calcutta 71* started with a statement by a 20-year-old boy who'd lived through history and, for a thousand years, had been living at the age of 20. *Padatik* started with an excerpt from a text on the city by the eminent British journalist James Cameron.

All three films were made in three successive years.

The lines, coming one after another made the beginning of *Calcutta 71*:

I am twenty.
For one thousand years I remain twenty.
For one thousand years I walk through squalor and death.
For one thousand years I breathe despair.
For one thousand years I see history of unending poverty.
History of poverty, of the exploited, of the oppressed and
    the wronged.

Just these lines, coupled with the voiceover, showed on screen and disappeared.

Then appeared the naked mannequin suspended by the neck, like a hanged man.

The suspended mannequin and the accused person featured prominently in an imaginary courtroom, presided over by a judge.

Accepting the validity of *anger* as a social entity, the trial scene came to an end.

Unexpectedly, the city, in a mad fury, appeared on the screen as it was in 1971. The maelstrom. In-between, as always, flashes of normal life.

Then appeared a young man, presumably 20 years old, from behind a back-street wall. He was being chased, he was on the run, a desperate run, from a narrow lane to a wider one, crossing a crowded street, running away from a village, through a forest, along the beach somewhere, the sea and its surging waves in the background, and finally, early in the misty morning, through the tall trees of the Maidan. Suddenly, guns firing—one . . . two . . . three. A flock of birds shrieks out. Then the deep voice of a newsreader on the soundtrack, 'A young man of twenty, unidentified, found dead in the Maidan, with three bullet injuries . . . '

The film carried three stories—the first by Manik Bandopadhyay, and the other two by Prabodh Sanyal and Samaresh Basu, respectively. All one-day stories, stories of everyday life, of subhuman existences, one after another: one in 1933, one in 1943, the third in 1953. The voice and the text of the eternally 20-year-old man appeared at the end of each story. And finally, a sequence capturing the turbulent 1971. At long last, the young man of 20, unidentified, found dead with three bullet wounds, appeared—young and vibrant—before the audience to speak his mind. As he spoke, he grew enormous.

Agit-prop stuff? Anybody's guess, not mine.

The release at the biggest theatre, Metro, was a big event, and the response was intense. There was a big rush for tickets every day. Many had to go back, disappointed. In the big city and in the suburbs, even in the smaller colonies. Those who'd lost their children and family, those who'd lost their friends, identified the young man of 20. Those who loved the film hated the system that was uprooting the hopes of the underprivileged.

But there were also those who had problems with the film. Some questioned its political credibility, others its aesthetics. Some said, it was oversimplified. Some felt it was hopelessly romantic. Some said it was gimmicky. I listened to all of them, and, on my own, identified my own lapses.

To my mind, any film growing and running at an incredible pace and generating tons of controversies shows its internal strength. It was an experience for me to watch the viewers talking to each other as they came out of the big theatre, day in and day out. Not all of them were as articulate as I would have liked them to be, but even a furtive look did not go in vain. That too told a story. Watching them, and talking to even the most talkative among them, I remembered Albert Johnson who spoke about *understanding the times and history.*

I still remember a particular incident. Two young men, fully charged, walked up to me. One of them, rather impatient, asked me when I shot the film. I remembered the first day of shooting and that was in the studios. That was when we took up the imaginary Court of Law. I said: 9 September 1971.

'That's not true—that's a lie!' he shouted.

I was taken aback. How could he say so, and in a manner so offensive? I took the other boy aside and asked him what had happened to his friend. Was he sick in the head? The boy said that they had seen a dear friend of theirs in one of the sequences—he'd been fiercely delivering a speech at Esplanade East. Later, that evening, he had an encounter with the Central Reserve Police (requisitioned by the state governments).

'Was he killed?' I asked.

'Yes,' he said, 'he was shot dead.'

Immediately, I walked up to the aggrieved boy and begged for forgiveness. As a matter of fact, I explained, I had been recording such events for a few years. The boy, killed only a few hours later, must have been captured by my cameraman during one such shoot.

Till this moment, I do not know who the boy was.

There were various stories, which I gathered every day. A middle-aged teacher told me that he had lost his job because one of his boss' moles had spotted him at a massive protest rally. A prominent Income Tax officer, South Indian, said that he and his wife had come to see the film in their own car. But after seeing the film, he was ashamed of getting into the car and driving back home—he was ashamed of owning a car. I asked him not to worry—I owned a car too!

An overseas story might not be out of place here. At Nyon, Switzerland, where I chaired a small festival jury in October 1972, the last day was named 'Indian Day' as a mark of respect to the Indian juror. Moritz de Hadeln, then director of the festival, managed to organize a good print of *Calcutta 71* from Venice where, earlier in August, I had presented it at the festival. On the last day of the Nyon Festival, after the award-giving ceremony, Moritz fixed up two important events—screening of *Calcutta 71*; and the presence of the Indian ambassador, who was to make a speech after or before the screening. He was Arjan Singh, formerly Air Chief Marshal, Indian Air Force.

The Air Chief Marshal was very cordial with me, and when his time came, he made a short and sweet speech. The film started within minutes. The house was packed, with many even sitting on the floor. Quite a substantial number had come from close-by Geneva, a mostly African and Latin American audience.

The show was over. And I was mobbed. A young sari-clad girl made her way through the crowd, shook my hand and then said that our ambassador was not happy. She was in a hurry, so she ran away—she was the daughter of the First Secretary, studying at Sorbonne. She'd come to spend a few days with her parents. The ambassador walked past me, this time not caring to stop.

In the large banquet hall, the big crowd waited to hear the ambassador's after-dinner speech. I was with Basil Wright, standing at the far end of the hall.

The speech, again very short, was bitter this time. In the ambassador's perception, the film did not show the truth about India, did not speak a word about its balanced economy, its surplus food and, importantly, its jet planes which it was now manufacturing.

The speech was greeted with catcalls and boos.

Wright was visibly angry. A couple of weeks later, when I was back in my city and the film was still going strong in the big theatre, I received a lovely letter from him. In it, Wright asked me not to take the matter seriously because 'there are always hardcore areas of chauvinism with governments and government departments, where the idea of a film even suggesting that their nation is anything other than an earthly paradise is viewed with horror.' He asked me to put my ambassador in the right perspective: 'at the wrong end of the telescope.' Which I did. In conclusion, he assured me that the event 'was really no more than a rather funny little episode, and was so regarded by those at the reception who bothered to listen to it.'

On receipt of the letter, I immediately sent a copy to Indira Gandhi in New Delhi. In addition, I sent a short report, my own: candid and, reading between the lines, a bit caustic. As a result, no damage was done to me or to my passport. With or without *Calcutta 71*, I continued to go wherever and whenever I had to.

In his letter, Wright did not spare even his own country. The documentaries made by him and his colleagues, whichever depicted negative aspects of the society, were never officially entered in foreign expositions. So in 1965, at the New York World's Fair, they set up a pavilion close to the official one and began to show their own films. The event was an immediate success, and the government departments became wiser and more careful.

Now, it was time to work on a new film. Dispassionately, I learnt my lessons from *Interview* and *Calcutta 71*. Watching the bewildering reality of the instant present, I learnt and unlearnt a huge lot. Then, withdrawing into myself, I felt an urge to make a film featuring a young man who would question himself. Who would even be ready to *go against the tide*. I had a quiet session with my friend Ashis Burman, and we jointly prepared a rough outline of what finally turned out to be *Padatik*. Doing a kind of reappraisal.

Once it was done and screened, Samar Sen, formerly brilliant urban poet and lately hardcore left-wing journalist, called it 'the report of a policeman'. Whatever it was, while making *Padatik*, I was aware of the fact that the line between self-criticism and slander is slender—but unbreakable. Unbreakable, because of the growth of *establishmentarianism* even on the Left Front. And whatever I was, I knew I was not a fence sitter.

Once again, a new film, a film with a starter—and I repeat the Cameron quote on the city, 'Every time I return to Calcutta, I find it an intimidating and even infernal city, unredeemed and probably doomed.'

Followed by the young man, on a desperate run along the city lanes. Lane after lane. The piercing sound of gunfire. A sharp cut to the big face of the young man filling the screen. The face with three bullet wounds, coming one after another, the face lacerated, burnt. On it, the title.

The story began—a story with a beginning, a middle and an end—all three in perfect order.

The man, a full-time political activist, was in hiding. The police lifted him from his hideout. Outsmarting the police, he escaped from the prison van. Then, again, in another hideout, from there to another, a posh apartment in a safer locality, the owner, a woman of his age, inheriting the property of her deceased father. By birth a Punjabi, once married to a man in business, but a man without scruples, now a divorcee, an executive in an advertising agency, living alone in her big flat with her ten-year-old son who was studying in a boarding school in a hill station. An ideal hideout for a fugitive. Totally cut off from his moorings, his political world, his only contact with the outside world being a young dedicated cadre who came every other day. A duplicate of the key was with him; the fugitive did not need one because he was forbidden to step out.

When the fugitive arrived, escorted by the cadre, the flat owner was out of town. A magazine lay carelessly on the couch. He picked it up—*Frontier*, edited by Samar Sen. Surprised, he gave a furtive look at the cadre. Yes, she happened to be a distant sympathizer of the party. It all started after her younger brother, a bright boy, was killed in a police encounter. No, not here, at Ropar, in Punjab. Ropar was also in ferment then.

She came. They introduced themselves to each other, and the matter ended there. Living under one roof, each remained tightly sheltered until, bit by bit, they came out of their shells. She felt sad about his parents. The mother was sick, bed-ridden. The father, a petty clerk in a commercial firm, was still hanging on. The younger brother, an amateur footballer, was yet to get a job. The father could not understand his wayward son, neither his manners nor his party. Quite often, whenever they met, they clashed on issues relating to his brand of politics as against his own when, way back, before Independence, he had been a freedom fighter.

When the fugitive was all alone in the silent apartment, he withdrew into himself, set aside the excess of political passion, and started asking questions—questions about himself, about the party and its leaders, about the people for whom they were fighting, and most importantly, about who were the *friends* and who the *enemies*, and how to mobilize the friends to build a front, a broad front, aiming at the broadest. These and a few more questions came crowding to him, but he had no answers. The only one close at hand knew only to *obey*—not to *question* nor to *answer*. The only alternative, therefore, was to write a letter, which he did, a long letter to the leader, sent through the cadre. A strong letter.

The answer came swift and sharp. The key to the apartment was returned to the owner at her office. The courier was mandated never to visit again.

In spite of the mandate, he did visit again, one evening. Came and went away, dropping a word: the fugitive's mother was critically ill. She was dying to see him.

By the time he got back home, the mother was dead. Ignoring the unkind look of the neighbours, the father took the son aside, away from the onlookers, and as if hiding behind a wall, told him a secret, a secret he kept to himself for the last two weeks. He did not want the mother to know about it. Why not? The father had wanted his wife to die in peace. Two weeks ago, a section of the senior employees was asked by the management to sign a bond— an undertaking declaring that in future they would not take part in any strike organized by the office union. He did not know what the others did, but he, the father, had not signed. He had refused. Overwhelmed, the son, estranged for so long, looked deep into the father's eyes.

A freeze.

A long freeze.

On the soundtrack, drums begin to beat. In the silence of the night, the distant sound of a police van approaching . . .

EIGHT

Deadly Discipline
When Trains Ran on Perfect Time . . .

Three films were made in three years—in 1970, 1972 and in 1973.
All three made on the big city with which, since my arrival, I had
developed a kind of love–hate relationship. In the first two films, I
made *statements,* unashamedly. I was forced to, hard pressed by
my own times, and with confidence coming 'not from always being
right but from not fearing to be wrong', as the painter Peter
McIntyre once said. In *Padatik,* the fugitive started asking questions, even *going against the tide.* When his questions were over-
ruled, he refused to accept that he had lost the battle. When it was
least expected, the father and the son arrived at a moment of truth.
For me, that was a most challenging moment. Handling a delicate
situation such as that one was pretty difficult for me. Hours of
talking it over with my actors would not lead us anywhere, because
it was a matter of intense feeling—not a matter to be argued. So I
sat with both of them, the father and the son, and told them a
story—the story of my previous cameraman, Paul Chatterjee.

The son of the civil surgeon in a North Bengal district, he
joined a revolutionary group, popularly known as Terrorist Party,
in the days of British rule. He was 16 then. Understandably, the
father was furious, threatened him a number of times and was even

ready to take drastic action. But for the intervention of the mother, he would have been thrown out of the house. One day, in the middle of the night, he was called to take part in a militant action. The action, however, fizzled out in no time and the entire group was beaten mercilessly and thrown into the prison van.

Next morning. The district hospital was surrounded by the armed police. The general ward was cleared to accommodate the arrested group, all in critical condition.

The civil surgeon came down the stairs and appeared before the door. He was required to report early. A tough man, on urgent duty! A man without any expression!

The doctor walked up to each and every bed, gave instructions to his staff, mostly monosyllabic, and walked out. Half a dozen policemen—officers and subordinates—followed him all the time, as if he too was under surveillance.

A minute passed, not more. The doctor appeared at the door once again, walked swiftly, this time there was no one following him, stopped at two or three spots, as if he was looking for an instrument he might have dropped on his round, and then, finally, stopped beside his son's bed. He bent and whispered a word or two. He seemed to be in a hurry.

'I'll resign,' whispered the enraged father and the next moment dashed back up the stairs.

I came to the end of the story and stopped.

I looked at the father and the son. They looked at each other, meaningfully. They looked resolute. I realized that the moment had arrived—the moment I was waiting for.

The shot was taken. It was superb. I embraced both of them, the father and the son—Bijon Bhattacharya and Dhritiman Chatterjee.

Now, it was time to think of a new project—a new film.

'What next?' asked Gita.

I looked at her enquiringly. 'You have had enough of such stuff,' she said. I should look for new pastures.

Kunal, 19, said neither this nor that.

In utter confusion, I toyed with ideas I had once nurtured but then laid aside. I glanced through books that came my way. But all the time, I felt dreadfully empty. I envied Charlie Chaplin who, talking to journalists at a pretty old age, said he would never be able to retire because ideas just kept popping into his head. I recalled Gabriel Garcia Márquez once telling me in an intimate conversation that 'ideas come to me through images'. And as for Istvan Szabo, the Hungarian filmmaker, there were stories scattered all over. But, silly me! I could think of nothing, see nothing. My mind and eyes grew weary.

Strangely, an idea had come to me once. Just once. That was in early 1974. One day, on my way to the Reserve Bank of India during peak hour, I was struck by an unusual spectacle: an unending, serpentine line of men and women, young and not so young, waiting patiently, unmoved. It was a huge queue, the like of which I had never seen before. I forgot about my appointment at the bank and walked along the line of countless people, watching them, talking to them. I gathered they had come from various districts to buy job-application forms. Jobs that were far fewer in number than them.

I set aside my own work and rushed to a friend of mine, Mohit Chattopadhyay—college teacher and eminent playwright, specializing in the theatre of the absurd. I told him about the spectacle and asked him if he would collaborate with me on my next script. It would be a huge crowd of 30,000 or the double that number or even more, waiting for days to collect application forms from a particular counter within a well-guarded fortress. Buying forms from a counter or two, then depositing the same, Law and Order remaining dreadfully active all the time. Until eventually the applicants turn violent and attack the impregnable fortress. The 'Chairman' of the fortress would then declare an Emergency.

Mohit gladly accepted my offer and the two of us began work on a satirical fantasy; we called it *Chorus* (1974). For right or wrong reasons, the film received the Golden Lotus, along with quite a few awards at foreign festivals, including Second Prize at the Moscow International Film Festival and the Highest Diploma of the International Federation of Film Critics Association (FIPRESCI), at the prestigious International Forum of New Cinema in Berlin. But it failed miserably in the domestic circuit. One evening, an angry group emerged out of a city theatre and, identifying me in the foyer, they rushed to me and asked if I could provide them with a subtitled print—because the film had been beyond their comprehension. The fantasy had gone over their heads. Such a reaction was not new to me; I was more than used to such encounters full of sarcasm about my work. I took it all as part of the game. But I wondered why I kept in check a beautiful line, which Lindsay Anderson, maker of the remarkable film *if . . .* (1968), a funny, bitter allegory, his all-time best, had once told me that 'today's fantasy would turn out to be tomorrow's reality!' How delightfully prophetic Lindsay had been!

The Emergency was declared in India on 26 June 1975.

Dark days followed. Press censorship was imposed. Hundreds of political activists went underground. Fear and tension ran high. Any sign of dissidence, direct or oblique, was immediately crushed. Even Tagore was considered suspect:

> Where the mind is without fear and the head is held high
> Where knowledge is free
> Where the world has not been broken up into fragments
> By narrow domestic walls
> Where words come out from the depth of truth
> Where tireless striving stretches its arms towards perfection
> Where the clear stream of reason has not lost its way
> Into the dreary desert sand of dead habit
> Where the mind is led forward by thee
> Into ever-widening thought and action
> Into that heaven of freedom, my Father,
> Let my country awake.

The Emergency came and bared its ugly teeth, affecting all our lives, though meaning very different things to different people in different contexts.

It all happened at the midnight hour when the *world* slept, as did I. As I awoke to life and my private freedom, I got the news. Big news, banner headlines! Effortlessly, I recalled another midnight hour, in 1947, when the father of the lady now prime minister asked the countrymen and the world to remember a tryst with destiny made 'long years ago' as he announced that 'the time [had come] when we shall redeem our pledge.' The father's moment had been a breakthrough; the daughter's, 28 years later, simply a bad break.

What followed between me and my world was, first, a large number of telephone calls, made and received, nothing substantive. Hours later, I went off to a friend of mine, cool-headed Dipendranath Bandopadhyay, sensitive novelist, essayist and editor of *Parichay*.

I rushed into his one-room office, pulled out a broken chair and sat down before him, as if it was he who had to answer for all that happened at that unearthly hour. To my utter dismay, he defended the promulgation of the Emergency. I was furious, he kept his cool. I wished he would get worked up so that I could be violent. All that I wanted was a verbal fight with him. Fighting him would have been, in a way, fighting the Emergency.

In impotent rage, I pushed back my chair, got up and stormed out. And vowed never to return. A year passed and, to my surprise, one day he paid me a visit at home. His face was full of anguish. He looked exploited, oppressed, wronged and deceived. In a few words, he apologized; it was a kind of a confession. I could see how intensely he had debated with himself all this while, and suffered unbearably. Years later, long after the Emergency was withdrawn, he died a premature death. Dipendranath was a gem of a man and a writer.

The Berlin Film Festival in those days used to be held during June–July. My film *Chorus*, good or bad, but winner of the Golden Lotus, was the official entry at the International Forum of New Cinema, and presented at the forum just a week after the Emergency was declared in India. When, after two hours, the curtain was drawn, Ulrich Gregor, director of the forum, led me on stage and got ready to start the question–answer session. A young woman, visibly excited, literally sprang out of her seat and spoke straight at me in immaculate English: 'I think I am correct when I say, hidden behind a satire, yours is a militant film. Now, Mrinal Sen, be brave and tell us how, in the context of the message of your film, would you relate it to the state of emergency imposed in your country?'

Frankly, I felt uncomfortable, and Gregor got upset. I had no choice but to ask him to go ahead with the translation of the question both in German and French. He was good at both. Earning a few moments while Gregor was busy doing the translation, I composed my thoughts and spoke with pauses between the lines. 'I am glad,' I said, 'that you call mine a militant film. And, true, much to my countrymen's discomfort, the Emergency has just been imposed in India. But, to be honest, I am not aware of the legality of the Emergency. So I do not know when and where I cross the boundary of law. Under the circumstances, I prefer to keep mum and not answer your question.' I repeated, 'Sorry, no answer from me, not a word.'

The hall was silent for a few moments. I did not know how it happened, but it did happen and I got a bit emboldened and said, 'Got my answer? Have you? I shall not answer. I hope I am clear.'

Instantly, there were cheers and applause. I felt important, and Gregor was relieved. The rest of the questions and my answers were innocent, simple, even indifferent.

At the end of an hour-long session, the person who came first to shake hands with me was the head of the local diplomats in the Indian Consulate in West Germany. Beaming, he heartily congratulated me for smartly handling the questions but expected me to categorically admit that the prime minister was my leader! There was another diplomat behind him who understood me very well; he looked quite intelligent and was the Indian ambassador to

GDR, coming from East Berlin. He looked at me and smiled a mischievous smile. I winked at him and smiled back. Diplomats, after all, are not all K. P. S. Menon or T. N. Kaul or their ilk.

A collection of essays by Satyajit Ray, *Our Films, Their Films*, was published around that time. I reviewed the book for the weekly magazine *Sunday*. In one of the essays, 'Renoir in Calcutta' (1949), about one of his three trips to the city prior to his filming *Le fleuve* (*The River*) (1951), Ray spoke about Renoir's annoyance with the American mania for organization—everything on time, everything going by the schedules, trains running on perfect time. Having said it, based on the conversation with the French master, Ray, with his penchant for humour, concluded, '[For Renoir], [t]he important thing, however, was to get away from the synthetic environment of Hollywood, and India was as good a refuge as any. [. . .] There will be no schedules to distract him, and [Ray uses Renoir's own words here] no checking and double-checking of inspiration. And, of course, out here, the trains never will run on time.'

Since I reviewed this book during the Emergency, I played innocent and wondered, 'Had the French master come now, would he have got the same freedom in India, as assured by Ray, when, from 26 June 1975, trains had all been running on perfect time?'

I said it, I wrote it, but before going to press, the editor asked me if he could strike off my last line from the review which was otherwise pretty good. I did not refuse. I did not feel like it. I could appreciate the problems the editor had to work with under the Emergency. The editor was M. J. Akbar.

The axe of the Emergency fell on me another time. A line was carefully plucked and summarily dismissed. The line, incidentally, was a quote from Nehru. He wrote it during the British rule in India and I used it during the Emergency. As I said earlier, I was made to realize that the truth meant different things to different people in different contexts. What he wrote and I quoted was, 'Law is but the will of the dominant faction and Order is the reflex of an all-pervading fear.'

The Emergency was withdrawn after a year and a half, or a bit longer. After suffering a jolt, losing an election and spending a night in jail, Indira Gandhi came to power once again. Before the expiry of her tenure and as she was growing from strength to strength, she was brutally assassinated. An act of ugly vengeance!

The dynastic rule continued, the son took over. But one fateful evening the son too was killed. Incomprehensible! The entire country poisoned by hate and suspicion. A cannibal time!

I made my film *Mrigayaa* (*The Royal Hunt*) during the Emergency, in 1976, the same year that Ritwik Ghatak died. Ray and his team were busy working on the essentials to start *Shatranj ke Khilari* (*The Chess Players*) (1977), based on one of the most powerful stories of Premchand.

For quite some time, Ray was being pressed by his art designer, Bansi Chandragupta, to take up *Shatranj ke Khilari*; to me, he'd recommended Premchan's *Kafan* (The shroud). That was Ray's first and only film in Hindi, in 1976–77, and he had a wonderful cast: Sanjeev Kumar, Saeed Jaffrey, Shabana Azmi, Tom Alter and others, and the outstanding Richard Attenborough. Being a perfectionist—and Bansi was no less—the materials to characterize the period were collected with extreme care.

Mrigayaa, made in 1975–76, was a take-off from an Odia story, the story of a young tribal and a senior British administrator. Nothing was in common between the two men to ever meet and understand each other. Nothing, but one common passion—hunting. To both of them, a big game was a big game, a prey a prey. That was probably why the young hunter and a loving husband reacted like a primitive hunter when the lackeys of the native landlord kidnapped his wife. He killed the landlord as the wild pigs are killed when they destroy crops or a tiger for lifting a child. Avenged, he brought his 'trophy', the most heinous game in his area, to the man who could understand him as a hunter. Finally, the Imperial justice gave the verdict. The tribal was hanged.

The text went that far, no further. In the film, the hanging was presented with customary fanfare, as done officially, a bit of a long-drawn process. But that was not all in *Mrigayaa*. Immediately after the act of hanging, as in the text, a sharp cut revealed a vast undulating tract, a massive hill with no vegetation but only boulders, huge, dominating the scene and the dawn moving in slowly. Scattered, the community of tribals, men and women, young and old, remained standing still, as if for eternity. To me, it was a kind of ritual which we, the filmmakers, composed. Not really a tribal phenomenon.

Almost all were first-time actors—Mithun Chakraborty, Mamata Shankar, Bob Wright and his wife, Anne, and a very old friend of mine, an IPTA activist from its formative period, Sajal Roy Chowdhury. All of them acted powerfully, all of them seemed to have an intuitive flair for what the roles demanded. And all of them got immediate attention.

When, on 24 December 1975, the members of the crew and I were having our last session before proceeding to location early next morning, there appeared Ritwik Ghatak at the door, aided by a young man. He was probably released from the hospital, or had forcibly discharged himself on a personal bond. He came to our apartment, and none of us failed to notice that he was gasping for air. Gasping, and talking, and laughing. 'Gita!' he shouted.

Gita came into the room and was frightened at the sight of him. He looked thinner than the thinnest, drained of all strength and vitality. He said he was hungry. Gita rushed to the kitchen and brought something for him to eat. He ate a lot. He said, 'I won't drink any more.'

But he was reeking of it all the time. He yawned and said, 'I won't live for very long now.' He asked Gita to sit beside him. She sat. He said again, 'I won't live for very long.'

Gita said, 'If you do not stop drinking, how will you survive?'

'I won't drink any more,' he said. Then he looked at me disdainfully, and turned to Gita.

'You know, Gita, Mrinal is a wonderful man, but his *Bhuvan Shome* . . . Phew!'

Then, that terrible night—6 February 1976. We had come back from location two days ago and were getting ready for the hanging sequence when, in the evening, I got a frantic call from Ritwik's daughter.

'Where are you calling from?' I asked. I smelt danger.

She was calling me from the hospital.

I knew he was fast approaching the end. I asked Gita to inform Ray and the others and I rushed to the hospital. The superintendent asked me to go upstairs and be there for the end.

I was beside Ritwik as he lay there, dying. His daughter and a family friend were downstairs, waiting.

Ritwik did not see me, but I was very much there. Two young doctors were trying hard to let him live for at least a little while. He and I, and two doctors. One after another, the young doctors continued mouth-to-mouth breathing in order to resuscitate their patient for temporary revival from imminent death.

He died. That was 5 minutes past 11 at night. Perhaps, by dying, he saved himself. The last few years of his life were one big unfortunate adventure.

Many years passed, but I still retain some blurred images of him from the days of Paradise Café. In thoughts, in ideas, he remained the same larger-than-life Ghatak, reckless Ghatak, heartless Ghatak, undisciplined Ghatak, inimitable Ghatak, and, above all else, the adorable Ghatak.

The wife and the son, the youngest of the three, came by the first train early in the morning. Lakshmi, his wife, was teaching in a girls' school about 150 km from the city.

NINE

Wherever I Go,
Things Keep On Happening . . .

Who said it? Something like this! Pablo Neruda? I think, yes, in his *Residence on Earth*:

> If you should ask me where I've been all this time,
> I have to say 'Things happen.'

Nothing could be truer than this. And this time it was in a village in Telangana, about 100 km from Hyderabad. A village where, in the Nizam's time, a woman labourer in a landlord's farm, begging for half an hour's leave to breastfeed her child at home, had to vouch for herself by squeezing her breast in the presence of the vassal's man. I found the village and the people absolutely right for my film. The only condition that I had to brave was that the film was to be made in Telugu, the language of Andhra Pradesh.

This script too was written in collaboration with Mohit Chattopadhyay—based on *Kafan*, Premchand's last story before he died in 1936. It all took place on a winter night in a village, where the son's young wife lay fainting in the throes of childbirth, which stretched into the next day. All that happened in the night was in the text; and whatever happened the next day came up in the latter part of the script. The beginning and the middle were our own, based on points offered directly or obliquely by the text. We called the film *Oka Oori Katha* (*The Marginal Ones*) (1977). They were three in the family—the father, the son, the young daughter-in-law.

Creating the script was a challenging job. Filming it was equally demanding, if not more. Premchand's story was set in a village in Uttar Pradesh. While writing the script, for obvious reasons, we could think only of the rural scene in Bengal. Finally, the film was planted in Telengana, in the south. We travelled a long way. From Uttar Pradesh we went to Andhra Pradesh via West Bengal. True, we had plenty of 'alien' features to familiarize ourselves with— outfits, food habits, local customs, rituals, modes of expression and, of course, the language, and so on. Not so simple to familiarize and fall in love with, until we could develop a kind of respect for the circumstances in which the characters lived, grew and also perished. But what we found strikingly similar—whether in the north, south and east, and whether biting cold or blazing sun—were the poverty and exploitation. Which is precisely what the story was about—the story of poverty, the story of exploitation—the same story everywhere, anywhere in the world.

However, the reaction of the author's son, Amrit Rai, admittedly, an authority on Premchand, was rather seesaw. He loved the film, found it a shattering experience, but could not agree with our interpretation. I had anticipated that, and told him that his father too, had he been alive, would not have agreed with our understanding of his story. I asked Amrit Rai if he had any regrets about allowing me to make the film. Rai said an emphatic no. He pressed my hand. That was sweet of him.

In the written text and in the film, like others in the village, the family in question was miserably poor. There was no lack of heavy work in the village, but the father and son turned their back on the *empty-headed* toilers who worked and starved. They pilfered and begged, they even borrowed but never paid back, and if they worked one day, they would take the next three off. People abused them, beat them, but they did not suffer. Totally free of worldly cares, theirs was a strange life. They conquered hunger and continued to pooh-pooh the handful of the privileged class who knew very well how to profit by exploiting the poor. The father was a sort of freak, the son his spiritual heir. We aimed at a devastating fantasy born out of a story of poverty and strange idiosyncrasy. The father and son being the absurd extension of reality, the young wife of the son struggled in stark reality.

We scanned the characters and redefined their roles. While filming, we discovered in the father a towering iconoclast. That was where Amrit Rai differed from us. Both he and the academics opined that he was the victim of a cruel society, dehumanized. Though he agreed that the father was played by a powerful actor.

To watch Vasudeva Rao play the father was quite an experience. He gave the impression of a prehistoric caveman appearing before the camera at our call. At appropriate places, he displayed a rare kind of sycophancy; and at suitably dramatic moments, he bubbled over with sarcasm and anger.

But he failed me once. Only once. At one past midnight—and that was the last shot of the day's schedule—I asked him to yawn between two words. He tried but failed. Tried again, he failed again. Ten times he tried. Every time he tried, he failed. I got furious. I shook him and shouted, 'Can't you yawn?'

Vasudeva was silent for a few moments. Then, forcing a smile, he said softly, 'I do not think I have ever yawned—I have worked all my life.'

I felt crushed. I embraced him.

At their leisure, Mohit and Vasudeva had a number of sittings. Mohit collected material to do the story of the man.

Vasudeva was born in a poor family, the poorest of the poor in the locality. He did not have any formal education, did not even go to a primary school. Failing to send him to school, his father handed him over to a village opera, Guppi Company, where he was to sing and dance and occasionally run errands. A helpless Vasudeva, as he prepared to leave home and his family, began to cry. With his head high, the father asked the boy to face everything that would come, and fear nothing. *Paroa nehi*! 'Worry not!' the father said. Since then, and till the time he came to us, that short, pithy expression was the son's watchword, his slogan to sustain himself. He said he had not realized that the father's parting advice could mean so much to him. Only when he was asked to yawn, he failed.

'I hang my head in shame,' he said to Mohit, despondently.

'Paroa nehi!' said Mohit, to cheer him up.

He looked up and smiled.

Vasudeva was a remarkable man. He died last year, died unsung.

Krishnamoorthy was another loveable man in our team, tall and dark and the same age as I. I did not know him at all, until, at my request, P. Sundaryya, the communist leader, sent him to our camp. I'd asked Sundaryya if he could put me in touch with someone who knew absolutely everything about that particular region and could stay with us for the entire period. That would be a great help to my team. The very next day we met, and Krishnamoothy made it very clear that the job would be his labour of love. He too never went to school. He'd learnt through experience, he said.

Krishnamoorthy was immensely helpful not only to me but also to all members of the team. Particularly to Mamata Shankar, who played the son's wife who, on that fateful night, frequently fainted in the throes of childbirth and was found dead early in the morning. With intense care and affection, he taught Mamata how to collect firewood, how to cook, how to wash dishes and clothes, how to keep the courtyard clean, how to lift water from the well, how to handle the grindstone. Pointing to a woman working in the field, he asked her to learn how to wear a sari. He taught her all this and many more things in their minutest detail, because quite often he had seen film actresses making a mess of everything and looking intolerably false. Mamata became totally dependent on Krishnamoorthy.

One day, when we were filming a sequence, Krishnamoorthy heard one of our actors, playing a farmer, speaking his lines. He had a problem with one line. He came close to the actor and asked him to say it again. The actor did so. Krishnamoorthy grimaced.

'What's up?' I asked, surprised.

Without mincing matters, he said, 'You have put a wrong line into his mouth.'

I looked at him enquiringly.

He said, 'It is about that old man, the father who *chews and eats and sleeps like a water buffalo.*'

'Right! That is precisely what we say,' I explained, 'to mean that so-and-so is lazy.'

'Lazy, you say?' Krishnamoorthy was shocked and surprised. 'That shows you people are city dwellers,' he retorted, 'You know, we, in villages, treat water buffaloes as our source of sustenance. They work so hard. Just as we do.'

As simple as that! Like film actresses always making a mess of everything and looking intolerably false! The line we put into the farmer's mouth did not conform to fact—it smacked of falsehood!

Mohit and I realized we had been wrong. With our urban upbringing, it was perhaps immoral on our part to go the way we did. Happily, we did not.

We packed up after 19 days of inspired filming, learning and unlearning, and, in the process, becoming more careful, if not more wise.

Back home, Kunal, standing at the door, was beaming. Was it because the Left Front in West Bengal had a landslide victory in the election and formed a stable government? No, not that. Kunal had fallen in love with Nisha. They acknowledged it just a week ago, and Gita made a day of it. And I got the news on my arrival. Great news! *Things keep happening!*

Rest and post-production work for around four weeks—then off to Algiers via Paris. I decided to have a stopover for a day in Paris and catch the onward flight the next morning.

In Paris, I had an appointment with a friend at Cinémathèque française. If not the largest, the Cinémathèque was considered the most prestigious of all the film centres, having one of the finest archives and a huge complex of diverse activities relating to world cinema. Even now it has retained its reputation and shine. That was my second visit to Cinémathèque, in 1977. The first visit, unforgettable, had been in 1969.

In 1969, I was in Venice with *Bhuvan Shome*. The evening of the first screening, I was quite nervous. In addition to the usual festival crowd, there were many distinguished people in the theatre. Next morning, I was woken up by a telephone call in my hotel room. The call was from Paris and the caller was Henri Langlois, head of Cinémathèque française, a living legend! I had never met him but had heard so much about him. So a call from such a man was indeed a surprise for me! The biggest ever! And why not? A man known and revered as the custodian of the treasures of world cinema—it was he! One who was answerable to no one, not even to André Malraux. For, whatever was done for Cinémathèque, it was Henri Langlois.

Introducing himself, Langlois asked me if, on my way back to India, I would come to Paris and carry my film along with me. If my trip had been planned differently, he wanted me to promise that the plan would be altered. It sounded rather like a command. But that was Langlois and his manner of speaking, as I gathered later. He was not a man of many words, I also heard.

I wondered how the news had travelled in but a few hours, between Venice and Paris, about an unknown film and an unknown me. But it did. I'm certain that Langlois' friends had been present at the screening; some of them may even have spoken to me after the show, and then one of them must have called him in Paris. I was curious who it was. I suspected either of the two women who had collected my hotel address room number: one was Madame Kawakita, the grand old lady of Japanese cinema, never tired of moving from one festival to the other even at her age, and largely instrumental in introducing Japanese masters to the Western world; the other, of the same age, was Lotte Eisner, wife of the famous composer Hans Eisner, a confirmed communist who, when in the United States, had a tough time with the House Un-American Activities Committee.

So from Venice, I went off to Paris. My film went through a different channel. On the appointed day and at the appointed hour, I reached the office of the Cinémathèque française, my first time ever. I was late by a few minutes. A lady, tall and heavy, Mary Meerson, was in her office downstairs. She saw me, stood up, came out and asked, 'I suspect you are Mrinal Sen, aren't you? Langlois is waiting for you. Go!'

Meerson gave me an unwomanly push. I was about to fall down the stairs, but I held on somehow. That was her way, I was told.

I had a fairly long session with Langlois at his office. Considering he was not a man of many words, I was ecstatic. And I hoped the encounter had not left him unhappy.

And, today, on 31 May 2004, I sent a mail to my publishers that 'I cannot but dramatically appear with an outstanding postscript to the colourful story of Langlois, which my son Kunal sent me this morning from Chicago.' The story was revealed in this year's Cannes Film Festival, which concluded on 23 May. I had no news of it—neither from the international media, nor a single word from the high-profile official delegation from India who cared only for the beach and glamour, and for an industry which they now call *entertainment*. Film critic Michael Wilmington, in the *Chicago Tribune*, penned this stupendous story. Here is a long excerpt:

> There is a canard afoot that festivals such as Cannes are simply snobfests. That is not true, and nothing proves it more than another great documentary (one being Michael Moore's top prize-winner, *Fahrenheit 9/11*) at this year's Cannes: Jacques Richard's *Henri Langlois: The Phantom of the Cinémathèque* (*Le fantôme d'Henri Langlois*). Only

one hundred or so people saw it at the screening in Salle Bunuel (named after Spain's Luis Bunuel), including Chicagoans Lisa Nesselson and Glen Myrent (who translated the subtitles) and Facets-founder Milos Stehik— probably because *Fantome* runs three hours and thirty-two minutes. Nothing I saw moved me in quite the same way.

The movie's subject, Henri Langlois, may be unknown to many—though it is a name any movie-lover should revere. Langlois, born in Turkey, was the longtime director of the Cinémathèque française, which he founded in 1936 (with filmmaker Georges Franju), nurtured under great difficulties through the Second Great War and brought to world prominence in the '50s.

Langlois decided, initially without government aid, to assemble a film library. At first he did it selectively, preserving what conventional wisdom considered the classics. [Finally] he decided that conventional wisdom might be wrong, that it was best to try to preserve and show as much as possible. The official critical establishment might have missed some classics.

It turned out that they had missed quite a few. It was largely through Langlois that the high French reputations of Howard Hawks, Alfred Hitchcock, Orson Welles, Buster Keaton, Luis Bunuel, Fritz Lang and many others were first made—he passed on those enthusiasms to the young Parisians who flocked to the Cinémathèque.

It was at the Cinémathèque's daily showings, beginning in the '40s, that a group of young French cinephiles— notably, future moviemakers—François Truffaut, Jean-Luc

Godard, Claude Chabrol, Eric Rhomer and Jacques Rivette (all quoted in the film)—got their movie education. The group above, who called themselves The Children of the Cinémathèque, haunted Langlois' theatre, most of the core crew jamming into front-row seats, and, when they could not get the prize places, lying on the floor before them.

[. . . Langlois's] Cinémathèque was founded on the idea that all films (initially) are created equal; the cream eventually rises to the top. Langlois had tastes and prejudices—he began his showings with his own personal pick of the 100 great films—but he showed everything. And he tried to save (almost) everything.

[. . .] A messy packrat kind of guy, big-bellied, moon-eyed and eccentric, his constant companion and Cinémathèque's right hand was Mary Meerson, another fanatic cinephile. They were an odd-looking pair and Langlois was very casual in his methods. (Many of the Cinémathèque's earliest acquisitions were illegal prints the studio owners probably would have destroyed.) Eventually, he ran afoul of the more orderly French political establishment who funded him—and who, in 1968, tried to choke off Cinémathèque funds.

To a man (and woman), the now prominent world cineastes, who owed him a debt of gratitude, rose up in protest in the Paris streets (including, crucially, many from Hollywood). Truffaut and Godard stood side by side with Nicholas Ray. They all saved Langlois's job and his Cinémathèque.

It was a debt well paid. For it was Langlois and Meerson who planted the seed for most of the cinephilia, which followed the film festivals, the archives, the whole video and DVD industries and even the cinematic new waves of numerous countries, beginning with Truffaut and Godard's France and then surging up in Eastern and Western Europe, South America, Asia, Australia and the US. It is one of the few stories about bureaucratic assaults that had a (temporarily) happy ending, and it is told by Richard with such passion and grace that time vanishes.

Another story was told to me by Louis Malle, then in New York, in 1982. Yet another astonishing anecdote about Langlois's idiosyncratic way of functioning.

After a retrospective of Ray's films at the Cinémathèque, which was a big success, Langlois decided to have a month-long screening of Indian films. A huge number were collected from official sources, and a few from here and there, all of which were previewed with adequate care. Not a single film was left unseen. Finally, as always, he had his own picks for the programme. And the strangest thing happened: he decided to open with *Baishey Shravan*, even though the last reel was missing for reasons unknown. Langlois felt that the session should start with the film of his choice—he did not care about the missing reel. Because of his knowledge of India, Louis Malle was asked to make the opening speech. Before the screening, Langlois made it known to his audience that they would not see the end of the film. I knew nothing about this until, in New York, Malle told me all about it.

Back to my Algerian tour! The trip was short and quiet. Unexpectedly, I met an expatriate Ethiopian, Haile Gerima, director of a long film, *Harvest 3000 Years* (1976)—a film on Ethiopian agrarian issues, which I had seen at the film institute at Pune and loved. He told me he could not make a second film due to lack of funds and so had moved to the US and was now teaching cinema somewhere on the East Coast. Med Hondo of Mauratania, whose film *Soleil Ô* (Oh, sun) left an impression on me, was also in Algiers. He asked me if I could send him a translation of a Tagore poem on Africa. I said I would, but did not. I was always, and still am, very liberal about making promises and keeping very few.

Outside the city boundary, I stood before the house of Albert Camus, who, when in Stockholm to receive the Nobel Prize in Literature in 1957, had an encounter with an Arab university student. The student accused him of not caring about the Arabs in Algeria, to which, Camus quietly answered: 'I must also condemn the blind terrorism that can be seen in the streets of Algiers, for example, which someday might strike my mother or family. I believe in justice, but I will defend my mother before justice.'

Standing there, I wondered how once, before he was killed in an automobile accident near Paris, Camus had said that there would be no death less meaningful than one in an automobile accident. His death reminded me of another freak death in my own city, Jibanananda Das, a poet of unusual strength and elegance, who, in 1954, was run over by a tramcar and died a few days later. Camus disliked cars, especially the ones driving at high speed.

Homeward-bound, I felt tired. I wondered why I had to accept each and every invitation that came my way. I should not, for various reasons. Waste of time, in particular. On the flight, I decided that I would be choosy in future—but it did not take me long to be otherwise. I got a call from the Festival Director in Delhi, asking me when my Telengana film would be ready for entry at the Karlovy Vary Festival in Czechoslovakia. I could have very well said that it would not be ready for the festival, but I did not. The film was ready just in time, it was entered on the dot, and I was invited for a week. And just two days before I was to leave, I received another call from Delhi, this time from the Chinese Embassy. As a gesture of goodwill, the Chinese People's Association for Friendship with Foreign Countries invited me and my wife to visit their country. The invitation was sent through their embassy in Delhi. The year was 1978, when the long-drawn Indo-Chinese impasse had just thawed. Gita was thrilled, and I was no less excited. More so, because we came to know that we would be the first to cross the border when ice had just started melting. There was no way I could trim the heavy schedule of foreign tours. Perhaps I did not want to.

As always, this time too, mine was a lone journey to Karlovy Vary. Just like I always did, except for two trips when I had company. Once, in 1973, when both Gita and Kunal travelled with me to the Mannheim-Heidelberg International Film Festival, where I headed the jury. Kunal spent his time visiting the department stores, trying to buy an electronic calculator against the meal coupons supplied by the festival. And a second time, later that same year, to the Tehran Festival in the time of Shah and Queen Farah, where Gita had been invited as the spouse of the juror. Gita loved the land and its people, loved the eyes and the songs of the pretty Iranian girls, and most importantly, greatly enjoyed the frequent displays of wit and humour, all very spontaneous, by another member of the jury, the great Frank Capra, Sicilian by birth but a non-Hollywoodian American filmmaker, director of *Arsenic and Old Lace* (1944), my most favourite. He was brilliant company. Once, during the screening, he told me he was feeling frightfully sleepy—because, right from the beginning, it was a bad film and it would end up no better. He asked me to wake him up if I found anything worthy of notice. When at the appropriate moment I woke him up, he literally jumped onto his seat to see what a juror should not have missed. Nothing of the kind. The show was over. Capra was relieved but also worried that the viewers might catch him as a 'sleeping' juror. He had been snoring—that was his problem.

The visit to China in August 1978 was Gita's third trip abroad, a trip both of us thoroughly enjoyed and which even prompted Gita, a non-writer, to write an intimate story, charming and moving, for the Bengali magazine *Drishya*—a cine-club magazine—though her text had nothing to do with cinema.

Hong Kong to Canton, by train, to the mainland, then from Canton to Beijing (Peking). Our journey began from there. First to the stupendous mausoleum of Mao Tse-tung, looking divine. An excerpt from Gita's story:

> We came to Mao Tse-tung Memorial Hall. We saw a huge crowd, gathered to pay tribute to the man 'lying in state'. We joined the line. Before and behind us, the waiting crowd, the slow-moving crowd, very slow, all Chinese, all uniformed young soldiers, all incredibly disciplined. There was silence all around, a silence punctuated by the soft footsteps of the crowd, a silence that was stifling, a silence that threatened to consume me completely. I stood before the man lying in state since the day he died. He looked clear and calm, unruffled. I looked deep into him. I remained unmoved. I remembered the dreary days in West

Bengal when, day in and day out, the young people chanting 'Mao' were mercilessly killed. Mysteriously, faces appeared before me, one after another, faces in front of me, faces behind me, faces whom I knew and whom I'd never heard of, a crowd of faces, a huge lot of them, asking the man and their 'Chairman': Why did they do it! What for! Suddenly, tears welled up in my eyes. I began to cry.

Ours was a tight schedule. Travelling to various places, visiting museums, schools, universities and film studios, attending seminars, answering questions, watching plays and films, and acrobatics too, and finally, on the fifteenth day, back to Canton. All in a mad rush.

And the last night with them. Another excerpt from Gita's story:

We were four in all travelling together from one end of the country to the other—we two, our interpreter and one old lady, very ordinarily clothed, wearing a three-quarter pyjama and an ordinary shirt, like we see in our city. And a pair of rubber slippers, like we say 'hawaii chappals'. She was always with us, officially instructed to answer all questions relating primarily to politics and history. We came to know from our interpreter that she was a very knowledgeable person and a full-time worker of the Communist Party. All four of us reached Canton on the last day to catch a train to cross the border, on our way to Hong Kong, early next morning. After dinner, the lady and the interpreter came to our room. She wanted to tell us something which, during the duty period, she had kept to herself.

For some time, she was quiet and then she opened up, told us her own story, bit by bit. We were Indians—that is why. That was what she said. When she was seven, she saw her father being buried alive by the marauding Japanese during the aggression. Her husband took part in the historic 'Long March'. In 1949, after the revolution, he became the governor of the province where we had visited the memorial of Hsiuen Tsang and where, to one side, our lady had silently shed some tears. That was where her father was brutally killed. Her husband came to India as the ambassador in 1956 and left in 1962. He had to. She was with him right through. Later, the Gang of Four's disgrace fell on him and he was sent to a deserted place in the midst of the hills. He died, fighting loneliness, in 1972. She said it all, gave a long pause, and said again, 'The only companion I have now is my little granddaughter.'

I did not know if she wanted to say more, but she could not. She burst into convulsive sobs.

What a woman! A woman endowed with dignity of a rare kind, and always keeping herself at a respectable distance! One so deeply immersed in politics yet so human! A distraught daughter, a dutiful wife, a loving grandmother—all in one!

But talking about China and dropping not a word about the Great Wall of China is like reading *Hamlet* without the Prince of Denmark.

Because of our nonstop two-week schedule, Gita grew tired and was having breathing trouble. In addition, her cardiac condition was not good. Even then, she was determined to go to the Great Wall. Two days before we were to leave for Canton on our way back to India, we witnessed one of the great wonders of the world, which at least at that time, was in a wonderful state of preservation. I advised Gita not to climb the wall and walk because she was not keeping well. She was in two minds—to climb or not to climb. Suddenly, she opened her diary and started scribbling. She loved scribbling. This was a quick note to Kunal.

'What are you doing?' I asked.

'Do you see the writing on the wall?' she asked me, quietly.

Gita's note to Kunal was precisely that: 'Not to climb the Great Wall is an act of cowardice.' Gita wrote it for her son and then got ready to climb.

From Canton we boarded a train, crossed the border and reached Hong Kong where we decided to spend a day. Next morning, Gita took a flight to return to her household, and, on invitation, I left for Los Angeles via Tokyo to take part in a weeklong, in-group global discourse on cinema and society. The event, not quite common, had been organized by the National Commission of International Archive of Cinema in collaboration with the American Film Institute. Frankly, it was not that we, the participants, grew any the wiser through such a discourse, but the fact that we, the few, met and exchanged experiences acted as a stimulant. It was a free-for-all kind of event which we enjoyed as we would an outing. Those invited were Michael Cacoyannis from Greece, Lindsay Anderson from England, Agnes Varda from France, Ousmane Sembane from Senegal, Youssef Chahine from Egypt, Susumo Hani from Japan and I from India. Seven in all. Talking among ourselves and also interacting with American directors, one or two every day. The grand old man of Hollywood, King Vidor, retired long ago, came one day and spent hours with us. His categoric refusal to accept some famous films made in

THINGS KEEP ON HAPPENING

recent times bore absolutely no malice. He had forgotten the title of a Japanese film, he said, which during the half hour that he watched it, showed more than ten variations of the sex act. I asked him if, by any chance, it could be *In the Realm of the Senses* (1976) by Nagisa Oshima. That was it! He patted me on the back and wondered if I had seen the entire film. He gave me a sly look. I smiled. He said—and he felt proud—that war films used to be made in the 30s, not any more. He kept his fingers crossed about a film which possibly would be ready next year—Francis Ford Coppola's *Apocalypse Now* (1979). His statements were unusually plain and simple.

At an evening party I met Tony Richardson (director of the 1962 film *The Loneliness of the Long Distance Runner*), one of the stormy petrels of British cinema. They were three, the triumvirate, when their cinema needed a radical change—he, Lindsay Anderson and Karel Reisz (director of the 1960 film *Saturday Night and Sunday Morning*). Richardson left his country and came to Hollywood in search of cinema, but drew a blank. In the boisterous party that evening, among all the familiar faces, he who'd run the long distance was a lonely man. He was on the verge of losing his faith, his soul was restless and tortured. I could see he was doomed.

When he died, he died unsung.

TEN

I Pull Myself by the Hair and
Force Myself to Look at the Mirror . . .

That was the time when I journeyed a lot, but never for pleasure.

Back home, the journey within.

June 1977! My team and I were in Telengana, filming *Oka Oori Katha*. That was when a new government came up in the state of West Bengal, a government of the Left. Hopes mounted, so did the excitement. But the leaders had no magic wand with which to work miracles; and so they could not wave away the ghost of inherited liabilities that continued to make inroads on the election manifesto. As a result, promises made with pomp and fanfare began to lose their sheen. Alongside, new problems continued to pile up. Slowly and steadily, popular hopes were belied. On the one hand, in some measure, large or small, deep-rooted problems were being solved; on the other, new problems continued to create bigger fissures. Yet there was no dearth of dreams and dreamers. Nor any dearth of self-complacency.

In the meantime, a friend of mine, Subhendhu Mukhopadhyay, gave me a big file, a cyclostyled copy, which he'd collected from his anthropologist brother, Sudhendu Mukhopadhyay. It was a comprehensive study of the pavement dwellers of the big city. With more than a hundred case histories collected by a group of young anthropologists under the supervision of Mukhopadhyay, the survey was highly revealing and presented an in-depth study of an aspect of the country's agro-economic scenario. Again, in collaboration with Mohit Chattopadhyay, the script had reality and fantasy inextricably entwined—a landless farmer coming to the city during the lean period between ploughing and harvesting, now in search of a place on the pavement. In the process, fighting in darkness and fighting with darkness—a kind of shadow boxing with a huge sandbag many times larger than him. We called it *Parashuram* (1979) (named after the sixth avatar of Vishnu who carries a battle-axe). He'd come to the city carrying an axe on his shoulder. He told people that he'd killed a tiger with the axe while he'd been in the forest, cutting wood. Partly impressed and partly in jest, an old pavement dweller had named him Parashuram, and narrated the story of the mythical man who took 'revenge by killing millions of adversaries with his axe'. It was a courageous project on the pavement dwellers of the city, based on Mukhopadhyay's anthropological study. The new government gave me the entire fund as well as total freedom to make the film. On the whole, however, it failed to turn out well enough at the boxoffice.

I felt like collapsing. Though only temporarily.

Once again, a trip abroad and then a swift return to the city.

Back home, I looked around me. Looked around and remembered a line from *Marat/Sade*, a play by the highly original Peter Weiss—'The important thing is to pull yourself up by your own hair to turn yourself inside out and see the whole world with fresh eyes.' I felt an urgency to seek silence, to withdraw within, to find the enemy within. So, now, much less of pointing my finger at the enemy outside and more at my own world, at myself. To cut myself down to size. Thus *Ek Din Pratidin* (*And Quiet Rolls the Dawn*) (1979). A new beginning.

The film was based on a short story by Amalendu Chakraborty, in which everything happened in one night. In an old mansion ravaged by time and let out to a dozen families living life at the bare edges of survival. It was about a family of seven huddled up in two small rooms and, more particularly, about the sole breadwinner of that family, a young woman in her mid-twenties, practically absent through the film until an hour or so before dawn, she appears on the scene, a bit tired. The story was about the night-long wait by the family because she had not returned home after her office hours. Something she had never done before, never ever. In the screenplay, a couple of minutes after the story began, a voice-over was planted, the voice of a commentator, and he, a sort of chronicler of history, in just two minutes, told the story of an age-old mansion, built in 1857, the year of the Indian Mutiny—the mansion that witnessed the rule of the East India Company and the subsequent governance by Queen Victoria, Empress of India, followed by political ups and downs; the partition of Bengal, preceded and followed by meetings, processions, riots, bloodshed, famines, exodus; as well as the uneventful life of the family of seven and the fateful night of the long and frightening wait.

Again, a little before the curtain was drawn and the family lost all hope of the girl's return, the second daughter in the family, still in college, had a fight with the mother—the two of them hurling against each other in dreadful frustration—and then indulged in what one could well call a monologue. Again, almost in the same tone as the voice of a chronicler, looking *beyond* and *building* history that would come *to be*—the story of the family, not of seven any more but six, moving out to a still-cheaper place to live in, when this college student would have no choice but to discontinue her studies and try for a modest job in some office. And then, one disastrous night, a similar story of a long wait would be repeated. A dead end!

Everything that happened in *Ek Din Pratidin* was set between the two—it was like treating the main story as an extension of a sociopolitical history that was and, as a prelude to another story, that would be *told*. After all, nothing can happen in a void, nothing can drop out of a vacuum, nothing can grow in isolation. The dressing, as I have just described it, was to help us put the film in a perspective that suggested the continuity of history.

On the surface, a simple story, with plot and incident de-emphasized, *Ek Din Pratidin* gave me immense scope to probe, to capture every movement of the arrow quivering in the flesh, and to expose the people's connivance in a male-dominated conformist society. The attempt was to point my accusing finger at the enemy within, at my own community. All quietly, unobtrusively, furtively, as though the characters and the crowd appearing in the film were all at fault.

To elucidate, a few excerpts from the script:

Night deepens, time passes, and the search goes on in the usual quarters—police station, hospitals, and even a mortuary. Topu, the son in his early twenties, and his friend with a scooter, go from one place to the other. No trace of Chinu, the sole breadwinner.

Night grinds on and the huge decrepit mansion continues talking in unceasing whispers—some with genuine concern, some with mock sympathy.

When, at last, the clock strikes three, the family loses all hope of the absentee returning. Shyamal, the neighbour upstairs, and his wife, who have been with the family for some time, now decide to leave them to themselves.

Shyamal and his wife are crossing the courtyard. He stops abruptly, as one of the elderly women lodgers appears, followed by others.

'You people . . . ? What are you doing here?'

'Is there any news?'

'Why are you so agitated? Leave them alone for a while, to themselves. Come on, let's go.'

The family, now numbering six, in the room. Gloom prevails. Poltu, the youngest, eight, half-lying in bed, propped up by pillows, his head bandaged. (In the beginning of the film, he had a fall while playing in the park. His friends took him to the doctor at the chemist's shop. The doctor did his job and prescribed a sedative for a good night's sleep.) The father seated at one end of the bed, Minu, the second daughter, on a wooden chair near the cot, the mother sitting on the floor, propped against the bed, and Topu, also on the floor, at the edge of Jhunu's bed. Jhunu (fourteen), lying in bed, crumpled. None of them is in a proper frame of mind, except Poltu and Jhunu.

FATHER: God only knows what's happened to the girl.

MOTHER: Minu, didn't she tell you anything at all before she left for office? Come on, don't hide, love!

MINU: For goodness' sake, Ma, why would I keep any secrets from you?

MOTHER: I just know she's never coming back.

MINU: Well, if you know so much, shut up about it.

FATHER: Minu!

(*Silence . . . Oppressive.*)

MINU: Dada, you threw up after you came out of the morgue. Amal-da told me you threw up.

Topu does not speak a word. The loud ticking of the clock can be heard.

MINU: Tell me, don't you feel like vomiting when you see this morgue? This room? This house?

Not a word from anyone in the room. A dreadful silence.

MINU: We've never spared a single thought for Didi until now. We've simply carried on like the selfish creatures we are. And today . . . today when she disappears in this fashion . . .

MOTHER: And scuttles us in the process . . .

MINU: Yes, that's what's really important to us, isn't it? That we've been cast adrift. A girl has been suffocating little by little every day, in this room, in this house. And today . . . we are thinking about her a lot, aren't we?

FATHER: Minu, what are you on about? This is hardly the time to be saying all this.

MOTHER: She's been saying whatever comes into her head. What is it you want to say?

TOPU: Stop it, Ma!

MINU: Ma, tell me, tell me the truth. Have you ever thought of Didi? Have you? Ever?

MOTHER: No, I haven't. You've been doing all the thinking.

MINU: No. We haven't thought of Didi. None of us. You, me, Baba, Dada—none! All we've done is to think of ourselves. And Ma, you've wanted your daughter to stay with you, here. Not to leave home.

MOTHER: Never . . . Never.

MINU: Really? Have you ever considered her marrying?

MOTHER: Of course, I have. I've always thought that once Topu is settled, we'll marry the girl off.

MINU: Once he's settled. You'll think of Dada's marriage and not Didi's?

MOTHER: What's got into you, Minu? Don't you know I've been collecting her wedding jewellery over the years?

MINU: But you knew very well that Didi doesn't want all that. All she wanted was to marry Somnath-da.

MOTHER: And what a fine state she'd have been in, if that marriage had taken place!

MINU: At least she'd have been fulfilled.

MOTHER: Fulfilled, is it? And spent her entire life in widow's weeds!

MINU: Tell me the truth, Ma. Had the police not shot him dead, would you have agreed to Didi's marriage with him?

MOTHER: He didn't have a roof over his head. He'd have spent all his time working for the Party. He wanted Chinu to earn a living.

MINU: She's doing exactly that even now, Ma.

MOTHER: And where would you be, if she didn't?

MINU: Yes, that's it! Say that. Speak the truth. That we actually needed her.

Throughout this heated exchange, Mother has been getting more and more angry at Minu's scathing comments. She now half rises, in fury, pointing her finger at her husband.

MOTHER: Why are you telling me all this? Tell that man over there! That man sitting so silently! The only thing he's ever done is to remain silent and leave everything to me.

Mother can no longer control herself. She hides her face and cries.

Looking blank, the father slowly stands up and silently walks out of the room.

Stony silence in the room except the sobbing of the mother.

*

Father stands alone in the middle of the dark courtyard. He sits on the step. Far away, the sound of a running fire engine is heard.

An hour later, when a taxi at the main gate calls out, roaring loudly, the entire mansion springs to life. Jhunu rushes to the gate, mother follows, as does the father, Minu stands at a distance—all at a time, all unsmiling, all seemingly unwelcoming. Jhunu pulls open the gate, the taxi door opens and reveals Chinu outside the door, safe and sound, but a bit tired. The lights on the upper floors came on one by one.

Safe and sound! A great relief to the family! But in an instant they are seized with a terrible fear. One after another, they disappear from the scene. The mother takes refuge in the hellhole, her room. All of them are frightened of the neighbours, as though the neighbours are pointing their accusing fingers at Chinu, at them.

In a few moments, Chinu is left alone in the courtyard. She has nothing to hold on to. To her, the crowd and the family looked unfamiliar and even hostile.

Chinu is in her room and Minu is standing at the door. Chinu draws her inside and shuts the door.

CHINU: What is it, Minu? Didn't you people want me to return home? Did any of you even wonder about what might have happened? Didn't you ever think that I might have something to say for myself? None of you asked me anything, no one said anything. Nobody gave me a chance to say a word . . . If I'd had an accident, you'd have had nothing to say . . . My God! I've become a stranger in just few hours . . .

MINU: Didi . . . Didi . . . You . . .

Suddenly, Poltu, with his bandaged head, opens the door and looks in Chinu's direction.

Across the courtyard, the landlord is seen coming down the stairs.

The last confrontation the family had was with the landlord who cannot be accused of being over-fond of his tenants. He was always trying to find an excuse to evict one or two or most of the families, so that new tenants could be got at higher rents.

The landlord calls the father and asks him to vacate the place as soon as possible because such goings-on will not do here. Topu, the younger brother, rushes to the landlord.

TOPU: What was that you said?

LANDLORD: I said that these disreputable goings-on won't do.

TOPU: What the hell do you mean disreputable?

LANDLORD: Don't you know what it means?

Chinu rushes out from her bedroom, closely followed by Minu.

MINU: Didi, where are you going? Didi!

CHINU: Please, please believe me . . . I didn't . . .

TOPU: Didi, go in now.

Topu turns to the landlord.

TOPU: Listen you, if you can't keep a civil tongue in your head . . .

LANDLORD: You're going to teach me civility, are you? The girl spending all night in some . . .

TOPU: You bastard!

Topu lunges for the landlord and takes him by the throat.
An ugly scene takes place between the two.
Mother comes running out and tries to drag Topu away.
Shyamal runs down the stairs.
Others crowd the scene.
Topu is still raging.
A battleground!

LANDLORD: What do you think you'll do?

TOPU: I'll smash your face in, you . . . I'll kick you in your respectable teeth is what I'll do . . .

175

They've had enough of it all.
Topu storms out of the house.
The landlord goes back up the stairs.
Everybody goes back to their rooms.
Not a whisper from any quarter of the mansion.

Inside, all six in one room, all six look shattered.

MOTHER: Minu, let her get some sleep.

MINU: Didi . . . Come on . . . let's get some sleep.

The father stands behind Chinu. Gently, he runs his fingers through her hair. Chinu finally bursts into tears. The mother is desperately trying to fight back tears.

Suddenly, a high-angled shot of the city. It is early in the morning.

As the day begins, the mansion erupts into activities of all sorts, all over the courtyard—washing dishes, washing faces, breaking coal for their stoves, bathing at the outside tank, lighting a coal stove, another stove, already lit, belches forth fumes. The soundtrack is heavy with all kinds of accompanying noises— a typical daybreak in the world of *Ek Din Pratidin*.

The mother appears on the ground-floor portico. She looks up, an aeroplane flies past. She looks as normal as always. She seems to be afraid of no one, as she was a couple of hours ago.

Through the bars of the window, the mother is seen lighting a coal stove. The stove is lit, it belches forth white smoke. Her face is partially covered. She is lost in thought, as though a great weight is pressing down upon her. Yet she is unafraid.

The first show. The house was packed at the big theatre, Metro. I was the first to come out at the end of the show and take my position at a quiet corner. While I found the crowd emotionally charged, as I felt too, the ones who came to me first were my old friends, all firebrand militants, now retired but still holding on to the fire within. They felt I had grown old, that I had mellowed with age. Which was why the end had been so full of despair. It was evident, they said, in the mother's expression.

'Despair, you say?' I asked.

'What else!' one of them said, confidently.

They saw only that—the face of the mother, sad and forlorn, and nothing of the inner strength behind the facade. Or maybe they did see but they could not feel. Sad for me, sad for them!

Very early in the morning, the mother stepped into another day. When the plane flew across the sky, it meant nothing but the beginning of a day like any other. When she lit the stove, she did not forget to gently shut the door behind her to prevent the smoke from going into the rooms. A daily habit. Nothing more, nothing less. Ordinary, as always. But the night had been very different. Throughout the night, the mother had faced chilling situations, one after another, and she had been drained of all hope. Yet she survived, and perhaps even emerged stronger. And that was the only logic of one's existence, that was the only hope for sustenance, that was the only way in which the mother and the rest of the family could still dream and look beyond. Fighting back with one's own strength. *With no promissory notes from the heavens!*

The release was well timed and in good theatres. The response was positive when the viewers could be seen identifying themselves with the characters. Meeting the friendly crowd at the foyer was wonderful. And, indeed, safe! But a large number among them had a question for me. The same question every time and everywhere: *What happened to her? Why didn't she come home? Where had she been?* And, interestingly, most of the ones asking the question were working women! Yes, they liked the film, they loved it, and yet they had the question. They were just curious, they said.

Just curious? Just that?

I was not quite sure.

Could it be that they wanted me to assure them that she did not do anything that would be deemed unacceptable by the conformist society? That she did not violate any social norms? That they wanted a certificate from me testifying to her good character?

One evening, when I was mobbed by viewers, the majority being women, a very respectable-looking man, presumably a thoroughbred Bengali and roughly my age, asked me in English, in a tone that was distinctly superior: 'Mr Sen, it is important that we know what happened to the woman.'

Sounding much less than superior, I replied in Bengali: *Dekhun, sir, amar to money hochhey, chhobi-ta ami apnar moton darshak-er jonnyei baaniechhi. Apnara dekhben aar jantrona paben. Jantrona paben karon apnara jobab paben na.* (See, sir, I have made this film precisely for people like you. You will watch and suffer. You will suffer because you will not get an answer.)

I added, 'If you ask me again, my answer will be: *I do not know. I do not want to.*'

I was surprised when, a decade later, a national daily, the *Indian Express*, carried excerpts from a letter from Ray to his friend—and reportedly not for public consumption—in which he referred to my 'I do not know' and said, 'Never before has the maker [of a film] shown ignorance about characters authored by him. I suspect Mrinal does not know either why the "professor" disappeared in *Ek Din Achanak*.'

(In an altogether different context, the 'professor' in *Ek Din Achanak* [*Suddenly, One Day*] [1989] left home, unprovoked, and never came back. I suspect Ray wrote that letter to his friend sometime in 1989, when I was making this film. *The Indian Express* carried the excerpts of his not-to-be-published letter on 6 October 1991.)

Honestly, Ray's suspicion was not untrue. But equally true was my reaction when I read the excerpts in the paper. I read it, and instantly saw before me the gentleman in front of Metro, speaking in a tone that was distinctly superior. I saw him reprimanding me, as if asking me threateningly, *Come on, don't keep any secret from us.* (I remembered the line of the mother.)

A simple answer to a simple question made years ago also came to my mind. Someone in Samuel Beckett's time allegedly asked him, Why did Godot not appear even once in his play? To which the playwright's instant answer was, 'If I knew, I would have said so in the play.'

Happily, Gita got a major assignment in the project—she was to play the mother, a very complex role. But she was not my first choice. I asked her how she felt about Tripti Mitra (one of the greatest actors in Bengali theatre). Gita said I shoudn't give my choice a second thought but simply go ahead and fix it with Tripti. When I met Tripti the next day, and we had an initial talk, she seemed thrilled at the thought of us working together and moreover to be working for film, not a medium that was essentially hers. We spoke for quite some time; she had her questions and I helped clarify as much as I could. At one point of time, she asked me which of the two roles—the mother or the college-going girl—was more important. I thought she was asking it casually, but no, she was very serious. In the context of the film, who would play the crucial role?

I felt terribly uneasy. I did not know what to say, and how to say it. For the time being, I evaded the issue. The next day, I told her on the phone that every time I thought about her question, I felt confused. Could she herself arrive at a decision on the matter. Whether to accept the role, or to refuse? To make things more complicated for me, she said neither yes nor no to my offer. Finally, I decided to put an end to this mother–daughter imbroglio. Since both of them would be under the same roof, from evening till morning, huddled up for hours, feeling jittery all the time, fighting at unpredictable moments and making life a hell, she would do good not to accept the role. A woman of intense sensitivity, she knew pretty well what the film would be stuffed with from the beginning to the end, and how the characters, the mother and the daughter in particular, would pass through an eternity of numb and mounting tension. She agreed. And that was the end of the matter. I suspect she was perhaps rather relieved.

To persuade Gita to act the mother was not that easy. Once she agreed, she kept asking me questions, wanting to know more about the character, day in, day out, and, on her own, suggested quite a few things of feminine importance. Later, Gita and Sreela— Sreela Majumdar, my favourite, who played a drifter on the pavements in *Parashuram*—built a fascinating rapport to help each other, even when, at the end of their tether, they fought fiercely.

The day after the film was released, Gita received a large number of calls. One call came from Tripti Mitra. She congratulated Gita, and then said, 'Had I played the mother, I would have been deprived of watching the performance of an outstanding actor.'

'She said no more,' Gita told me, deeply touched, 'She did not give me a chance to speak a word. She cut the line abruptly.'

'Are you sure it was not a technical fault?' I asked.

'No, it was not,' she said, confidently.

I realized, just as Gita had, that there had been so much passion in Tripti's words.

A thing such as this rarely happens in life!

ELEVEN

The Nineteen Eighties!
A Decade, Every Inch Worth My While . . .

May 1980, Cannes. An unforgettable festival. For Gita too, because she was the principal actor of my film. Because she was born to the role. To be reckoned with, that was also the time for a group of young film lovers, Swiss and Dutch, who formed a team—Cactus Film—which had its base in Zurich. All of us— Indians, Swiss and Dutch—worked together at Cannes, we worked hard and we worked wonders.

Outside its national boundary, Cactus opened its account with *Ek Din Pratidin,* and around the same time, with Yilmaz Güney's *Yol (The Way)* (1982). I was what I was. As for Güney, he started as an actor in Turkey and eventually went on to become a director. Being a man of Kurdistan, many of his films vigorously upheld the cause of life and freedom, many were about the persecuted Kurds, about resistance of one kind or another.

My involvement with Cactus Film was rather ordinary. And, by and large, accidental. One of the Cactus group, Eliane Stutterheim, organized for herself an invitation to the International Film Festival of India. She came to India in January 1980, saw my film in the Indian Panorama at Bangalore Filmotsav, loved it, discussed relevant points with her European contacts who were then also in Bangalore—most of them journalists, the rest filmmakers, all invited to the festival. Getting their fullest support, she asked me if, on its acceptance by Cannes, she and her friends at Cactus Film could be allowed to act as my agents. I considered the generous offer, and soon after we became good friends. Both Gita and I realized our friendship would last long. Later, in Cannes, the entire Cactus team, five–six of them, and Gita and I—we became like a big family.

Güney's, however, was a different story. Allegedly involved in a murder case, the man was imprisoned in Istanbul, with no idea when he would be released. Nobody knew, not even the insiders. That was a prison of a very special kind, where the prisoners, Güney in particular, were free to move about within a protected area. Meticulous plans were made, both inside and outside, to somehow bring him out into the open, beyond those confines. Hazardous, but made possible at last, and the prisoner managed to escape. Climbing up and down the rugged surroundings, he reached the shore and crossed the windy creek by night. He was not alone, there were reportedly two more to conduct the operation and give him adequate protection. After a day or two of hiding at the Greek border, they travelled on fake passports through a cumbersome route and finally reached Paris. Then it was more or less smooth sailing. Political asylum was sought and granted in a few days. Paris was where he would now stay and take on the post-production work of the film *Yol*. The rushes of the film, travelling by another undisclosed route, were expected any moment. Elizabeth Waelchli, the Swiss editor, who also worked with me five years later, was waiting for the rushes. It was sometime in the autumn of 1981 when the work finally began. At breakneck speed.

While Güney and his skeleton team were working in Paris, the entire laboratory work was done in Zurich, the home of Cactus Film. Paris and Zurich worked hand in hand at a frenetic pace, and *Yol* was at last ready for Cannes 1982.

When we were at Cannes—Güney was still in jail—we heard unbelievable stories about him from Cactus, about his days in the special prison in Istanbul, about his plan to film *Yol*. They had many more secrets to strictly preserve because, for reasons known only to the Turkish authorities, that was when prison restrictions involving him were growing even more stringent.

Gita sprang a delightful surprise at Cannes Festival in 1980. There were three official screenings of *Ek Din Pratidin* during the festival, and two more on viewers' demand. The responses were very positive, and Gita was paid glowing tributes. Sreela too. We missed Sreela very much, as did Eliane who'd met her in Bangalore during the Filmotsav. Referring to Gita, my friends and viewers asked me, 'How could you keep her in hiding all these days? And why did you?' They asked her, 'What have you been doing all these days? Acting as a housewife? Just that?' Gita's favourite answer was to good-humouredly recite a popular Bengali proverb: *Gnayer jogi bhik paye na*—the nearest approximation in English being, 'The neighbourhood genius always goes unnoticed'.

Interestingly, Sreela, sweet and dark, was a great favourite among the young men who'd come from Senegal to sell coloured beads and shells. During the festival, it was a common sight to see them squatting on the pavements, their colourful merchandise spread out before them. Whenever Gita would shop from them—and she loved to try out her Indian-style bargaining skills—those who'd seen the film, just a few, never failed to recognize her as 'the mother'. They would also tell her how much they'd liked the performance of the daughter and asked if she would be coming to the festival. Gita was sad that Sreela could not come, that we simply could not organize her trip. All she could do was to buy a few beads and shells for her 'daughter'.

Apart from the well-attended official press conference, Cactus organized plenty of interviews, most of which went off pretty well. I was happy, but Gita, speaking endlessly on the same subject, grew quite bored of it all. Cactus, busy with promotional work, did the running about all the time. Whether at the press conference or in the interviews, questions were restricted not only to the film under scrutiny; there were also questions on India politics, on ethnic diversity, on senseless bigotry, on population explosion and, most particularly, on my city of glaring contrasts. It was only my city that I felt comfortable speaking about, both the good and the bad, and not necessarily treating it as a holy cow. Naxalism was another subject that frequently came up because, according to quite a few, it was an issue I had specialized in. Honestly, that is not entirely true. And I said so. To say I had specialized in Left philosophy would be too much of a claim. Though, yes, I have always hated sitting on the fence. And I said that to them too. A certain journalist from *L'Express* asked me which of the Marxist varieties I belonged to. It was clear he knew my city was home to more than half a dozen Marxist parties. I said that since discretion was the better part of valour, I preferred to remain a private Marxist. There was instant laughter. Which showed that I had been taken in the right spirit, that they realized my statement was in jest. Unmitigated? Perhaps not! Perhaps I also wanted to say that I was no card-carrying member of any party. However, in the next issue of *L'Express*, there was a short write-up with a photograph of mine, under the headline: 'Mrinal Sen, Marxiste Privé'.

As I recall my story at Cannes, I remember what Jean-Paul Satre said when he declined to accept the Nobel Prize: 'The writer must therefore refuse to let himself be transformed into an institution, even if this occurs under the most honourable circumstances [. . .] I do not wish to be institutionalised in either East or West.'

After Cannes, I was invited to two more events—one in London and the other in Paris.

In London, the National Film Theatre (NFT) organized a weeklong retrospective of my films. For obvious reasons, the concluding film was *Ek Din Pratidin*. Followed by the customary Guardian Lecture at the NFT—a long conversation with Guardian critic Derek Malcolm, and then a question-and-answer session with the audience. The event drew a fairly large crowd. But one desperate militant Indian, living in England for long years without caring to revisit India, asked me a couple of irritating questions. I felt uncomfortable, even disgusted. But instead of reacting to his questions, I started asking him amusing questions of my own, in order to more fully know his background. The result was a big laugh in the theatre. He was angry, I was happy.

Similar questions were reportedly raised again at NFT when, two years later, in 1982, it was Ray's turn to answer questions. The problem with Ray, however, is that he took the question seriously, got provoked and made an unkind comment about me. The editor of the *Sunday Observer*, Vinod Mehta, called me from Bombay and asked if I would be interested in writing a rejoinder, so that it could be put out the following Sunday. Mehta left nothing undone. Under his instructions, a local representative of the weekly rushed to my place and handed me a copy of the current edition. I read the story and saw Ray's comment in the headline: 'Mrinal Sen Always Hits a Safe Target.' Ray must have been referring to my films, my so-called political films, about which a question may have been raised by someone in the audience. Without getting too worked up, I wrote a few lines about funny audience members who always have a stupid question or two. I concluded my so-called rejoinder with a line I thought Mehta might use as the headline. I was right. The next issue of the *Sunday Observer* came out with my comment as one of its headlines: 'Ray Has Hit the Safest Target, Me.'

The Paris event was organized by a group of Scandinavian women. First, there was a special screening of *Ek Din Pratidin*. Then, an hour-long discussion on the position of women in India. The viewers-cum-participants were of Scandinavian nationality, living in Paris. I was the only outsider. Not really a very comfortable spot to be in!

The film was well received. Informal and well intended, the question-and-answer session that followed was livelier than in London. At the end, just before we were to leave, I said I had a question related to what we had seen and what we had been discussing since then.

My hosts were curious.

'I believe yours is the most permissive of all societies,' I stated. 'Am I right?'

'Perhaps,' one said, somewhat indifferently. The others laughed.

'How could you like the film, then?'

'We liked it, we loved it. Didn't we?'

The others nodded in approval.

'Didn't it ever occur to you that I built the film on a trivial incident?'

'No, it did not,' answered a lady.

She smiled, looked around, and she said, clear and sharp: They had come to watch an Indian film. Set in a strictly Indian milieu. Watching the film, they could perceive a multidimensional society within the confines of an Indian set-up. Also, the multiplicity in familial relations. All within the framework of a society vastly different from theirs. Despite the constraints of a male chauvinistic society, the family's sole breadwinner suddenly decided to stay out for a night. Good enough reason to raise a commotion! No, she had no problem understanding the central issue of the film, she did not feel distanced at all.

The lady looked at me. The others did not speak a word. And I, listening to the lady and watching the others, began to realize that she—indeed, perhaps all of them—had been touched by a certain commonality that ran through diverse cultures.

Suddenly, a couplet by an unknown folk poet of rural Bangladesh came to my mind. He may never have travelled far from home, but he had a beautiful observation about the universality of man:

Nanan baron gabhi-re bhai ek-i baron dudh,
bhuvan bhromia dekhi ek-i ma-er put.

(Cows are of many colours, brother, but their milk is
    coloured the same.
I go round the world, I see children, mother is the same.)

They loved it. I took a piece of paper and wrote it down—the original and the translation, both.

Now, it was time to leave for the hotel, pack my bags and then rush to catch my flight.

'What is your next film?' they asked.

'A film within a film,' I said, and added, 'Come to Berlin next year, in February 1981. Only if it's accepted, though.'

7 September 1980. A group from Calcutta, a film crew, travels to a village to shoot a film (about famine). The village is called Hatui. The name of the film, *Akaler Sandhane*.

This is how, with a voice-over, my next film began—*Akaler Sandhane* (*In Search of Famine*) (1980). In truth, on 7 September, the whole team went to a village called Somrabazar—and not Hatui, a fictitious one. When our convoy of crew and cast and equipment got there, we realized that word had spread about a film company coming to shoot a film on famine. I got out of my car, and took a walk, alone, into the village. What happened in the next couple of minutes was terrific. And that was possibly how I was greeted. An aged farmer, his body nothing more than a bundle of bones, suddenly spoke up, rather loudly, and almost in jest, 'Hey, look, they've come from the city looking for famine. But here, we are the famine—it is present in every pore of our being.'

A cruel taunt and a heartless jest!

I had never met a man like him before, never heard the like of him, none of his kind, who had learnt to survive by virtue of their own peculiar logic. The man said those words and gave a rather guileless laugh. But I was shaken. Two days later, when we took our first shot, it was of an old man, played by an actor picked from my own unit, speaking those same lines, speaking the same way and laughing the same guileless laughter. He never appeared in the film again.

Akaler Sandhane took a look at a young director's effort to portray, with commitment and honesty, the terrible famine that ravaged Bengal in 1943. Equipped with all that history had offered, including the researched details 37 years after the event and in a village setting, the young filmmaker came up against a famine of a complex kind that had been carrying on, relentlessly. He was faced with a community of elders that resisted both reality and cinema. In the event of a continuing conflict between the past and the present, the task became irretrievably difficult.

There were two sets of actors in *Akaler Sandhane*. Those who acted the *actors* retained their own names and had their role names too. Such as Smita Patil: she played an actress having her own name (located in 1980); and she had a role name when she played a village woman during the famine (in 1943). Obviously, she and the others had to continuously shuttle between two periods—1980 and 1943. Those who played the *villagers* had been given their role names. The rest—the technicians and the production staff of the film within the film—were shared by the actors and my unit members, all retaining their own names. Besides, there were real villagers who played themselves, played bit roles. The only exception was the actor who played the *director*. Of course, he had a specific job—that of directing the film—but remained unnamed.

With a huge cast and an equally huge number of actors and locals, and with situations that continuously evolved, the film only partially followed its written script. For the rest, it recorded whatever happened during the shoot—assembled, rejected, selected and reorganized naturally at the editing table. A challenging job, indeed, was keeping our eyes and ears open all the time.

A note on connection: As a rule, going back to the past and looking into the present, one is likely to find a logic that connects one with another. Whether in *Akaler Sandhane* or in my earlier films, there had been a running theme. For me, history had never been an irregular series of accidents. I have seen history as a continuous, growing phenomenon, marching almost imperceptibly into the characters of my own time. *Akaler Sandhane*, as clearly evident, was rooted in the uneasy, uncomfortable, irresistible and inevitable connection between past and present. As an example, I could see a connection between the character of *Akaler Sandhane*, Durga, the village girl with a child and a disabled husband, and the young woman in *Baishey Shravana* whose life was embittered as much as her old husband's during the dreary days of famine. Similarly, one could find a logic that connected the urban guerrilla in *Padatik* with the young filmmaker in *Akaler Sandhane*. Living the life of a fugitive, the urban guerrilla raised disturbing questions about himself, about his party and his leaders. And when the past walked into the present, the filmmaker in *Akaler Sandhane* faced a severe crisis. And that was how a theme ran through my films, one after another, forming links and touching continuity and contemporaneity at the same time, through a coexistence of past and present.

Connection, as always. Forming links. But, strangely, a subtle connection was determined by the choice of the actor—one singular actor—once playing an urban guerrilla in *Padatik* and then, seven years later, playing the filmmaker in *Akaler Sandhane*—Dhritiman Chatterjee. Was the choice carefully considered? To be honest, no! It was just accidental.

Partly out of my love for ruins and partly to accommodate the vast number of people and even, at times, to shoot the sequences in and around it, we requisitioned a huge feudal mansion. It had tall pillars and broken walls and decayed arches, but was still comfortably habitable; nothing threatened to collapse in the near future. That was where we lived a kind of convivial life.

191

An excerpt from the script:

PRODUCER: This is your palace.

DIPANKAR (actor): Palace indeed.

PRODUCER: The place for kings like you, for a month.

DIPANKAR: That's great.

PRODUCER: But there is no electricity.

Evening. The sound of a conch shell blown somewhere nearby.

DIRECTOR: What's up, Jayanta?

JAYANTA (manager): That's another story . . . A lady, and
her invalid husband, paralysed for the last ten years.
Living upstairs, at the north. The last of the old stock.
Their only daughter, married off four years ago, to a
village schoolmaster. The village, not far. The estate is
hundred years old. Split up into bits among the later
descendants, till they all locked up their individual
shares, a room or so for each, and went off with their
keys to Calcutta, Bombay, Delhi, all over the country,
one even to the States . . . Twenty-six rooms, and
seventeen owners. Can you guess how long it took me
to trace them and get hold of the seventeen keys to
open the rooms?

My unit settled down comfortably in the 26 rooms of a near-
abandoned *palace*. Now turned into an island of abundance,
totally cut off from grassroot reality. It all seemed to be good fun—
at times, unit members would be looking at photographs of the
famine, almost like a parlour game, at the same time as they discussed the menu for dinner—fried rice and chicken curry or something else. Empty cigarette packets of the imported variety were

soon seen scattered all over the village. The villagers were getting increasingly annoyed because the prices of vegetables, fish and everything else began to go up in the market, all because of the *outsiders*. They had come to take pictures of a famine, and had ended up sparking off another famine, reminding the elders again of 1943. Various instances of rural culture generated mirth and humour among the city folk as cycle-rickshaws announced the screening of *The Guns of Navarone* (1961), with the world's most beautiful woman Anthony Quinn (*queen!*) in the lead role. Of course, it was all in good fun, though perhaps bad taste. It wasn't all jokes, though. There was passion too. Passion that had brought them there. And faith, with which they had begun. But the gap was widening every day. The gap widened, the problems mounted, the crisis deepened. And the wizened old farmer came to mind—how he had laughed at the cinema-babus—how he had flaunted the famine that was in every pore of their beings.

Finally, one day, midway through filming, we were forced to stop.

The schoolmaster appeared. The grand old man of the village. A man of profound wisdom. A man who'd once come to a farmer's courtyard to watch our shoot. To see how fiercely the starving farmer turned down the moneylender's coaxing. To watch and bless the *director*, and Smita playing the farmer's daughter-in-law. To wish them success and hope they brought glory to the country. Who, at the end of a shot, walked up to the actor playing the moneylender, patted him on the shoulder and said, 'There are still people like you in our village.'

Now, when the *director* and his team felt utterly confused, and the producer was shouting in impotent fury, the grand old man insisted they better go back. Back to their studio to do the rest of the work peacefully.

193

Some excerpts from the script:

Deeply hurt and disgusted, the schoolmaster moves towards the door.

Smita, the actress, is revealed in a corner, listening.

The schoolmaster stops for a moment, looks reverentially at her and then leaves.

Smita Patil standing still.

From the balcony upstairs, a lone woman watches the whole show.

The wife of the invalid husband, widowed a fortnight ago, is left to terrifying loneliness.

Slowly the camera zooms in on her.

She—a picture of desolation!

An extreme top view of the huge courtyard, members of the film unit scattered all over it.

The unit get busy with its pack up.

The camera keeps moving in and out, capture the hectic activity.

The vans are loaded, the cars are filled with bags and equipment, the unit gets ready to leave.

Everyone walks silently towards the cars and vans waiting outside.

Jayanta is the last to take his seat inside one of the cars.

Before the lady upstairs, the courtyard is laid bare, desolate, melancholic.

The exterior of the mansion.

The time-worn pillars look on in despair.

A dog moves about in the strange silence.

From behind a pillar, a little village girl, an empty powder tin in hand.

The silence is suddenly broken by the roar of the automobile engines, one after another.

The cars and vans set off.

The little girl with the powder tin rushes out.

Darkness.

Out of the darkness emerges the face of Durga, the village girl, in close-up, looking blank.

Dissolve to Durga, looking blank, in mid-close shot.

Follow by several dissolves, one after another, of Durga wearing the same blank expression.

Mid-shot, mid-long shot, long shot, extreme long shot and finally a dot.

The dot fades out.

On successive dissolves is heard the voice-over:

A few days later, Durga's child died.

Her husband is missing.

Durga is all alone.

The voice sounds lifeless.

As the dot fades out, the title appears: *Akaler Sandhane*.

The 20-page manuscript by Amalendu Chakraborty, out of which the script and the film emerged, comes to mind. It ended with a certain Durga in 1980, asking the heart-rending question: 'Where did you run off to, you babus? Hadn't you come to make a film on a famine?'

A year later in February 1981, at the end of a press conference in Berlin, an unknown journalist cornered me outside the conference room. At the press meet, he had not said a word. Now, like a doubting Thomas, he asked, 'Would you say cinema is a myth-making technology masquerading as the mirror of reality?'

I had no ready answer for him.

Two years later, in July 1983, I had an accidental meeting with Cesare Zavattini, the most uncompromising defender of neo-realism. The way he put across his ideas was splendid—so simple and yet so profound. An example here: 'It is but a common practice to *invent* a story, *insert* the same into reality in order to make it thrilling and to comfortably escape from it . . . We are aware that reality is extremely rich—all that we require is to learn how to look at it.'

After our most enjoyable conversation, he pulled out a paperback from a leather bag he was carrying, wrote something on a blank page and lovingly passed it to me. 'For you, Sen,' he said. A book in Italian, *La Verita'aaa* (The truuuuth), a collection of his work, named after a film he made or wanted to make.

Then, suddenly, his expression changed. A wounded Zavattini confessed unabashedly, 'I, now, tell you a truth—I have lost faith in cinema. It has nothing to offer me now.'

The wizened old farmer came to my mind. I told Zavattini about him, about how he had laughed a guileless laugh at the sight of the cinema-babus. His eyes brightened. I told him about the unknown journalist in Berlin and his question. 'I know', he said, and nodding, and he walked away.

I wanted to ask him a few more questions, about his loss of faith in cinema and about myth and reality. But he left, and I never could find him again. A friend of mine who'd been watching us from a distance said, 'He's grown senile.' It was cruel of him to say so. I immediately dismissed his words.

Back to Berlin, 1981. Ours was a four-member team—Smita and Dhritiman, the actors. One playing a double-role—an actress (1980) and a peasant woman (1943); and the other playing the director, and I. Always moving together and watching films. The fourth, D. K. Chakraborty, the producer, spent most of his time in the casino, making money, losing money but always remaining cheerfully casual. And, as it happened at Cannes the year before, Cactus was doing the running about and organizing exclusive interviews. As we returned from the festival, we carried a basketful of delicious stories for Gita, Sreela and Rajen Tarafdar, all actors playing the *lonely widow* of the big mansion, the *village girl* with disabled husband and child, and an *actor* of the village opera, now retired, respectively. A film director himself, Tarafdar was persuaded to act much against his will and he acquitted himself with remarkable skill. So much so that all three, including Tarafdar, were whisked away by Shyam Benegal for his film *Arohan* (The ascent) (1982).

When Gita was away at Shyam's location, I was scribbling quick notes for my next, *Chaalchitra* (*The Kaleidoscope*) (1981). Just notes and a few details. Nothing more.

Akaler Sandhane was one of my most awarded films, both nationally and internationally. In *Chaalchitra*, the principal character, an aspiring journalist, was commissioned by his editor to do a story of the city—to chase the dramatic in single-day situations, to collect the diversities in small events, to trace the trivia which are no good for media agencies. All in a frugal storyline, or no story at all, with no invention.

I looked for my main actor and found one, Anjan Dutt, theatre activist, and by profession a journalist looking for roadside stories. Anjan was the man for me, playing the pivotal role. To give him moral support, Gita was to play his mother.

That was the time when I was always on the move. Before I could start filming, I took a few days off and rushed to Oberhausen to act as juror in the prestigious short-film festival. I returned after seven days and immediately got onto the job.

Chaalchitra was quickly shot, quickly edited, quickly mixed and rushed to the Venice Film Festival in August–September 1981. The actors acted very well, but despite some positive reviews in the Italian press, which could be used as quotable quotes, the film failed to fetch much attention. I wish I could treat the film as a dress rehearsal and make it all over again. Had it been taken up again, it would have been a delightful and a meaningful film for sure.

Again on the move. From Venice, Gita and Anjan, empty-handed, went back to India, and I left for New York to join a six-member Indian delegation comprising Smita Patil, Shyam Benegal, Girish Karnad, Govind Nihalani, Kumar Sahani and I, and an official, unlike most of the officials who used to care more for routinism, Prabodh Maitra—a likeable person and, indeed, very helpful. In New York, we filmmakers showed our films and held unceasing discussions about the same. Every day was a remarkable day with our highly enjoyable sessions during which we contradicted ourselves and corrected our own conclusions as often as we wished.

But my trip to the States had to be cut short to catch up with my filming schedule, a new venture.

TWELVE

Take Chances!
I Wish You All a Very Tough Time . . .

About a quarter-century ago, the following, more or less, was what I said to the students at the film institute in Pune. Whether or not it meant anything to them, I don't know, but the exact text of the concluding lines of my convocation speech was:

> Remember, when you touch your multifaceted medium, you touch man. As you serve your medium, you serve your conscience too. And as you walk into the world, you take chances or play safe. By taking chances, you achieve or perish. By playing safe, you merely survive. The choice is yours. Till the time you choose, I wish you all a very tough time.

I too had been having a tough time all through, plagued by financial worries and in a state of constant insecurity, both physical and ethical. All the time, I debated with myself, if it would ever be a feasible proposition to strike a balance between creativity and commerce. Some said no. Some said yes. Example? *Pather Panchali.* A fabulous success. Creativity and commerce walked gracefully, hand in hand, and shook the world. But *Aparajito,* Ray's second, and to my mind his greatest, was a commercial failure, a flop everywhere except in festival circuits around the world, starting with the Golden Lion it received at Venice. An issue, always controversial, defies any conclusion. Yes or no, remembering my quarter-century-old convocation address, I chose to serve my conscience. Fortunately, neither Gita nor I had sought an apartment with a lot more air and space; nor did we look for a new car every seven years. Kunal and Nisha got happily married in 1980. As long as they were in the big city, we lived together. They lived in one room, Gita and I in another; the third was our living room. We lived a modest life. It was a happy home for all four of us. But in the eyes of an interior designer, it may have looked dull and conventional and downright unattractive.

Frankly, I did not care. Never. Not even after the *Chaalchitra* experience, when it drew a blank at Venice except for two minor unofficial awards. As we came back to my restless, nervous, unpredictable, intimidating and infernal city, I got back into myself, picked up a story by Ramapada Chowdhury and bounced back with an unsparing critique of the middle class, the class to which I essentially belong. Severe from the beginning to the end, the film was to have hardly any relief. There was no scope for it anywhere. With Anjan Dutt and Mamata Shankar in the lead roles, *Kharij* (*The Case is Closed*) (1982) went into production in a ramshackle studio, Aurora, which in its heyday did a pioneering job and was still remembered.

Anjan and Mamata were a modestly comfortable couple with a young son. As far as anybody could see, the first names were also the names of the actors. Because the parents were busy and the son needed care, and because they needed someone to do the domestic chores, they engaged a full-time worker, Palan, aged 12 or so, to live with them. The boy lived in a village near the city; his father turned him, his youngest son, over to this urban family in exchange for a monthly salary, settled upon after the usual bargaining.

The city was in the grip of a cold wave for a few days—a rare phenomenon. The boy was meant to sleep under the stairs on the ground floor along with another boy of his age working in another apartment. Because of the cold, Palan went to the kitchen, tightly shut the door and fell asleep next to the still-burning coal oven. In the morning, the door was broken open and the boy was found dead.

The doctor was called, the police was informed, the body was rushed to the morgue for a post-mortem. A curious crowd continued to collect outside the house. The only absentees were the father of the deceased and members of his family; they were still in the dark.

No one was criminally to blame. But different sorts of blame and guilt were underscored by the death. Also underscored were the conditions that made the poor father lease out his son, as well as the police and how they operate, concerned more with regulations and less with sympathy. Most importantly, following the cruel death, the focus was on the young couple. First came shock and pain which, under pressure of the secret guilt, changed to self-protection, tinged with aggressive defence. So much so that one started hurling against the other for reasons unclear to both of them. Unclear, because both of them were civilized, both possessed exemplary sensitivity, both were living a happy marital life.

To quote the eminent American critic Stanley Kauffmann: 'The real closing of the case is the closing of the family circle, the clan against the world.'

An excerpt from the script:

Anjan is in a senior lawyer's consulting room. A respectable neighbour is with him. They have come to seek his advice and find a way out to escape complications.

LAWYER: You just said that the boy was like a member of the family, didn't you?

ANJAN: Yes.

LAWYER: That's just talk! Do we give them their legal rights? Or acknowledge any moral claims they might have?

Nobody speaks a word.

LAWYER: How old was he?

ANJAN: Who, the boy? Twelve or thirteen, I suppose.

LAWYER: In other words, a minor.

ANJAN: But it was his father who brought him here.

LAWYER: What choice did he have? At least there'd be a salary each month, and the boy would get two square meals a day.

ANJAN: But was it our fault, really? I mean, you tell me . . .

LAWYER: If you look carefully at anything, at anything at all, you'll find the whole world is at fault, morally. And we lawyers . . . Do you see those law books? We suppress the moral truth with those law books. The legal lie must prevail over the moral truth.

A short pause.

LAWYER: Anyway, let's see what the post-mortem says.

The post-mortem said that the case was not of asphyxia but of carbon monoxide poisoning.

When, to fetch the father, Anjan and Mamata were looking for somebody who knew the village, the father came on his own to collect his son's salary for the month.

The body was released the following day. The police issued a permit to cremate the body. The body was cremated in the early hours of the night. In the presence of the father and his relatives and his friends. They were quite a few, all boy-servants from Anjan's locality. The boy working upstairs was constantly beside Palan's father. His employer gave him a leave of absence for the day. To ensure a peaceful ending and no undesirable trouble, Anjan and his respectable neighbour spent some time with the father and the teenage pallbearers.

But the peaceful ending was yet to come. Those returning from the crematorium were to perform rituals at the threshold once crossed by a dead body. They came to the house, about a dozen boys, headed by Palan's father. They came at midnight to have a touch of purifying fire. There were a few knocks at the door. The insiders woke up. One of the insiders, an elderly woman, carrying the purifying fire, climbed down the stairs and opened the door. The others came and watched, frightened. Palan's father entered first. The others followed. The rituals over, the father quietly climbed a few steps, looked for Anjan and Mamata and their lovely child. Those were tense moments, moments of breathless fear. Waiting, scared—both the insiders and the outsiders. Without raising his voice—and he had hardly any strength to do so—the father bid goodbye to everyone with folded hands and turned towards the door. The others followed, except one—the one who kept looking—the one who, from now on, would sleep alone under the stairs.

That was how the film ended, and that was when a section of viewers felt utterly disappointed. And disgusted. Hardcore militants, all of them, who hated the 'incredibly tame' ending. On the other hand, Lindsay Anderson was deeply impressed by the 'quiet dignity of the victim'. He said so in a letter to me. I wrote back and told him about my brief encounter with the people who would have possibly loved to see the father, the victim, slapping or punching the young employer. As a matter of fact, one of them, an old friend of mine, told me that is exactly what he would have liked. Softly, I said to him that the slap had indeed fallen—on all our faces. On the faces of our entire class. I did not allow him to find an escape route. My friend was sad to see that my talent had gone to waste! I said all this to Lindsay, because I knew he would enjoy the story. In reply, in a manner that went well with him, Lindsay asked me to choose one book from my bookshelf—the one he'd written, and given me when we met in Cannes—turn just one page and then read what he'd written for me. I read it and in a way I got his answer to my letter, infinitely sarcastic:

> For Mrinal . . .
>> 'Are we intelligent enough to survive?'
>> (And thank you for understanding.)
>>> *Salut!*

The book was called *About John Ford* (1981): 'aggressive and defensive in about equal measure [. . .] gentle and irascible, bloody-minded and generous, courageous, uncompromising and endlessly evasive [. . .] fiercely anarchic [. . .] one of the great poets of humanity in our time.' With masterpieces, like *Stagecoach* in 1939, out into the open air of America's past, told in a masterly narrative style, it is the account of a trip through New Mexico, and *The Grapes of Wrath* in 1940, based on John Steinbeck's story, dating back to the exodus during the 30s' Depression, it captures the disintegration and eviction of the farmers' families who left everything and went to the south to pluck grapes. I still remember a line from the novel: '[T]he line between hunger and anger is a thin line [. . .] and the anger began to ferment.' Ford was considered one of America's great film directors, and Lindsay unabashedly called himself 'truly Ford-intoxicated'.

Born in a 'foreign' city, in Bangalore, and made in England, Lindsay Anderson died a sad death—he had a heart attack while swimming in a countryside lake in France. Tony Richardson, his comrade-in-arms, whom I met at a boisterous party in Hollywood, died unsung. Karel Reisz is probably still alive in England, but has lost his bite long ago. But there was a time when all three of them made themselves intensely felt in British cinema, when they became an institution by themselves. Sadly enough, they could not go too long a way.

The trinity disintegrated, and the only one left at the post, to quote the man himself, was Lindsay Anderson, 'standing on the burning deck', antagonizing big producers like David Puttnam and his kind. While Puttnam was producing money-spinners like *Chariots of Fire* (1981) and later was even knighted by the Queen of England, Lindsay stuck to his guns and continued to make funny, bitter, provocative and playfully roguish films, sparing none, not even the Queen Mother in his *Britannia Hospital* (1982): the hospital staff was on strike, but the official visit of the gracious lady could not be put off. So she was quietly brought in, concealed in a coffin!

Coming back to *Kharij*, barring a few short sequences, the film was shot entirely in the studios. The young man who built the set had never tried his hand at set designing before. But he did a wonderful job, and the illusion of perfect solidity possessed by the structure was brought out with utmost accuracy. The facade of a fairly old building and its three floors were constructed piece by piece, but put together at the editing table, the 'house' had a lived-in feeling, and looked very real and adequately weathered. Since he had no experience at all, not the least, I gave him a long time to do his job. After that the young man, Nitish Roy, never looked back. In a few years, he became one of the best art designers in India.

An idea of the storyline was given to Nitish. Also a bit about the quality of life the couple lived and about the apartment on hire. The first thing that Nitish asked me was about the nature of their marriage. Was it an arranged marriage—arranged by the parents of either party—or a marriage strictly by the couple's choice?

Arranged or not, would it make any difference to an art designer? I wondered.

For Nitish, furnishing the apartment was all that mattered. In case of marriage by choice, the in-laws would remain aloof, so the apartment, in all fairness, would be modestly furnished.

At once I realized that he would be the right man for me and would go a long way in his new profession.

One day in January 1982, while we were shooting, Eliane Stutterheim of Cactus Film brought about a dozen friends to the studios. Some were critics and some historians, most from Europe and the rest from the United States and Canada. They had come to the city as guests of the festival, the annual 12-day-long event popularly known as Filmotsav. I knew all of them, I had met them so many times at various festivals. The ramshackle studios carrying stories of the old days fascinated them. They loved the team I was working with, and they loved the time they spent with us. Before leaving, Gene Moskowitz, a particular friend of mine from Paris, took me aside and said, 'Mrinal, I am smelling a good film here.' I was touched. I pressed his hand. He pressed mine. I knew he was suffering from cancer.

We met a month later, in February. I was on the jury in Berlin, and he, as usual, was doing the coverage for *Variety*. It did not escape me that he was looking quite pale. Now, in Berlin, whenever I met him in the foyer of the festival theatre, I helped him take off his overcoat because he found it too heavy. I used to carry it up to his seat. We parted at the end of the festival to meet again in May. I would be in Cannes to act on the jury, and he, as usual, would be doing his job for *Variety*.

By the time we met again in Cannes, barely three months later, he was in a wheelchair. But he never missed a film, never failed to send off his article. Always on time, always in a wheelchair. By the time of the last film, he could watch it for only a few minutes. Then, disgusted, he said, 'Damn it, it's a television film!'

This time the festival authority packed him off to Paris.

On our way back, we had a stopover in Paris. Gita and I saw Gene at the American Hospital in Neuilly. He said he wanted so much to meet both of us in Cannes. He left messages at our hotel. He realized the jury business kept me busy. But he was happy that we had made it to Neuilly.

We had taken along a few stills of *Kharij* for him. He took the package lovingly and remembered his own predictions about the film. He was more or less certain that the studios he'd visited had, by now, been condemned. As he said it, he was scanning the stills and perhaps remembering the time he spent in those studios.

'You remember what you told me?' I asked. 'You said you could smell a good film.'

'Yes,' he said, without raising his eyes from the stills.

'Wait until next year,' I said, 'to see how good or bad the film truly is.'

We sincerely believed that he would live to see it next year, either in Berlin or Cannes.

We took the next flight back to India.

A few months later, much ahead of the next festival, Gilles Jacob, director of Cannes, called me from Paris to say that the festival committee had unanimously selected *Kharij* in the competition section. I was happy. I asked Jacob about Gene. 'Still alive,' he said.

Months passed. On 14 May 1983, my birthday, the film was presented at Cannes with a pre-title card: 'In Memory of Gene Moskowitz'.

The news of his death came through Eliane. She and I immediately decided that the film should be dedicated to the man who'd meant so much to all of us. To me in particular. I remembered it was he who, long ago, in 1960, wrote a beautiful piece on *Baishey Shravana*. He'd seen an un-subtitled version of the film at Venice, and loved it even without the benefit of understanding the spoken words. And without knowing who I was.

THIRTEEN

An Old Letter,
and a Few Things, Here and There . . .

A few things remain unsaid, left behind.

On 24 September 1980, around midnight, I wrote a letter to Gita from Somrabazar—a village, roughly three hours' drive from our big city. There, in September–October, my unit and I had based ourselves in a weather-beaten feudal mansion to shoot *Akaler Sandhane*. The letter was mostly about improvisations. Entangled was the story about the making of another film, *Baishey Shravana*, shot 20 years ago. Shot in another village and in another ramshackle house, dilapidated and derelict, about 70 km away. The name of the village—Mankar.

An excerpt from the letter:

> Do you remember Mankar? And those unparalleled ruins of the landlord's house where, once upon a time, the viceroy came to dine? Last night, I dreamt of the broken mansion. In my dream, I saw the old man, the last of the old stock, now paralysed and only half alive. Looked after by his graceful wife. You know, it was with that man at the back of my mind that I've been creating the 'husband' of yours in *Akaler Sandhane*. In my dream, I saw him

stand up. With an expression of absolute terror on his face. Staring at me. After a while, he asked me, 'Who are you, my child?' And that was when my dream ended. And I woke up.

Strange! The old man and the entire ambience of that ruined house came back to me so clearly after twenty years. Perhaps . . . why perhaps . . . I am certain that the old man at Mankar is no longer alive. Just thinking about it makes a shiver run down my spine!

The first thing I did early in the morning was to write a hasty note about a new sequence—a sequence that was not in the script. The improvised sequence was more or less thus:

In the morning, the elderly men of the village come for a last look at your paralytic 'husband' who died after midnight—the last descendant of a once-powerful feudal estate. There, they strike up a conversation with the film unit. Their talk is all about your dead 'husband'. Then appears Smita, 'the actress'. Ever since your 'husband' died last night, she has spent all her time with you, 'the wife'. Now she walks up to the production manager and says, 'Jayanta-da, the lady is insistent. She's refusing to let go of her husband's body until her daughter comes home from her in-laws. She is crying a lot. Keeps saying, "Let her come and see her father just this one more time." '

The 'director' asks the villager, 'Where's her in-law's place?'

The villagers standing around say, 'It's quite a long way off. At least sixty miles.'

'Are the roads motorable?'

'Yes, yes. Although not as good as the city.'

The 'director' steps forward and says, 'Give us one of your men to show us the way.'

He asks the production manager to spare a car to fetch the daughter.

The sequence, as improvised, was shot beautifully after breakfast. We made up the dialogues as we went along. The whole affair went off fairly well.

You know, Gita, last night's dream caused a miracle. Mankar appeared before me, and a host of things about *Baishey Shravana* came crowding back. I remembered that day, twenty yearsago—an overcast morning. We were shooting in the yard of the broken-down mansion. Suddenly, I noticed one of the owners—Dulal Kaviraj. A man weighed down with the burden of impoverishment. Running about frantically. I went up to him and asked, 'What is the matter, Dulal-babu?'

Dulal-babu was looking for a cycle-rickshaw. His wife was in labour. She needed to be rushed to the hospital.

'How far is the hospital?' I asked.

'It's in Panagarh, 14 km away.'

'To Panagarh by cycle-rickshaw!' I exclaimed.

I asked him not to worry, had a word with my production manager and immediately packed off the pregnant lady along with her husband in one of our cars.

The incident from twenty years ago helped me build the sequence that was shot in the morning—the old lady, meaning you, begging for the girl to come, sparing a production car to fetch her, et al. How spontaneous! How close to life! How compassionate! How easily experience metamorphosed into art. No end to surprises when you're making a film!

Autobiographical?

Yes, it is, in bits. The whole thing will never cease to amaze me.

Now, as I write to you, I am struck by a thought. How about Smita, 'the actress', coming to meet you, walking into your room? How about your half-dead paralytic husband, lying on the bed, mumbling? Trying to tell you something? And then how about you telling Smita that you are the only one who can understand him, no one else, not even your daughter? I think these words will do well as your lines, won't they? But believe me, Gita, these are not my words. These are to be borrowed, lifted from the mouth of the old lady at Mankar and put into yours. She said it about her husband when I'd gone to Mankar. And last night in my dream, the same half-dead paralytic husband stood up and spoke to me clearly, 'Who are you, my child . . . ?'

Unbelievable!

This is just an excerpt. I wrote a longer letter. I wrote about the heat and dust and mosquitoes. Gita did not speak a word about the letter—for the simple reason that it did not reach her. Once, not very long ago, I discovered it under heaps of useless papers, periodicals and letters, piled up in a corner. Written with care, it was not posted nor delivered through a messenger. Why, I cannot recall.

Anyway, in the course of filming, I introduced new sequences and even deviated from the written script as and when I had felt the urge. Correcting my own conclusions. Such things have always been a fascinating game for me, and highly enjoyable. But I would never recommend such operations for others, for the simple reason that I cannot ever vouch for them.

In this connection, I would like to refer to an informal conversation, held at Los Angeles in January 1970, with Federico Fellini—a poet, a magician and a genius among filmmakers, occupying centre-stage. The young filmmakers groomed at the American Film Institute who were present were very interested in Fellini's methods of improvisation, particularly in how he got his actors to come up with their lines. So much so that the students said they considered scripting as somewhat of an unnecessary adjunct to filmmaking.

Scathingly, Fellini said:

> That is stupid gossip. It is absolutely impossible to improvise. Making a movie is a mathematical operation. Art is a scientific operation. What we usually call improvisation is, in my case, just having an eye and an ear to available happenings during the trip of the picture. To be strictly faithful to what you've written four or five months before is a little bit silly. But that is not improvisation.

'What is it then if not improvisation?' I ask myself. It could be possible that Fellini played with semantics just to keep their enthusiasm in check. As far as I understand it, if it is *a little bit silly to be strictly faithful* (to the text), the additions/alterations/deviations or, more importantly, whatever is constructed extempore during *the trip of the picture* can be nothing but improvisation, clear and simple.

Still unsaid are a few more things, here and there. To recall them, I take my pick from random entries made in my festival notebooks.

That was when, all over the world, large-scale protests no longer broke out thick and fast, when the wind started shifting slowly, shifting back, and when I smelt much less madness in the air. And much less fire, within and without. That was when, in a quieter atmosphere in 1976, snow began to fall and people got ready to celebrate Christmas. That was in Leipzig, in erstwhile GDR. As usual, I was on the jury.

The number of entries in the festival was insufferably huge—films both short and long. Out of the total number, a few managed to be logical, beautiful and adequately effective; we could not but sit up and take notice. The rest could be seen and forgotten.

The jury worked hard throughout the week. We discussed the films, argued, differed and finally arrived at a consensus. Not an exciting finish, to be frank; it hadn't been a good beginning either.

One day in a coffee shop, I met Carlos Alvarez and his charming wife Julia. Accompanying them was their friend and colleague Manuel. As they introduced themselves, all three names sounded familiar to me. Had I heard of them before? Certainly I had. Suddenly I recalled a day in 1972, when at Nyon, after the festival had ended and most of the jury members had rushed back to their countries, I was the only wretched of the earth, waiting impatiently for my flight back to India the following day. Back to my city, where my film *Calcutta 71* had been running to full houses for several weeks. Early in the morning, I was woken up in my hotel by a telephone call from Moritz de Hadeln, the festival director. He told me he had received an important letter from an unexpected quarter and needed an immediate session with me. Within an hour, we sat deliberating on the mysterious letter.

The letter was from a man called Carlos Alvarez, written from a jail in Colombia, Latin America, and successfully smuggled out. It was an appeal to all lovers of cinema all over the world, giving information about him and his wife and six other colleagues, all in jail, all facing military trial. The world must know about them and organize world opinion in their favour. Alvarez, the Colombian filmmaker, appealed to the wider world: 'Save my colleagues, and me and my wife,' he said. The news must be circulated, and help put pressure on the military regime.

We were four—Moritz de Hadeln, Erika, his wife, I and noted Belgian director, Henri Stork, the one who made the famous documentary film *Misère au Borinage* (Penury in the Borinage) (1934)—about the mining workers, now considered a milestone of political filmmaking—along with another outstanding documentary filmmaker, Joris Ivens. We drafted two very strong telegrams: one on behalf of the jury; and another on behalf of the International Association of Short Filmmakers. Stork contacted the executives of his Association scattered all over Europe and collected their consent. I also did the same by speaking to the other six members of the jury on the phone. We then sent off both the cables—one to the military government of Colombia, and the other to UNESCO as well as various other agencies. In unambiguous terms, we said that persecution such as this was nothing short of fascist aggression on culture. After four years, the same people—the whole batch, headed by Alvarez—who had once been destined to be ruthlessly liquidated were in a coffee shop in Leipzig, meeting friends and planning their future action. Great!

Another incident comes to mind—involving Patricio Guzmán of Chile. In 1973, the year after the Nyon episode, I was invited to chair the jury at Mannheim-Heidelberg International Film Festival. Gita and Kunal accompanied me.

At Mannheim, we members of the jury decided that we would draft a resolution and read out the text on the concluding day of the festival, condemning the military authority of Chile for keeping the filmmaker behind bars. Our declaration assumed tremendous significance when Guzmán's *The First Year* (1972) won the Special Jury Prize at that same festival. The award was given in absentia. *The Battle of Chile* (1975–79), Guzmán's monumental three-part documentary, of which possibly *The First Year* formed one part, or was perhaps, the prelude to the mammoth documentary, were all shot under the shadow of the impending fall of President Salvador Allendé's government (the first democratically elected socialist leader in world history). Not every sequence was shot in Chile; some were also shot elsewhere, in extremely difficult conditions. Of very special notice, not only in Chile or Colombia but also all over Latin America, except in the free territory of Cuba, was a particular theme manifesting itself in films in the 70s: *colonialism and violence.* 'We have been taught a false history and false economic beliefs,' the filmmakers asserted. Their films projected all these in diverse ways and in diverse forms. The sociopolitical reality all over colonized Latin American countries was more or less the same.

In this context, it may not be out of place to recall a short speech made in my big city sometime in the mid-50s, or even earlier. Cheddi Jagan, prime minister of British Guiana, and Forbes Burnham, the education minister, had come to my city. In the office of the Anti-Fascist Writers Association, the education minister, a brilliant young Black man, who later became prime minister himself, said: 'In our schools, we were taught that the British Empire is an Empire on which the sun never sets. Now, as we come of age, we have learnt that the British Empire is an Empire where the blood never dries.'

If not at Mannheim, it was at the DOK Leipzig Festival three years later that Guzmán was presented before the international audience amid thundering applause. Better late than never!

One evening at Leipzig in 1976, tired of watching substandard films, we came to the coffee bar of the hotel. Others joined us, mostly Latin Americans. We were all there, some talking animatedly, some narrating gruesome experiences, others silently listening. In the crowd of anecdotes, someone dropped the name of one Glezier, kidnapped in broad daylight from a busy street of Buenos Aires and never seen after. I heard the name, and instantly Glezier's face appeared before me. 1973, at the Berlin Festival. He had been distributing handbills, running from person to person, inside the Berlin Forum's permanent theatre, Arsenal. I walked in, he came forward, a friend of mine introduced him as a director from Argentina. Glezier pushed a handbill into my hands, and waited. The text had information about the trade unions in his country. I looked at him, a bit surprised. I did not hide my curiosity, and he embarked upon a blatant confession: filmmaking was not his first love, he said. I understood him and had no problem making the obvious connection. *The Traitor*, which I'd seen the day before, was his first film, about a trade-union leader who was chased and killed.

Glezier, so I was told, had been kidnapped and never seen again. Not quite strangely, the same had happened on my city streets—not one kidnapping but many, around the same time. The connection was clear and simple.

A Brazilian cleared his throat and mentioned Glauber Rocha. Just the name, and that was enough to charge the atmosphere.

Rocha, a great filmmaker and, admittedly, the most original thinker of Brazilian cinema. With six criminal charges against him, including the charge of subversion, he was forced to leave his dear motherland. Living the life of a fugitive, he moved from one country to another, always sad and lonely, always an outsider. In exile, he made films, reportedly not very stirring ones. At last, one of his well-wishers and a film producer, brought him to Africa where he made *Der leone have sept cabeças* (*The Lion Has Seven Heads*) (1970), a Franco-Italian production. The film failed to create waves even among discriminating viewers. The critics were not particularly enthusiastic; they missed the bite that was so typical of Rocha's films, particularly in his all-time best, *Antonio das Mortes* (1969)—using the moral and psychological behaviour patterns of the peasants, and their poetry, music and language, it is a saga on the Brazilian life of the underdogs—which he'd made while he was still in Brazil.

I, on the other hand, missed none—neither his bite, nor his rhythm. *The Lion Has Seven Heads* is one of my favourites among Rocha's body of work. He was a cult figure in Brazil, an institution. I never met him and so could not ask him why, when he worked abroad, such as in Africa and, later, in Spain, his admirers were distracted. Was it because he felt ill at ease working in a foreign country? Quite possible, I said to myself. For a man like him, such problems as I thought of made absolute sense.

A short flashback, again!

While at Berkeley at the University of California in 1975, Tom Luddy, the man behind the Pacific Film Archive and a particular friend of mine, gave me a letter to read. It was Rocha's letter to Tom, written from Paris. I read it and could clearly see that he had been passing through a period of depression. He needed a job, he wrote, he needed money to make a film, he needed someone who would understand him. What he needed most was to communicate. I never met the man, but reading the clumsily written letter, reading between the lines, I realized he was acutely distressed—by the infinite splendour of Parisian life on the one hand and his inner confinement on the other.

Rocha sent a new script along with the letter, and asked my friend if he could find funds for another film, this time set in the United States. I read the script and found it exceedingly well-conceived, although loaded with metaphors, the like of which I had read in some measure in his *Lion Has Seven Heads*.

Understandably, Tom could do nothing much about Rocha. And I never asked him if he'd sent him a reply. Probably not.

Rocha returned to Brazil and died a few years later. Died unsung—the man, the rebel, the worker of miracles, the one who wrote an unprecedented piece: 'The Aesthetics of Hunger' (1965).

Interestingly, such unexpected meetings and anecdotes were almost always with and about the Latin Americans, always outside their own countries, always dramatic and mostly brief. The briefest encounter was once in the late 70s. I hurriedly came out of a Moscow hotel to get into the car ready to take me to the airport. An LP record in hand, a man in his mid-thirties rushed over to me. 'My friends and I saw one of your films at the Carthage Film Festival,' he said, 'and we liked it very much.' He gave me the LP and said, 'It's the album of my film's music. It's for you.' I saw my name written on a patch of white space, given to me *with love*, with his signature at the bottom—Jorges Sanjinés.

Sanjinés—that intrepid young Bolivian director! The album carried the music of his film, *Yawar mallku* (*Blood of the Condor*) (1969). That one singular film of his that depicted the inhuman conspiracy of birth control and sterilization on the natives, the Indians, by the American Peace Corps, brought him instant international acclaim. But when it was shown in the countryside, with all peasants as the actors, 'we realized it did not work,' admitted Sanjinés. That was a global problem! I saw it somewhere a year ago, and I loved it.

My meeting with Fernando Solanas of Argentina took place after the screening of *Oka Oori Katha* (1977) in a Cannes theatre. The meeting was dramatic, but not brief. That same evening we met in a coffee shop. He told me about the indignity of his position as a fugitive. He had run away from his country after the coup, and was waiting for a favourable climate to ensure his safe return. The least that could be said, as much as he could understand, was that a communicator, in order to communicate to his people effectively, must have a favourable base.

Agreed. But what was the base Solanas was looking for? A healthy people's movement? Awareness on national scale? A tolerant system? What?

Essentially, a base to protect and inspire, the communicator must be an absolute necessity, in the absence of which creativity, sooner or later, would exhaust itself.

Solanas has survived, so have many others, but there were plenty of activists who are no more in the news and who have been totally eclipsed. It is possible that the system kept some of them alive—hale and hearty, because the system these days will not show up in the classic fascist style; it would rather prefer to practise *repressive tolerance*. Which perhaps was why Solanas, in his *La hora de los hornos*, said, 'We fear peace more than war.'

Right or wrong, in 1968, in the midst of aggressive manifestations and inflamed passion, the students at the Sorbonne made
a big noise in May. Right or wrong, Jean-Luc Godard lost no time
in leading his friends and admirers and *invading* Cannes Festival.
Chanting Mao, they made history by paralysing the 12-day long
programme. Just a year later, when Sorbonne withdrew from the
scene and Cannes came alive, Lindsay Anderson's *if . . .* bagged the
big prize. For reasons, right or wrong, the delegates and film
enthusiasts and even the critics attending the festival had
straightaway connected the verdict of the international jury with
the previous year's ferment at the Sorbonne. Thirty years later, in
1998, Venice made a tasteful gesture to honour the Sorbonne incident. The Venice Biennale and the Venice Film Festival, in collaboration with the National Film Archive at Rome, planned to
celebrate the thirtieth anniversary of the event. To pay tribute to
the event and to lend a historical perspective, they marked out 1965
to 1975 as *the decade of protest.* They organized a retrospective—
a selection of world films befitting the protest theme—all produced
during these ten years and all shown in Venice. India's *Calcutta 71*
was one of the films. At the 1998 festival, they presented only one
film in the main section, that of Alexander Kluge, the guiding spirit
of New German Cinema. The film that was presented was the one
which got the big prize in Venice in 1968, *Die Artisten in der
Zirkuskuppel: Ratlos* (*Artists in the Big Top: Perplexed*). It was
decided that the National Film Archive would carry the
retrospective to the leading universities of Italy.

I was invited to Venice for the event; the ticket was sent well
in advance. But on the flight, an unforeseen incident occurred,
compelling me to cancel the trip. It was all very funny though also
a bit nightmarish. The evening flight to Bombay was inordinately

delayed due to a major technical snag. When at last we were about to land at Bombay airport and had fastened our seatbelts, the plane began to circle—and continued to circle. Time was passing, and I was going to miss my international flight! Suddenly, amid the passenger's confusion, anger and impatience, the voice of the captain was heard: 'Attention, ladies and gentlemen! This is your captain speaking. For unavoidable reason . . . we have to go south-ward . . . to Hyderabad.' At Bombay airport, due to the heavy monsoons, the runways were under water. In the middle of the night, we landed at Hyderabad. Finally, an unscheduled flight was organized the next day for the stranded passengers, which flew first to Madras, further south, and then to Calcutta after midday.

A few days later, I heard that the man, a Venetian 'rebel', who had authored the idea of celebrating the *decade of protest*, had a fight with the apex body of the Mostra (the festival) on ideological grounds. The fight came to such a pass that the man had to ultimately resign. I knew nothing about him except his novel plan. His life at Mostra was very short. That may be one reason why! And such stories of entrances and exits are not uncommon at the Mostra. Even today.

I had no knowledge of what happened afterwards. For myself, I closed that chapter.

FOURTEEN

The 'Delicious Liar' Continues to
'Tell the Tale' Left Untold . . .

'You are a delicious liar, Mrinal,' she said, smiling a sweet smile,
and embraced me.

It was February 1982, at the Berlin festival. Both of us were
on the jury, she and I. She was the chairperson. Out of the nine
jury members, except the chairperson, there were three of us more
or less likeminded souls—David Stratton, distinguished cineaste-
distributor-exhibitor from Sydney; Helma Sanders-Brahms, the
Berliner, maker of many award-winning films, quite a few with
feminist concerns; and I. Among the others, not all were unbiased.
One, an old-timer from Domkino, Moscow, was good at multiplying problems. At the final stage, all of us got bogged down with
a tough debate over a film. An unending debate. The opinions were
sharply divergent. The film under scrutiny was one of the two contending for the Golden Bear. When the debate ran wild, and there
was no sign of restoring sanity, the chairperson intervened and
argued against the division of the best film award. To ensure a
possible unanimous choice, she felt that the warring members
needed a breath of fresh air. She announced a break for half an
hour to give relief to our jaded nerves. I went to the coffee counter
along with a few others. The chairperson joined us. As soon as she

stood beside me, I detected a pleasant aroma. I looked around and sniffed the air, trying to figure out the source.

The chairperson came closer and whispered, 'Perfume.'

She was smiling a bewitching smile. She looked so beautiful that she took my breath away.

I said, 'No, I can't believe it.'

She was still smiling. It appeared she was reading my mind.

Amazed, I added, 'You haven't changed!'

'No?'

'No. You remain the same.'

'Since when?'

'Since the day I saw you first. Long, long time ago . . . Rebecca!'

She chuckled gleefully, and said, 'You're a delicious liar, Mrinal.'

I could see she loved saying it. She embraced me.

With nothing to hide, neither of us felt embarrassed.

Joan Fontaine! Whom I first saw in 1941. With Laurence Olivier. In a Hitchcock film.

Once a Hollywood star, and now, after long years, heading the jury of a prestigious film festival!

The session resumed with renewed vigour and the debate continued unabated. Finally, as always and as everywhere, after a great deal of verbal acrobatics, we had no choice but to vote for and against the films. And, as always and as everywhere, the verdicts were controversial, resulting in applause and boos when they were announced.

Three months later, in Cannes, I met Gabriel García Márquez for the first time. Now, after 21 years, in 2003, as I write this book, his first volume of a planned three-part autobiography comes to my hand—*Living to Tell the Tale*.

Gabriel García Márquez was on the jury at Cannes in 1982. As was I. As was Georgio Stryler, the famous producer of the Italian stage and once a close friend of Bertold Brecht; Sidney Lumet, a prolific filmmaker from New York, his most satisfying work being *12 Angry Men* (1957); Suzo Cecchi D'amico, an eminent writer of screenplays; Jean-Jaques Annaud, distinguished filmmaker from France; and Geraldine Chaplin, esteemed actor and daughter of Charlie Chaplin; and two others. Here, as in Berlin, we were nine in all.

Gita and I came to Cannes a day before the festival began. The first one to greet me in a cafe was Humberto Solás, my friend from Havana, then at Cannes with his film *Cecilia* (1982). He'd taken the morning flight from Rome and arrived an hour earlier. I was happy to meet him and I introduced Gita to him. We managed to occupy a table. Suddenly, I think he realized he'd better avoid meeting me while the festival was on. He excused himself, said he was in a bit of hurry and rushed out. Until the end of the festival, I did not see his face. I was on the jury, which was probably why he made himself scarce. His understanding touched me, but I was sad that I missed him.

One morning, we came out of the theatre, Gita and I. Márquez called out to me. We turned. He and his wife walked up to us. He took me aside. 'Did you like the film?' He meant *Cecilia*, Humberto's film, which we'd just finished seeing. A complex story of love set in the colonial period, the girl being Cuban, and the man, a high-ranking officer from Spain.

'Did you like the film?' Márquez asked again.

'I'm sorry, I won't agree with you,' I said.

'I've not told you whether or not I liked it, have I?'

'Your question! What else! Your question suggests your dislike for the film.'

Márquez nodded, and patted me on the back.

Whether in Cannes or elsewhere, we knew that selecting films for awards would always be a complicated job. To make it less complicated, we decided that, as in any other festival, we would carefully shortlist the films. To judiciously eliminate a few on first viewing, we decided we would sit once every three days, having had just a few films to touch upon. For a possible second viewing, we agreed we might call back one or two for further discussion. All these to correct our own conclusions, to check and double-check our shortlist, to be doubly sure of the finalists. Such precautions notwithstanding, for all the confusions, known and unknown, more often than not, problems would always crop up and the final verdicts had seldom been regarded as noncontroversial in any competitive festival, not just Cannes alone.

In the first session, I was ready to take up the case of *Cecilia*. But no one seemed to be interested in it. None of the members spoke a word about it. I, for one, liked it, though I would certainly not rave about it. So I let go of it. In the second session, before going to the meeting room, Geraldine Chaplin raised a particular film sky-high. I drew her aside and made it known to her that I too liked the film but it was certainly not one of the filmmaker's best. Even then, I sincerely believed that the film deserved a serious discussion; unlike some other entries, it had a distinctive quality. I said I would take it up in the meeting, and I hoped she would give me adequate support. The meeting began and did not last for more than an hour. The chairman was nice to me and at my request allowed me to start the discussion. I briefly presented a case for the film. I felt I spoke rather well. But looking around I realized I had not been able to impress anyone. What was more, not for once did Geraldine even look at me. She appeared to be busy doodling on a piece of paper. So I could see that I was a minority of one. And since the majority will always prove a point, I immediately withdrew from the scene. Coming out, Geraldine pressed my hand and made a clean confession: 'What a shattering job it is to be on a festival jury!' she said. She looked visibly upset. I told her not to worry; neither she nor I, nor a minority of two, could have salvaged the film. We better forget it, I said, and look ahead.

Here, an incidental note. Once I received an email from Kunal, in reply to one of mine, to make a point. Speaking only in general terms and citing examples, I touched upon the occasional hazards of democracy. Kunal agreed and gave an example of his own: 'If astronomical principles had to be decided democratically,' he wrote, 'we might still believe that the sun revolves around the earth.' I hugely enjoyed Kunal's argument and, going to an extreme, I quoted a familiar dictum: 'the tyranny of collective mediocrity'. Kunal loved it and said it had an unfailing bite. This is how we used to keep in touch, my son and I, always via e-mail, a game, so to say, a continuous come-and-go. In the process, I got to know his world and mine increasingly better. And the bottom line arrived at by both of us through this particular exchange was: that democracy had its limits.

So, in a democratic setup, whenever I had to act on a jury, whether in Cannes or elsewhere, I had no choice but to take such limitations for granted in that context, and operate with extreme caution and understanding. And what was true of me was also true of others. As for the final verdicts, there was no way but to take chances—all the time. The last resort—voting for and against, and counting numbers.

Back to Cannes, 1982. Despite creating a shortlist of films, and checking and double-checking it, the final session of the jury was unusually long. It started after breakfast in the big suite of a central hotel, and went on till two in the morning. A nonstop session, with breaks as required. There was no way to reduce the time. The films to be examined and rated and finally selected for particular awards were marked on the shortlist (which was not really that short). To name just a few that made the cut: Michelangelo Antonioni, Werner Herzog, Jean-Luc Godard, Costa-Gavras, Wim Wenders, Taviani Brothers, Ettore Scola, Alan Parker, Zerzi Skolimowski, Karoly Makk and Yilmaz Güney. Almost all outstanding film-makers from Italy, West Germany, France, UK, Poland, Hungary and Turkey. Some of those eliminated were award-winners to be reckoned with. Lindsay Anderson, to name one, with his *Britannia Hospital*. True, the masters were not always obliged to make masterpieces. But, again, who would decide which would be the masterpieces and which not? Who would draw the line between the *better* and the *best*? And how? Could there be any yardstick? Yes or no, all of us came to the conclusion that each of the contending films had been critically examined. The information I collected after the results were out was that the verdicts were, by and large, generally acceptable, and the catcalls and boos in just a few cases were mostly feeble. Further, to our satisfaction, most of the major announcements brought the house down.

Even though the verdicts were well received on the whole, every one of us had our own doubts about one particular award or the other. But that was how it happened everywhere, in all festivals, big or small. Cannes was no exception. One thought this was great, and the other thought it was not. In the ultimate analysis, none of us had anything to do but gracefully accept the *democratic decision*. Numbers game!

Oddly enough, Márquez had a problem of a different kind. To start with, for four hours or so, we took films, one after another, and continued to interact in diverse ways. There were the effusive variety, talking loudly. A few were soft-spoken and mostly reserved in speech, and some others chary of giving their views openly. Márquez was pleasantly discerning and a man of few words. During our lunch-break, he asked me to come out to the balcony overlooking the sea. There, when there was no one else around, he spoke.

'You said you liked *Cecilia*, didn't you?' he asked.

'Yes, I did,' I said, 'But why?'

He said he was sad that nobody had mentioned the film. I could not understand why, because he himself had not liked the film. I reminded him of what he asked me and what I said when we had come out of the theatre the other day. He admitted that the film did not deserve any prize. But all that he wanted was a sort of *mention* by the jury, which could safely pass as a modest tribute to Cuban cinema.

I wondered why he insisted on such an absurd claim, and particularly within the framework of this festival. I tried to convince him that, for reasons known to both of us, *Cecilia* should be forgotten. Forgotten, I ventured to say, like *Britannia Hospital*. As far as *Cecilia* was concerned, I could see that Márquez had no problem forgetting it. But to forget Cuba—well, that was difficult. So, not to accommodate *Cecilia* but to respectfully remember Cuba, he came out with a kind of citation: 'The jury to pay tribute to Cuban cinema on the occasion of the presentation of *Cecilia* by Humbarto Solás.'

To be honest, I was not impressed.

'At least we can open a dialogue, can't we?' he asked, defensively.

Giving up, I said, 'It is entirely up to you.'

But Márquez wanted *me* to raise the point. Being so close to Cuba, he felt he had better keep off the issue. Unwillingly, I agreed.

The post-lunch session started. Addressing the chairman, I raised the point. The members felt uncomfortable. The chairman of the jury felt confused. He asked the secretary to have a word with the president of the festival, Robert Fabre le Bret. The secretary rushed to president's office. And Fabre le Bret lost no time in appearing on the scene. Fabre le Bret, the grand old man of the festival, presiding over the Cannes events for a decade, listened to the proposal as presented by the confused chairman. Strangely, Fabre le Bret felt neither confused nor uncomfortable. He raised his voice and asked, 'Who said it?'

I lost no time in raising my hand: 'It was me!' Fabre le Bret, looking like a patriarch and talking likewise, gave his instant verdict and made things absolutely clear: 'Mrinal,' he said, 'do not forget that you are asked to give an award to a film—not to a country. To a film, understand?'

So saying, he left, and we got back to our work.

Gita, alone in our hotel room, was receiving calls from known and unknown people who believed she might know a bit about what was going on in our secret meetings. Something may have filtered through and reached her is what they hoped or imagined.

The closing ceremony was held the next day, in the evening. The theatre was packed but for one notable absentee—Gabriel García Márquez. But his wife was very much with us, Gita and me, until the event came to a close.

The 12-day event was over, the Riviera was left to the tourists, the Cactus group was on their way to Zurich, and we, on our way back to India with a short stopover in Paris.

My unit was waiting for my return. The post-production programme of *Kharij* had been prepared to accommodate my travel plans. We took a few days to finalize the schedule. The final edit and dubbing took us four weeks. For the background score, B. V. Karanth, theatre activist and also a filmmaker, came down from Bangalore. That was the third time he composed music for one of my films. To work with him was a sheer delight. The laying of just five tracks took us four days. My editor and I left for Madras to do the rest of the work. K. K. Mahajan, my cameraman, came from Bombay to do the final grading. The laboratory struck out the answer copy in the first week of August. The censor certificate, obviously without any cut, was obtained the following week. A corrected copy was made in the next two days, followed by a third copy the day after. That was the copy which went to Cactus Film. Cactus organized three screenings—one for themselves, one for the Berlin preview committee because Moritz de Hadeln, director of the festival, wanted to see it, and another for Cannes because Gilles Jacob, director of the Cannes Film

Festival, had his eye on it. Both of them liked the film, both of them wanted to programme it for their competitions, both of them called me—and neither was prepared to hear a 'no'. I spoke to the producer, and the producer asked me to decide. I left the choice to Cactus, because neither Cannes nor Berlin made any difference to me. Finally, much to the annoyance of the Berlin director, the film was booked for Cannes 1983 much ahead of the festival time.

All these days, the members of my production team had been itching to get involved in a new project. The man to produce my next film was also growing impatient—he said he had waited long enough and would wait no more. He asked me to find a subject of my choice—he was ready with the money. He even suggested a couple of ideas in the hope that I might like one or the other. He was desperate.

'Unbelievable', said a close friend of mine, a German film-maker, Reinhard Hauff, who was making films in West Germany long after I had begun. By then, with perhaps his first feature film, *Die Verrohung des Franz Blum* (The brutalization of Franz Blum) (1974), he was quite well known all over the world. Reinhard's is a remarkable career with a good number of award-winning films and a production company, Bioskop Film, founded by him and a couple of his friends, including Volker Schlöndorff, maker of the 1979 film *The Tin Drum* (an absurd fantasy based on Günter Grass' eponymous novel—about a three-year-old German, who refused to grow up in protest against the Nazi regime). Since early 1993, Reinhard has been the president of German Film and TV Academy in Berlin. When I told him about the producer of my next film, about how impatient he had grown, Reinhard said, 'Unbelievable!' He could not believe how daring my producer was, to turn his back on established standards of success and desperately attempt to make an *independent film, like the ones I was making.*

I was a lucky man, Reinhard said. Knowing my producer and the family for long years, I thought this was just normal. His father, Babulal Chokhani, one of the leading producers of the country, and a trendsetter in many ways, had made a large number of popular films since 1931. The most notable being the beautiful musical, *Alibaba* (1937). To my mind, it was India's best musical, starring Sadhana Bose and her director-actor husband Madhu Bose. As co-actors, it was their best too, playing Marjina and Abdulla. He had called it a day with his last production in 1956. Now, 25 years after he made his last film, the son walked into production and found me to be the right man to start. Choosing me to make a start! 'You are a lucky man, I repeat,' Reinhard said, and laughed. 'You cannot find a producer like him anywhere in the world, for sure!'

Looking at our films, Reinhard's and mine, we did not appear to be kindred souls. But both of us found a commonality in the idea of cinema as provocation. That could have been one of the reasons why, two years later, in 1984, Reinhard, basically a feature filmmaker, took a short break and playfully made a long film on me and my city. During his ten days in my city, he spent a couple of hours with Jagadish Chokhani, my new producer, and built a short sequence on him too. With a huge portrait of his father over his head, Chokhani answered Reinhard's questions in a relaxed mood, sitting on a thick mattress spread on the floor, leaning against a huge bolster. Chokhani looked like an Indian landlord, but without the arrogance. He spoke pretty confidently too. In reply to Reinhard's question on the commercial viability of offbeat films, Chokhani said: 'A new wave will be required, because every industry requires it. Take, for example, the textile industry. If in the clothing industry, the designs are the same, they cannot have the market only on reputation—they have to change the designs. Similarly, the film industry also requires changes all the time.'

Now, back to my search for my next film for my desperate producer. For me to come up with an appropriate subject at the appropriate time had always been a nerve-wracking exercise. Istvan Szabo, Hungarian director of *Mephisto* (1981) (wherein an actor of unusual talent, corrupted by greed of power in a fascist society, finds it is too late to return to himself over again) and many more outstanding films, could not agree with me. It was as simple as collecting a shell from the sea beach, Szabo said at Cannes once. But I had problems finding an idea to work with. Nerve-wracking, every time. Even now. Then, one day, I woke up in the middle of the night and for about an hour could not get to sleep again. I got up and walked into another room which had a large wooden cabinet covering the wall beside the door. The cabinet was full of books. I pulled out a chair, sat down and stared at the books. One particular title seemed to be staring back at me, an anthology of short stories by Premendra Mitra, with slimmer volumes of his poetry beside it.

I pulled out the book and read one story again at that unearthly hour, read it for no reason. I had read it so many times over the last 40 years but never thought it could be filmed. That night, at that desperate hour, I read it again, and for the first time I glimpsed the cinema hidden in its lines and between the lines. For the first time, I discovered Telenapota in a manner I had never done before. And, strangely, 'Telenapota Abishkar' (Discovering Telenapota) (1941), like Marienbad of Alain Resnais and Alain Robbe-Grillet in their *L'Année dernière à Marienbad* (*Last Year in Marienbad*) (1961), was a figment of the imagination, entirely unreal. The worlds they held, however, were vastly different, one situated far away, at an unreachable distance, or, to put it in another way, anywhere, nowhere. In the words of Robbe-Grillet, the renowned nouveau-roman writer who collaborated with Resnais: 'This is precisely what makes the cinema an art: it creates a reality with forms. It is in its form that we must look for its true content.'

This is how the story of Premendra Mitra begins, and how the reader locates Telenapota:

> When Saturn and Mars come together, you too might discover Telenapota. In other words, when you have unexpectedly been granted a two-day break from the suffocating pressure of work, if someone comes and tempts you, saying that somewhere there is a magic pool filled with the most incredibly simple-minded fish anxiously waiting to swallow any bait, and you have often spent unsuccessful hours angling without a catch, you may suddenly find yourself on your way to discovering Telenapota.

Regardless of age, angling was a favourite pastime in Bengal in those days, though perhaps not any more. So when I decided to make my film based on 'Telenapota Avishkar' (Discovering Telenapota), the man was no more to be an angler—he was made a professional photographer, sort of my alter ego. In my script and later in my film *Khandhar* (*Ruins*) (1984), the photographer was first seen in his studio, working in his dark room, the photographic paper under the thin layer of the liquid in the sink, all under the red glow of the light, being handled gently, delicately. The image on the photographic paper grew slowly, became sharper till it defined itself—the image of a young woman set against the ruins— a picture of desolation. At that point, the lines of the text were rewritten and replaced by the voice of Subhash, the photographer, in the strange silence of the dark room—a monologue of sorts:

The city and its mad bustle, its hubbub and jostling crowds, all the hassles of work and the thousand problems . . . There are times when they get you down. But if, all of a sudden, you are granted freedom for a couple of days, and you are lifted out of the suffocating tedium, a gust of wind that sweeps you away somewhere, far from the world known and familiar, when time seems to have come to a stop, when a dear friend of yours comes and tempts you, then you too can take a trip along with him and another of your friends, to the ruins . . . photographer's paradise.

'Photographer's paradise,' said Dipu—the one who'd coaxed the other two, Subhash and Anil, to come to this place. Once upon a time, here stood a huge palace symbolizing power, glory and arrogance. Where, once upon a time, Dipu's forefathers reigned. Where all the grandeur was brought to dust by a host of common insects—the mosquitoes, the malaria bearers. All that was a 100-year-old story. A devastating epidemic destroyed it all and left a graveyard in its trail. Those who survived left the place and settled elsewhere. Their children went off even further, in search of jobs. And Dipu, belonging to one such generation, inherited a small portion of the ruins. Looked after by a farmer from his father's time. In the silence of that desolation lived Dipu's aunt with one of her daughters; the other one, with her husband, living a comfortable life in a town. A family of two, mother and daughter, heirs to another small portion of the derelict mansion. The mother was sick, paralysed and blind, surviving on the hope that a distant nephew would come one day and, as promised, marry the daughter. But the facts were otherwise—the man who'd made the promise continued to live a settled life in the city with his wife and a child. The daughter, Jamini, knew the truth but kept it to herself; she did not let the mother know. *Not to tell her, never to let her know.*

A short excerpt from the script:

Jamini is seen walking through the ruins to meet Dipu, her first cousin. There is something she would have liked to talk to Dipu about. They meet after long years. There are others around, busy cooking food amateurishly. Or, may be, lavishly. They come away—Dipu and Jamini. They are seen emerging from a dark passage into the open. They walk, they sit, they talk, they see the plaster peeling off somewhere. Dipu listens to the problems that the aunt creates all the time. He tries to view the situation with sympathy. At the same time, he feels terribly scared of getting involved. After all, he and his friends haven't come here to meet them. He looks stern. It does not escape Jamini, but she takes it calmly.

DIPU: What does your sister say? . . . and your brother-in-law?

JAMINI: They send a hundred and fifty rupees every month. They show a great deal of concern for us. They even send us clothes from time to time.

DIPU: They never ask you to go and stay with them?

JAMINI: They do quite often. But . . .

DIPU: Then why don't you go?

JAMINI: That is what I am saying. Mother doesn't want to go. Everything is gone, but her pride remains. She won't stay at her daughter's house.

DIPU: So she'll just stay here and wait for . . .

He sounds a bit impolite.

DIPU: Shall I tell her the truth?

Jamini says a quiet but firm 'no', and that is all.

'What a problem!' said Subhash, the photographer, when he heard the story. To which Dipu said, 'My aunt will not survive the shock if she knows the truth.' None of the three could say how the story would end. And, true, it was none of their business, either, to play any role other than leaving the mother and the daughter to the ruins. And, all the time, lumps of plaster continue peeling off here and there.

Earlier, walking through the looming pillars and unending roof-less corridor, braving the broken walls and decayed arches, all threatening immediate collapse, Subhash crept out without being hurt. 'Photographer's paradise!' Suddenly, he became incredibly philosophical, and shouted, 'Time, the hand of time. Time, the destroyer!' And all this before Subhash knew anything about the mother and her daughter.

A cruel story was built in two and a half days. Thrown into an awful situation, the visitors and the daughter are forced to go through a dreadful exercise, acting a dreadful play and giving an absurd impression to the mother: that the photographer among the visitors was the one who once promised to come and marry her. Finally, all three visitors return to the city, go back to their respective posts. Just before leaving the ruins, Subhash, the photographer, and the daughter have a brief encounter. He clicks a photo of hers and utters a mute *thank you*. What follows appears one after another—the visitors on their way back to the city, the mother lying in her unusually large bed and possibly dreaming, the daughter standing at the door, afraid to cross the threshold. Finally, the myth that kept the mother alive so long is ruthlessly shattered. Back at the studio, Subhash is seen busy with his professional engagements, with a a blow-up of Jamini standing amid the ruins hanging behind him on the wall.

Shabana Azmi played Jamini and Naseeruddin Shah the photographer. Pankaj Kapoor and Annu Kapoor played Dipu and Anil respectively. All of them, among the best of actors in Indian cinema. Gita played the paralysed and blind mother.

The film was mostly shot on location, all amid the ruins, for three continuous weeks, working seven days a week, for ten hours every day, sometimes more. The rest was shot in the same ramshackle studios over five days. In less than five weeks, it was all over. The post-production work would start three weeks later. So, after four weeks' hard work, rest for three weeks for everybody. But for my production manager and chief assistant and me, only two weeks. To rest, to relax, to think of nothing.

Suddenly, a surprise attack came from Gita. At the breakfast table, with just the two of having our breakfast. She asked, 'What is going to happen next?'

I was not prepared for such a question. Since Gita was playing the mother, I asked her to answer her own question. Frankly, I was a bit confused.

From what she said then, slowly and straight from her heart, it was clear that what she asked was not her question but her musing as the mother who had just come to know the truth. She said, 'For the next few days, the mother and the daughter will not speak a word. The daughter will carry on with her chores, will take care of her mother, bathe her, feed her, dress her, turning her over to her side and do everything that she had been doing everyday. Then on the sixth day or the seventh, or sometime some day, the mother will quietly ask the daughter to sit with a paper and pen and write a letter to her sister in the name of the mother. To tell her that they have decided to leave this place and go and stay with them. Does that not make sense?'

Incredible! Her family pride, so ruthlessly protected all these years, was suddenly shattered! All by herself! And all so quiet and calm!

I was overwhelmed. This was what humanity and humanness were all about. When humans faced reality. Once the garb of fantasy was lifted. Confronting reality once the first shock was overcome.

Gita said, 'For the last two days, I have been thinking of the mother in *Ek Din Pratidin*.'

That was it. With the break of the dawn in *Ek Din Pratidin*, she was not the same as she had been throughout the film.

I was really proud of Gita.

The year rolled on to 1983, the new year . . .

FIFTEEN

Nineteen Eighty-Three!
Going Places, Meeting the World . . .

'Meeting the world!'

The phrase reminds me of an incident that took place a long time ago when, late one summer afternoon, Kunal, my son, just five then, and I had an accidental meeting with the world. A frisky meeting.

That was a cloudy day, the sky overcast. We were sitting in a public square in the south of my city. A raging nor'wester—*kal baishakhi*, as we call it in Bengali, when the furious wind unsettles all that is calm and quiet until it blurs the horizon and subsides soon after—was imminent. Suddenly, the stormy wind was heralded by a terrifying flash of lightning. Kunal stared at the sky, amazed. So did I, frightened. It was tremendous in scale, stretching from one end of the northern horizon to the other. The little boy turned to me and exclaimed, '70 mm screen!'

I was taken aback and yet extremely intrigued.

My grandfather, at the same age as Kunal's, would have compared a similar streak of lightning to perhaps a huge mythical bird, Garuda, spreading its vast wings. Or a Muslim grandfather, to Jibrail, the messenger of Allah.

242

But, now, with science and technology dominating the social and cultural scene, Kunal used an expression that had come so spontaneously to him and which belonged essentially to the modern world. Interestingly, he had been exposed to the 70 mm screen in a city theatre only a week ago, which explained his immediate association arising out of that newly acquired experience—an expression which is no nation's exclusive possession. That was obviously a new addition to his lexicon, and had no barrier—regional, cultural, or linguistic. Kunal and I, both incorruptibly Indian, found it as anyone anywhere else in the world would. At that very moment of Kunal's exclamation, I realized that *the world had come to our doorstep*, and that too with a terrifying bang. The sudden flash—and the instant realization!

Now, back to the time when I took a pause.

A year passed. Having completed the five-year tenure (1977–82) with not enough success, the Left Front in West Bengal came to power again for another five years. With promises to keep, as always, it stepped into the second year of its second term, 1983. Keeping my fingers crossed, I continued to go my own way, proceeding with the post-production work on *Khandhar*. In-between, I made brief trips, not quite productive, within the country and also abroad. One of these days, I received a call from Rome inviting me to be on the jury for the ten-day festival at Venice (August–September). I asked who else would serve on the jury with me. Out of the seven of us, Gian Luigi Rondi, director of the festival and a veteran journalist, told me, four had so far agreed: Agnès Varda (France), Nagisa Oshima (Japan), Ousmane Sembene (Senegal) and Bernardo Bertolucci (Italy). Since I would have loved to spend more time with them again, and this time as one group and in the same hotel, I agreed. With my acceptance, Rondi had five confirmations.

Soon after, Eliane of Cactus Film insisted that, on my way back from Venice, I make a quick trip, just a couple of days, to Toronto where *Kharij* had been programmed. I was a bit uncertain, and so I kept it in abeyance. The post-production work continued swiftly; to get the best of effects, my editor Mrinmoy Chakraborty and I had to be constantly on the run. Rushing from one place to another, to Bombay and Madras and back. And suddenly, in great hurry, a day's trip to Delhi, unavoidable, to have a quiet lunch with the French Minister of Culture, to discuss a particular proposal: an Indo-French co-production. The exact nature of the project was yet to be clarified, said the minister. His name was spelt as Jack Lang. Why 'Jack' and not 'Jacques', I asked. After all, the little I knew him, he was an incorruptible Frenchman. His wife came to his rescue, because the minister's English was much less communicable. What I gathered was that the father of the minister had been with the resistance fighters when, during the war, the Boche (the German soldiers) had infiltrated France. 'Jack' came from the father's admiration and gratitude for the Allies.

The production, as suggested by the minister, within the framework of the Indo-French protocol, was taken up two years later. Two more countries were involved—Belgium and Switzerland. But, considering me and my handling of a production, it was not a big-budget project.

I rushed back home and got busy with *Khandhar.* But Cannes, where I was to present *Kharij,* was closing in on me. So I left the job unfinished and got set for a weeklong trip. Anjan Dutt and Mamata Shankar, playing the couple, were in Europe already— Anjan was in West Berlin for a month-long theatre workshop, and Mamata was travelling through England with her dance troupe. Even if for a day, both of them agreed to come and join me. In the meantime, Gilles Jacob, the delegate-general, invited Gita to the festival in the hope that she would wish me the very best all the time and lend her moral support. 'Besides,' Jacob said, 'Isn't Gita your actor and wife?' Wife, true, but didn't he know, I asked myself, that she appeared in *Kharij* for less than two minutes, not more?

All in all, I still remember how stimulated I felt about the press conference that followed the special press show of *Kharij*. To my mind, the event was the best so far in my career. There was more of perception and feeling, and just a few questions. There were journalists, a whole lot, in front of me. All of us discussed the film. They said a lot and I learnt a lot, and said a lot as well. And there was no surprise attack from the press, nothing of the kind.

Just one example, to elucidate. It was how the session began. Not with a question but with a perception. The perception of a senior journalist. He said he could read something on the furrowed lines of a haggard face. He meant the face of the poor father who came to the city with his 12-year-old son. The father who'd been compelled to lease out his son, turn him over to a civilized urban couple, to live with them as a boy-servant. On the lines of the haggard face of the father, he saw the picture of rural economy, devastated. As though he saw it all outside the frame of the camera!

The journalist said it, and in a flash a serpentine queue appeared before my eyes—a crowd in front of a counter of a pawn shop. Waiting for their turn to come forward and do as required. At the head of the queue, Antonio, the principal character, had just got the token and gone to another counter to collect his money. The camera, holding the crowd waiting outside, kept steady for a little longer. Watching through the counter. The one who now came forward was a middle-aged man, his face rather longish, unshaven, exhausted and distraught. He had come to get money in exchange for his binoculars. To convey that much, just that, surrendering the binoculars to the man behind the counter, and not a frame more than what Vittorio De Sica, director of *Bicycle Thieves* (1948), required. Just enough to record how devastating the economic situation was in post-war Italy. It was clear that the man was pawning his binoculars under tremendous economic pressure. Never before and never after was that man seen in the film. A master-touch by one of the great masters of the post-war world cinema!

Earlier, in 1942, Sergei Eisenstein, in his brilliant essay—'Dickens, Griffith, and the Film Today' (1944)—described this point with astonishing clarity. Elsewhere he said, 'When I use typage, I look for a face, I find a face, I film it and I do not distort it. On the contrary: I try to capture it as it is.'

To make a statement about the particular time, or, to put it precisely, to characterize the post-war period, De Sica looked for a face, found the face, filmed it, captured it as it was—a typage, so to say, pulled out from the social fabric. Just a touch, and what a master-touch.

In this context, it might not be inappropriate to mention Friedrich Engels—his letter to Margaret Harkness about her 'brilliant' fiction *A City Girl* (1887/88), which he had read with 'the greatest pleasure and avidity'. While praising the work with profound compassion, Engels did not fail to point out a lapse (which, in a way, related to what Eisenstein called *typage*):

> If I have anything to criticize, it would be that perhaps, after all, the tale is not quite realistic enough. Realism, to my mind, implies, besides truth of detail, the truthful reproduction of typical characters under typical circumstances. Now your characters are typical enough, as far as they go; but perhaps the circumstances which surround them and make them act, are not perhaps equally so.

Three examples from three stalwarts in their respective areas—Engels in 1888, Eisenstein in 1942, and De Sica in 1948—comparing favourably with each other. All three in three distinct periods but linked aesthetically by *typage*.

A short question from one of the journalists: 'Isn't yours a film about child labour that is rampant in your country?'

This was my precise answer: 'I wish I had made a film on child labour which, true, is rampant in our part of the world. But as far as this particular film is concerned, the focus was on my own class—the society to which I essentially belong.'

On further questioning, I said the film was intended neither to be on child labour nor on the suddenness of an unfortunate death. My crew and I had been undemonstratively trying to do a ruthless post-mortem of my own society. A slap on my face, on the face of my class.

'The performances were very impressive,' someone said. 'There was hardly any acting,' said another, as if replying to his colleague, and added, 'The actors just behaved—they did not act.' But, more than a year later, when *Kharij* had its American premiere in New York, Stanley Kauffmann, writing in the *New Republic*, analysed how the actors made the most of their talents. Here, a significant quote:

> The principal actors [. . .] heighten our own feeling of espionage into interiors with the confidentiality of their performances. It's a kind of acting that precludes display and is thus easily underrated as mere *behaving*, which it is not. Theirs is a close parallel between the acting here and the look of the film itself—the actor needs skill—enough skill to ignore skill, to concentrate on congruence with the character, on permitting us to peep and eavesdrop rather than to project at us.

I am unashamedly tempted to quote one more of Kauffmann's lines: 'To make a film this way requires a lot of experience, and not just of filmmaking.' A friend of mine, Udayan Gupta, journalist and cineaste, living in New York, called me up only to read out this line. It left me at a loss for words.

14 May 1982. Cactus made a day of it. Immediately after the evening screening at the main hall of the festival building at Cannes, Eliane dragged me and Gita, on either side of her, up the stairs, and threw us on to the sprawling terrace. The spectacle before us was the biggest of all big surprises—a birthday party for me! A huge party! Huge enough to put me to unbelievable embarrassment! So many people kept pouring in and wishing me many happy returns. Countless! Later, Gita and I came to know from the Cactus group that not every guest had been invited—many had come on their own. I wished my actors had been with me. None of them could finally make it—one from England, and another from West Berlin—not even for a day. When, after midnight, we came back to the hotel, exhausted and relieved, Gita told me that I had never looked so nervous and awkward. It was not that I did not realize that. Yes, of course, I did!

The last day of the festival. A glittering evening. The razzle-dazzle of the concluding event. We were just a few backstage, eight or nine in all, the chosen ones. One of them was Carlo Saura, the Spanish filmmaker, famous mostly for his operatic films, with whom I had a quarter-dozen meetings on similar occasions. Among those whom I met for the first time was Shohei Imamura, bagging the big prize, both for his film, *Narayama Bushiko* (*The Ballad of Narayama*) (1983), and the leading lady. It was a remake of an earlier Japanese film, but this particular version highlighted the more disturbing aspects of the tale through its harsh realism, of a woman left abandoned to die on a sacred mountain top, far away from the village. It was an experience to watch the film and to know what it meant to be Japanese, what their rituals were like. To me, it was a cruel film, and, indeed, typically Japanese.

Andrei Tarkovsky was also there as an award-winner for his very personal film, *Nostalghia* (1983), initially called *The Italian Journey*. He seemed to be a very private person, withdrawn, like his film. I met him for the first time there. His first major film, *Ivan's Childhood*, fetched him the big prize in Venice (1962), but, from the very beginning, he was in the bad books of the high-handed insensitive bureaucrats of the Soviet cultural scene. Finally, he was left with no choice but to leave the country, never to return to his homeland. And, most eminently, the man I was dying to meet and at last did manage to meet—the grand old master of French cinema, Robert Bresson. He was the man for whom I had the profoundest love and admiration. He was sitting in a corner back-stage, waiting to be called.

He called me to sit beside him. I pulled a chair and joined him.

'Have you seen my film?' he asked, quiet and serene.

'Yes, indeed, I have,' I said, enthusiastically.

'Which show? The evening show?' he asked.

'Yes, when you were ceremoniously presented after the show.'

'Did you hear the catcalls?'

I could say neither yes nor no. How could I say no? How could I turn a deaf ear to the ear-splitting noise? Ear-splitting and heart-less! Now, sitting beside him, I could not look at him, I didn't.

'Tonight they will scream again,' he said. Said it almost to himself.

Bresson's turn came. He was called to appear on stage. Standing in the wings, I heard the same uproar—applause and catcalls, both. The man and the master braved it all and disappeared with the trophy. He did not even say a single word to the audience, unlike the convention at the concluding ceremony at Cannes.

At the end, when the curtain was lifted for the last time, and the awardees seen arrayed in a line, some waving their hands, Bresson was not there.

Yes, indeed, *L'Argent* (Money) was the last film by Bresson. Had he possibly made another? Not that I know of.

Remembering the savage uproar that evening, which I heard from behind the wing and also the catcalls after the screening of the film, and knowing myself as I was, I paid my tribute to Bresson in the *Statesman*:

> Being a habitual viewer and a regular filmmaker, I now see that a passionate cineaste does not have to speak necessarily, like his counterpart in literature, only of his anxiety to change the society, of his protest, of his challenge to the world difficult to accept; but also of the confusion, of the anguished search, of the inherent contradictions, which are beyond easy resolutions. Brilliant patches of such anguished searches and of human situations in total disarray, and finally, of love, of its purity and innocence are seen to manifest themselves in Robert Bresson's films, one after another.

The rest of the post-production work of *Khandhar* was taken up immediately on our return. It was certificated soon after, in August, a year after *Kharij*. Around the same time, Kunal got was accepted by the University of Illinois to pursue his doctorate in electronics and computer science, which he was already doing for some time at the Indian Statistical Institute. Nisha, his wife, after finishing her postgraduate degree in nutrition science, was conducting research on reproductive biology. She had just finished her thesis but was yet to organize her degree requirements. At my end, I was busy getting ready to leave for Venice where I would have to act a juror. At the last moment, Gita decided not to accompany me because Kunal was to leave for Chicago some time in the second week of September. And she wanted to be there when he left.

Suddenly, I was struck by an idea. I allowed Gita to leave her options open—either to see off Kunal at the Calcutta airport with tears trickling down her cheeks, or to receive her son in a country thousands of kilometres away from home with a broad smile on her face. After all, Chicago would be a short journey from Toronto. And Kunal would be happy to see his mother there. Gita was delighted that, without having to spend her own money, she would be able to go to Chicago and spend a few days with her son. All that I was to do was to put Toronto on my agenda and inform Eliane accordingly. I called her but she was not in Zurich—just an hour ago, she had rushed to the airport to catch a flight to Madrid. She had to be in Valladolid on time to receive the Gold Spike for *Kharij*. She would be back after the evening ceremony that night, or the next day.

Venice was my fourth visit, and Gita's second.

While in Venice—watching films, talking films, arguing about films, with Bertolucci acting as chairman of the jury—I received an urgent call from Munich. From Reinhard Hauff, whom German television had assigned the production of a fairly long film on me. Why on me alone, I asked. Why not on the big city as well, my El

Dorado! Reinhard insisted we meet and discuss the matter. We planned to do so immediately after the festival at Venice. The itinerary was finalized within a couple of days, and we fixed a day for a nonstop session at Bergamo. At Bergamo, a friend of mine, Davide Ferrario, film buff and lover of Indian cinema, organized a three-day-long mini-retrospective of my films. We were to stay in this small town for two days, with one day reserved for Reinhard.

As everywhere, in Venice, at Lido on the Adriatic Sea, we had a hectic programme. There were good films and not-so-good films. Opinions differed, as always. At last, it was time for the final marathon session to prepare our mandatory recommendations. We, along with with our wives and/or companions, went on a hour-long lovely 'cruise' down the Grand Canal until we arrived at a faraway island. The pre-lunch session lasted three hours, during which our companions went about the picturesque island and enjoyed the scenery. Once lunch was over, they were packed off to the Lido, and we, the jurors, continued to argue for and against the finalists until, after four hours or so, the list of award-winning films was prepared and the motorboats, driving at full speed, took us back to our hotel.

The finale was no less sparkling as anywhere else. Jean-Luc Godard bagged the big prize for his *Prénom Carmen* (*First Name: Carmen*) (1983). The eternally controversial director, yet 'the most elegant stylist', Godard presented a Godardesque treatment of the familiar Carmen story in a modern set-up. But the one who left a lasting impression on me was a young director, Euzhan Palcy, possibly, in her mid-twenties, for her first film, *La Rue Cases-Nègres* (Street of the houses of negroes, alternatively titled in English as *Sugar-Cane Alley*) (1983), a thoroughly unpretentious film on the simple life of her people, suffering and yet living an intense life. She was from the French island Martinique, in the Caribbean. In Paris she had been mentored by Jean Rouch.

The next day, we went to Bergamo, by car. Reinhard was already in town. We had no time to rest, hardly enough to sleep. The first day spent with David and his retro, and Reinhard now and then; the next day, exclusively with Reinhard, discussing his plan. Then we left for Toronto via Rome, and Reinhard rushed to Munich. For me and my city, Reinhard's two-member team—he and his cameraman—would arrive October. The rest of the crew, at most two or three, would be picked up from my unit.

Another David, David Overbey, a dear friend of mine, a critic and a writer specializing in Italian postwar cinema, received us at Toronto airport. The festival team was small but the organization was perfect. And they were nice people, warm people. We ran on perfect schedule and reached Chicago a day before Kunal was to arrive.

That was a reunion of an unusual kind in a foreign country. I recalled a day many years ago when Gita and I took our son, three and a half, for admission to a school. He cried a lot when he was left left behind. This time, after long years, we accompanied him and left him finally at the university gates. This time, Gita's eyes moistened but neither Kunal's nor mine. And all the time, all three of us missed Nisha very much. She was still in our city, finishing her thesis.

We returned soon after and got ready with adequate material for Reinhard Hauff. Then, sometime in the beginning of October, Reinhard arrived with his friend and cameraman, Frank Brühne. We sat and we spoke, he spoke and I heard, he and Brühne scanned the city streets for a whole day and, then, overnight, he changed his plan of action. The filming started the next day, started from somewhere, from nowhere, outside the pages of his notes. The filming ended without knowing how it would end and where. All in ten days, and he called the film *Ten Days in Calcutta: A Portrait of Mrinal Sen* (1984). Filming the city and filming me, and collecting plenty of clips from my films, and from one of his own, *Messer im Kopf* (*Knife in the Head*) (1978), on my insistence. I had a keen interest in *Messer im Kopf*, primarily because it was the story of a teacher and a student, both involved in students' unrest and, in a complex situation, both under police surveillance. Which in a way was not far from Indian reality. Since the post-production work would be done in Munich, Reinhard left the city after a couple of days. I travelled with him up to Bombay, where he took a meaningful interview of Smita Patil. She had acted in my *Akaler Sandhane*.

Suddenly, it happened a few days after Reinhard had left the country—Ray had a heart attack. A massive attack. The news spread like wildfire. A second attack followed five months later. Two successive attacks, and a bypass surgery in Houston cruelly cut short his working day. Earlier, he would spend more than 12 hours every day in his work chair. In his own words, 'Not very exciting.' Tremendous willpower, coupled with an unbelievable love for his work and the courage of his convictions brought him back to the same chair despite his failing health.

I recall that memorable cultural event in Calcutta, when in April 1987, I released Ray's book, aptly titled, *Stories*, an English translation of the stories originally written in Bengali for the monthly *Sandesh* over a period of 25 years. Along with this edition by Seagull Books, two simultaneous editions were released by Secker & Warburb and Dutton in London and New York, respectively. Interestingly, some young Soviet filmmakers who were present at the occasion revealed that they had taken the initiative of forming a film club named after Ray in a Soviet city.

In 1990, Ray made a film, *Ganashatru*, based on Ibsen's 1882 play *An Enemy of the People*. Later in the same year he made his next, based on his own story and called it *Shakha Proshakha* (*Branches of the Tree*) (1990). The third, made in 1991, was a gigantic leap taken from a short story he had written ten years ago, *Agantuk* (*The Stranger*). And all these three years, an ambulance used to wait outside the studio all the time. Eminent cardiologist Dr Bakshi was always at hand on the sets.

In-between, I had a quiet session with him, a long one—he and I, no one else. At a certain point I asked him, 'Don't you feel lonely at times?' He said, 'Terribly!'

One year later, on 23 April 1992, nine days before his next birthday, he died. The man who, barely two hours before his first heart attack in 1983, had told a television interviewer, 'I am too busy working to worry about death.'

A candid man, a man of unusual courage!

SIXTEEN

Nineteen Eighty-Four
The Year of 'The Ruins' and Back and Forth . . .

Before the commercial release of *Khandhar,* its producer Jagadish Chokhani, also a long-time distributor and owner of the Navina Cinema in my city, wanted to present the film at a couple of festivals, one in the country and the other somewhere in Western Europe. It so happened that the official festival in India, held in Bombay that year, selected *Khandhar* as its inaugural film. That was a glittering event when, on 3 January, the film was shown to an international audience. Strictly modelled on the Russian format, as always, there were speeches first, all acceptably short, and then the screening.

Talking about the Russian format, I have not forgotten about one in particular, a stupendous parade of pomp and grandeur in Moscow. That was the year when the festival started with Francis Ford Coppola's *Apocalypse Now* (1979), shown outside the competition. Coppola brought with him a team of technicians with their very special gadgets, and they worked through the night to ensure the perfect reproduction of sound. The big theatre was packed to the brim. So was the stage, with the high-ups occupying the front seats. On the dot, the all-powerful Philip Yermash, chairman of the State Cinema Committee, stood up amid deafening applause. He began his speech—and we feared it would never end. Amid thunderous applause, the speech at last did come to an end. The grand old King Vidor, living a retired life by then—and I was sitting beside him—remained unmoved during the speech. Only once, when the speech was over, he adjusted the strap around his wrist and glanced at the time. I was watching him. He looked at me and asked, 'Do you follow Russian?' I said, 'No.' He nodded, and said, 'Do you know the minister spoke for 59 minutes? 59 minutes! Without any translation.' Beneath the external calm, King Vidor, once one of the great Hollywood directors, was evidently annoyed.

The turning point in King Vidor's career, which would go onto span 67 years, came with *The Big Parade* (1925), one of the highest-grossing films of the silent era. He made a large number of films during his amazingly long tenure—made and left in-between. He has quite a few well-known films: *The Fountainhead* (1949), *Beyond the Forest* (1949) and *War and Peace* (1956), among many others.

Indian speeches, on the other hand, even now, are never long, but the rituals and sundry items, typically Indian, should in all fairness be drastically trimmed or, better, eliminated without doing any damage to *Indianness*.

Anyway, all said and done that evening, *Khandhar* made an impact on the audience. And those who spoke to us after the show, quite a crowd, said they loved the film. Many of them wanted to know when it would have its general release. The producer sounded confident as he said he would wait and see how it would turn out in a bigger festival abroad. I felt that was the right approach. Interestingly enough, this is the film which bagged the largest number of international awards.

Within a week, we came to know that Berlin, holding its festival in February, had just previewed the cassette and found it rather old-fashioned. The producer was terribly shocked. I asked him to take the news calmly. Just like Ray had to take it when in 1965 his *Charulata* was considered unacceptable by the committee at Cannes. I said so to my producer in the hope that he would not feel upset any more. But to tell the truth, I said it to myself. Last year, much to the annoyance of the director at Berlin Festival, *Kharij* went to Cannes 1983. Now in 1984, Berlin found *Khandhar* old-fashioned. So, happy ending for them! As simple as that.

Soon after, the film was released. In the meantime, Cactus had a talk with Gilles Jacob's secretary. The lady asked for a print, and Cactus rushed a copy to Paris for an early preview.

So far my films had failed to draw crowds to cinemas for continuous weeks, and none till now had been anywhere near a blockbuster. True, nobody would have been happier to see that at least once in my lifetime one of my numerous films had achieved a big success at the box office. It had never been so; it was not to be. As a result, my clientele had always been restricted to the moderate group of *minority* spectators. By accepting the reality and knowing that filmmaking costs a lot of money, the only alternative and a demanding action would be to look for similar discriminating groups scattered all over the world. Thus, by mobilizing moderate groups of minority spectators outside the domestic circuit, my agents could eventually fetch a wider figure, if not the widest. Very simple arithmetic, true, but certainly not that simple to execute. Even then, that was precisely why filmmakers of my kind had been found to care so much for festivals abroad. Primarily for recognition, and undeniably for circulation. Just for sustenance and, indeed, to guard against gradual erosion of our hard-earned beliefs.

Khandhar had a reasonably respectable run in my city and elsewhere. And those who liked the film loved it passionately. The press reviews were by and large flattering and, yes, dignified. But one simple statement, short and personal, surpassing all the adulatory comments came from the octogenarian author, Premendra Mitra. He drew me close, pressed my hand and said, 'Now I can die in peace.' The words came straight from his heart.

Next morning I went to his house, unannounced. He said, 'I am happy, Mrinal, you have kept your promise. You will remember that I gave you the rights strictly on one condition. Just one. That you will show me your film before I lose my eyesight. And, sadly, it has been deteriorating rather fast. Had I lost my sight, I couldn't have seen the *rotting ruin* of the house, the *ugly nakedness* of decay, the *dark crumbling staircase* and the *shrivelled old woman, wrapped in rags.* I saw all these, clear and vibrant, and saw the young woman, Jamini, placed in this setting, with a look that is *distant and sad.*'

While he was saying all this, he had one of his books of selected stories before him, particular pages unfurled, the phrases all underscored. He told me he had done his homework after his return from the screening. While he was speaking to me, he read out those phrases one after another. I was overwhelmed.

He leafed through the pages. He stopped at one and then held the book out to me. It was the last page. He asked me to read out the last lines. Also underscored in the same manner. I had read them a number of times before I had thought of filming the story. Since he asked me, I read them over again. He asked me to read it aloud. So, I acted the 'reader' and he played the 'listener'.

. . . Meanwhile, unknown to yourself, your mind will have undergone many changes. Telenapota will have become a vague, indistinct dream, like the memory of a fallen star. Was there ever such a place as Telenapota? You will not be sure. That grave, austere face, and the eyes that were far away and sad—were they real? Or, was she, too, like the shadow of Telenapota's ruins, just another unreal, misty dream dreamt in a moment of weakness . . . ?

I stopped for a little while before the end. One more line to complete the text. I read the line:

Telenapota, discovered for one brief moment, will sink again into the timeless abyss of night.

I remembered that night when I'd bumped into the story, read the lines, read between the lines, and rediscovered Telenapota.

'On my way home last evening,' he said, 'I remembered the lines.'

I was happy I had kept my promise.

As I was about to go, Premen-da asked me, 'What's his name?'

'Who?' I asked.

'The angler?'

I felt a bit uncomfortable. Even then I clarified the error, 'In the film you saw a photographer, not an angler.'

He looked askance at me—a momentary look—and then he nodded his head, 'Hm!'

Freudian slip?

Suddenly, if not the topic, the mood changed. He was then in no mood to again ask me who the man was.

Perhaps, he did not like the change. Perhaps he had no opinion. I did not want to know. I did not want to invite unnecessary complications between us. All that I might have possibly done would have been to pull a parenthesis out of his text and playfully ask, 'You have often spent unsuccessful hours angling without a catch, haven't you?'

To which, with a delicious kick, Premen-da might have said, 'If someone comes and tempts (me), saying that somewhere there is a magic pool . . . '

And I might have rushed to drown his voice and read out the rest of the text:

> [That somewhere there is a magic pool] filled with the most incredibly simple-minded fish anxiously waiting to swallow any bait (and you have often spent unsuccessful hours angling with a catch), you may suddenly find yourself on your way to discovering Telenapota.

And that might have been a wonderful play of words between us, built entirely out of his own text.

Anyway, that was a wonderful time we spent, talking and feeling.

Premendra Mitra died four years later, in 1988.

A week passed. Gilles Jacob sent me a long cable. Followed by a call from Eliane of Cactus. Good news! The committee liked the film very much. The visuals were very strong, they felt. So was the emotion. The choice, Gilles said, was unanimous. And the selection confirmed. But the committee proposed to have it shown out of competition and strongly hoped that I would not turn down their proposal. Why 'out of competition'? Gilles explained why.

Ray's first film, *Pather Panchali*, was in Cannes in 1955. On its 30th anniversary, in 1984, the festival authority had decided to pay tribute to Ray with his *Ghare-Baire (The Home and the World)*. More so, because they felt that after his massive heart attack and subsequently with his failing health, *Ghare-Baire* would perhaps be his last film. Considering all this, and to pay homage to the master in a most befitting manner, the festival authority decided that there should be no other Indian entry in the competition. Gilles strongly hoped that I would appreciate their sentiment and, at the same time, I would gladly give my consent to show *Khandhar* out of competition.

In so many words, Gilles said the same thing over again in his long cable, and asked me not to withdraw my film under any circumstance.

That was not all. The very next day, Gilles called up from Paris and thanked me profusely for not rejecting their proposal. At my end, I assured him that Ray's tremendous willpower, together with his unbelievable love for his work and the courage of his convictions, would sooner or later bring him back to his work chair.

As always in Cannes, on 14 May, my birthday, *Khandhar* was shown and well received. I did my job heartily—answering questions. Cactus did its job competently—negotiating sales. The first deal, signed and sealed, was between Cactus and the prestigious Swedish Film Institute. Happy beginning!

I left Cannes after a six-day stay. In those six days, I had no rest—talking about myself, about my Indo-French project, and, most particularly, about Ray and his film. His team was yet to arrive. I met them at Delhi airport, briefly—they on their way to Cannes. Understandably, the most notable absentee in the *Ghare-*

Baire team was Ray himself. He was still physically unfit and had been medically advised to go slow.

In Montreal, *Khandhar* bagged the second-best prize, and a month later, the first prize in Chicago. In Montreal, I was present to receive the award; in Chicago, Kunal collected it on my behalf. Nisha was visiting Chicago at the time and she was invited as well. According to her, Kunal looked the perfect Bengali babu in his traditional Bengali outfit, quite unlike his usual self and very much unlike all the others. But with the shawl round his shoulders, and fidgeting with the unmanageable yards of fabric, he also looked terribly awkward. They sent a couple of newspaper clippings to me, and one of them even had a photograph of Kunal holding the trophy. He looked quite smart, said Gita.

When I called Nisha, I asked her, 'Why are you unkind to your husband?'

'I am not,' she said confidently, and laughed. 'Remember the day, 20 February 1980?' she added, and continued to laugh.

Nisha was right. That was the day of their wedding. Occupying centrestage as the traditional groom and made to perform a series of unending rituals, Kunal had looked delightfully nervous. I had enjoyed the scene that day as much as Nisha did his apparent awkwardness at the Chicago event.

A flashback. Ranjit Mullick, the job seeker in *Interview*, had also been clad in white dhoti and kurta and looked the perfect Bengali babu. Coincidentally, 13 years after *Interview*, Kunal, still a university student in Chicago, had nothing formal to wear to the official event. Just like Ranjit, he had no choice but to wear a traditional Bengali outfit. Playfully, with two characters before me, one fictional and the other real, both thrown into an identical situation, I wondered if a long-winded pandit, dealing with aesthetics, would be prompted to comment on fantasy and fact, on *illusion* and *reality*.

All of a sudden, the name of a book comes to mind, *Illusion and Reality* (1937), a book I'd read way back in the early 40s. I read it with great pleasure and avidity. It had been published posthumously; the author, Christopher Caudwell, had been killed in the Spanish Civil War. Those were my formative years when, with every onward movement, as if climbing a steep hill, my horizon kept on changing.

Christopher Caudwell. Educated at the Benedictine School at Ealing, he dropped out at sixteen and a half and worked for three years as a reporter for the *Yorkshire Observer*. Then he returned to London and joined a firm of aeronautical publishers, first as editor and later as a director. He invented an infinitely variable gear, the designs for which were published in the *Automobile Engineer* and attracted a good deal of attention from several experts. He published five textbooks on aeronautics, and, amazingly, seven detective novels and some poems and short stories, all before he was 25. Soon after, he wrote his first serious novel, *This My Hand* (1936). He also wrote three other provocative and stimulating titles: *Illusion and Reality*, *Studies in a Dying Culture* (1938) and *The Crisis in Physics* (1939), though these were all published after his death. When the Spanish Civil War broke out, the Communist Party of Great Britain had raised adequate money to buy an ambulance, and Caudwell was chosen to drive it across France. After handing it over to the concerned unit, Caudwell went to Barcelona and joined the International Brigade. Among the 'brigadiers'—intellectuals in diverse fields—were Ernest Hemingway and Norman Bethune, to name just two. Caudwell was in illustrious company. He was killed in action in February 1937. Killed before he was 30.

What a world we had left behind!

Inadvertently, I travelled through time, back to the past, an unforgettable past, a past which in its own way had given me plenty of nourishment. Then, I came back to the present. Back to 1984.

An Orwellian time?

A letter came. From Chicago. A letter from Kunal—to Gita.

Gita was busy cooking in the kitchen. She asked me to read it out. I pulled out a stool, sat on it, opened the envelope and started to read aloud:

> Ma, I am writing this letter in a hurry. Writing from our University Library . . .

In his letter, Kunal recalled a day many years ago when Gita had taken him, then a little boy, to see Ray's *Aparajito*. He remembered that Gita had cried a lot. Watching her, he too had been close to tears.

> I had forgotten all this, but last night, it all came back to me. In the evening, some of us friends, including Nisha, went to the university film club. To see the same very *Aparajito* again. My third viewing, or the fourth. The others' too. The film left a deep impression on all of us. Every time we see the film, we love Apu more. Watching the film, I felt I was him. Everybody felt the same. But, even though many of us completely identified ourselves with Apu, some of my friends felt somewhat uncomfortable. Those who had decided to stay on here, in this country, had a bit of problem with the mother. Walking back, all of us came to our small apartment and a debate began. They advanced their reasons, and said, 'Doesn't her son have a right to his future? *Will the son keep himself tied to the mother's apron strings . . . ?*'

Kunal's was a short letter, but since he knew this particular film was my favourite among Ray's films, and by my definition the most 'contemporary', he wanted me to know about the 'debate'. To my mind, contemporaneity is determined, by and large, more by attitudes and much less by time. That is why I have always considered Carl Dreyer's *The Passion of Joan of Arc* as one of the most contemporary films ever made.

In Chicago, staying far away from the likes of Apu's mother, Kunal and his friends saw the film. They saw how, balanced between adolescence and youth, Apu suddenly matured into an adult, how his world began to expand, his horizon widened, and how he refused to pursue his father's profession—priesthood. When Apu thought of the impossible, thought of crossing barriers, when he became restless, even vocal, and finally walked into the world, the big city, Sarbojaya, his mother, remained calm and unperturbed. Calm and unperturbed on the surface but deep within she was suffering a terrifying loneliness. What had afflicted some of Kunal's friends, I guessed, was a sense of guilt. What else?

Kunal did not speak a word about how the debate ended. All he said was that he would not stay there for a day more than was needed to complete his work. He would come back and that was for sure.

Glancing at the letter again, I understood he had written it in a hurry, in-between his work, and dropped it into a post box on his way home. But why did he have to write in haste? And why the urgency? I wondered! Leaving Gita alone in the kitchen with her son's letter, I came out. And I started to think things over:

A story taking place way back in the late 1920s and early 30s. A film made in the mid-50s, made strictly within the timeframe of the text. Seen by a bunch of young people of today who have a right to their 'future'. Seen far away from their home in the mid-80s. In 1984, to be exact.

Surprisingly, while viewing, all differences of time and space disappeared—the timeframe was smashed without their knowing, and, without their knowing, *Aparajito* became a contemporary phenomenon. The viewers took their stand, clear and firm, arguing and exchanging views on a delicate issue.

A question crossed my mind at an unguarded moment: Would Kunal keep his promise? Or, some time or other, changes would come upon him? And his priorities?

Those were mundane questions, both for me and Gita.

Things kept on happening. Kunal and Nisha kept on coming to see us once a year. At times, twice. We too made quick trips abroad, once in a while. Later, they used to call us at regular intervals. And, as days went by and we continued to age, they called us every week, each call lasting even as long as half an hour. Besides, at an incredible pace, the e-mails kept flowing to and fro. Life went on, and my filmmaking too.

A letter came from Kunal, as they often did, but this time it was 15 years later, on 28 December 1999. In the middle of the night. Before going to bed, I opened my laptop and checked my mail. And there it was. A letter which, in an unusual context, and in a few words, said a lot about everything that had been haunting all of us over the years—*promises and priorities*. Kunal said, 'The fact that I will not be able to come to Calcutta during the New Year is finally sinking in. I feel like sharing the story with you.'

The first part of the story, as told by Kunal, ran thus: 30 years ago, when he and his friends had been in the last year of school, and for some there was another year to go, they made an adolescent promise—to meet somewhere in the city on the eve of the new millennium.

Those were exciting times. Not long ago, we witnessed the first man to walk on the moon. From Gagarin to Apollo— it took only ten years. It was not too difficult to imagine what the next thirty years would bring. And *2001: A Space Odyssey* concretized that vision. Through our young eyes, we visualized a city and a world that will be glittering and new.

How would they select the meeting point? In 30 years, the city would be nearly unrecognizable. They needed a meeting place that had not been 'bulldozed to make room for the brave new world'. The unanimous choice of Kunal and his friends was: the north gate of Victoria Memorial.

During the next ten years, we shared our plans with others. We invited new friends, any number of contacts whose paths crossed ours. For me, it was often a way of saying: you matter to me. Looking back, I cannot even remember the names and faces of all those who have been invited.

Over the next two decades, some of us drifted away. Still, each time we met, we talked about the millennium meet. Earlier this year, when I was in Calcutta, I was walking towards the Gariahat crossing one evening. As I was going past Triangular Park, I tripped on something. After recovering my balance, I looked down to discover that it was the same crack on the pavement that had tripped me up thirty years ago.

Everything was going for them as arranged in talks and dreams. Suddenly, at the beginning of December, Kunal got an offer from *Encyclopaedia Britannica*. He could neither turn it down nor ask them to wait until the new year because, in terms of his discipline, the job that was offered compared favourably with the options he could think of. He accepted the job and joined in a week's time. He joined, and his millennium dream was brutally crushed. Then this letter, which we received sometime in the middle of the night on 28 December. Kunal concluded his story saying:

> I do not know how many of us will be there. I do not know what they will do. But I do know now that though Calcutta has not changed much, I have—as have my priorities. And it is not about others. It is not about failing to keep my promise to someone else. It was a promise that I made to myself, and those are the ones that are hardest to break.

That was where Kunal's email story came to a close, but the finale was still to come, on 31 December 1999, the Millennium Eve.

Outside Victoria Memorial, at the North Gate. I was there at sundown, at 5.30, on the dot. That was the time they had all agreed on. I stood there with a number of them, many of them with their wives, some with their children too, and amazingly, several couples, then divorced. I was with them to represent the proposer of the dream-plan made 30 years ago. All of them looked their age, 30 years older.

That night I called Kunal. I told him that, as planned by him, I had spent a lovely time with his friends. As long as I was with them, I felt I was younger by 30 years. And they, older by 30.

Kunal was quite comfortable with his new job. Being at *Encyclopaedia Britannica* for a couple of years and getting to know more about its various projects and, more importantly, about his growing responsibilities, he found his last position as an executive closest to his heart. 'Creative, challenging and independent' is how he described it.

Nisha, specializing in early-childhood education, joined the University of Chicago Laboratory School and had been teaching at the nursery and kindergarten levels.

But their financial situation was rather dire: Kunal's monthly salary was 500 dollars as a research assistant, out of which $300 was spent on rent for their single room. Nisha's babysitting, coupled with knitting for a local store, and, later, a scholarship and free tuition is what helped her take up the full load of courses at university.

That is how they started and that is how they were growing. And that is how the four of us interacted with one another over the years. In all this time, have we ever missed one another? Of course, we have and do even now. But we have never felt distanced. Not yet. *Matadeo,* borrowing a title from one of Kurosawa's last films and paying tribute to the master! The old man in the film collapsed a number of times at his *dieable* age; his students kept rushing to their dying teacher. But every time, fighting a tough battle against death, he came alive, forced a sweet smile on his face and said, *Matadeo!*—Not yet.

Back to *Khandhar* which I had laid aside. To complete its dossier on the festival front, the biggest recognition came from the widely respected annual, *International Film Guide*, edited by Peter Cowie, which, as every year, selected top ten films of world cinema,

1983–84. *Khandhar* was one among those top ten. Among the nine others were *Under the Volcano* (1984) by John Huston (USA/Mexico); *Napló gyermekeimnek* (Diary for my children) by Márta Mészáros (Hungary); *E la nave va* (*And the Ship Sails On*) by Federici Fellini (Italy–France); *Coup de foudre* (At first sight) by Diane Kurys (France); *Un dimanche à la campagne* (A Sunday in the countryside) by Bertrand Travernier (France); *Paris, Texas* by Wim Wenders (West Germany–France); and Italy's *Kaos* (Chaos) by the famous Taviani Brothers who, right through their lives, made their films together, and that too unusually creative works. Now, looking back, I see, like in Cannes 1983, I was in august company. True, for this particular recognition, I had ample reason to feel proud, but, honestly, on the whole, the collections at the box office was much less than encouraging. Ironies never cease to be.

Sometime, at the beginning of the next year, Reinhard Hauff sent me a cassette of his film, 80 minutes long. He had done a first-rate job and captured the city in perfect rhythm. With the materials scattered across the city, in and out, shot in only ten days, and with clips carefully selected from my films, Reinhard, and his editor Heidi Handorf, restructured the film by playing with the visuals and sound in a manner he had never thought of while shooting. Not a conventional documentary on a city or on a city dweller. Later, in Munich, I saw the film *Ten Days in Calcutta* in a big theatre where a special screening had been arranged. David Robinson of the London *Times* was with me. I told him candidly, 'None of us in India has ever captured the city with as much authenticity as Reinhard seems to have done.' Robinson said, 'You can't see the tip of your nose, can you?'

271

What then about Louis Malle? I argued within myself. And Günter Grass? Reinhard had a genuine love for the city and its people. Even for the people on the pavement and in the slums. I watched him all the time, when he was working, even when he wasn't. Right through those ten days. And that was the chemistry!

That same day, in the evening, in Munich. Eliane of Cactus called my hotel from Paris and left a message. I called her back and we had a long talk. She wanted to discuss my Indo-French co-production. She said that a French company, Scarabee Films, had been formed; the Swiss concern. Cactus Film, had joined it as well as a Belgian outfit, Le Films de la Dreve. All within the framework of the official protocol. All this sounded like the film would be a big affair, but in truth we had an extremely tight budget. Eliane asked if I had made up my mind about the Indian partnership, and how soon I could send the screenplay for distribution among the three parties. She said all the three parties had liked the synopsis which I had sent her a month earlier. Now we needed to have the full script and an idea about the cast. The budget needed to be worked out too, at the soonest. And, most importantly, had I managed to get official clearance to 'rehabilitate' the rather odd location which three of my unit members and I had accidentally discovered in Rajasthan. All of us must hurry up and start work right away. At the same time, I was warned that it could not be a mammoth project. Involving four characters, only four, speaking Hindi, restricting the screenplay to somewhat of a no-man's land, frightfully desolate, where, long years ago, God's disgrace had fallen on once-prosperous farmers for reasons only God knew. My plot was loosely based on a short story by one of West Bengal's liveliest writers, Samaresh Basu. Once again, Mohit Chattopadhyay collaborated with me. Even at the risk of annoying the writer, because the script was a distant echo of the original, Mohit and I rebuilt the story with the feel of an easygoing parable:

There was always a choice—or, so it seemed. If you wanted to eat, to work, to have water, to survive, you could s up and give them your thumbprint and then stay in line. Or . . . you could leave the world and live on the margins, as did a weaver and a farmer. The two of them refused to acknowledge a master, and preferred to scratch out a living in the sprawling ruins of a lost village on the edge of a desert. The drought had thwarted the efforts of the farmer, and the weaver had made a deal with a trader. In exchange for enough to eat, the weaver turned the trader's raw wool into quality fabrics. The weaver and the farmer had developed a relationship of mutual respect and survival.

They saw no one but the trader who, from time to time, arrived on his camel with his goods, leaving behind food and wool, and then went off to faraway towns to sell the fabrics. Thus, the two built their own world in the middle of those weatherworn, time-forgotten ruins, and lived with what they believed was independence and freedom, with no master to tell them what to do and what not to.

Then a woman appeared in their world. She had been wandering, trying to escape her own past of floods and deaths because she was sick of death. When she was greeted with understanding, she stayed, and the hopeless look she had brought with her slowly dissolved. She realized she had a home at last.

Once dreadfully desolate, the village then began to throb with life, even if it was the throb of only three hearts.

One snake or two were of no concern to them because they were not unfriendly to one another. Planting was done and there was the promise of a crop. Clothes were washed and mended, meals were joyously shared. Even the trader seemed pleased that life had begun again in that dead place. The presence of the woman had brought a great deal of good into the lives of the two men, but the foundations of their relationship had begun to crack.

Two men and one woman! Simple arithmetic for the trader to be happy about.

Both the farmer and the weaver desired the woman. Both entered into a game of continued seeming closeness. The woman resisted at first but eventually gave in from a sense of gratitude.

The trader clearly saw what else was happening to them. At the same time, one day when the two men went to a local fair in the nearest town—a day's walk from the village—they saw they were being cheated by the trader. They rebelled, but the trader enticed them back into his web by giving them cash. Suddenly, the two men were telling each other that they didn't need to sleep to dream, for the money would buy dreams.

They earned, they dreamt, they nurtured their thoughts and desires in private. The woman felt acute distress as she saw what was happening, but was powerless to restore the old trust and love.

The trader saw the crop flourishing. He saw all three of them working hard, he also saw a crack widening.

The woman became pregnant.

The farmer and the weaver were now full of possessive rage. In naked fury, they attacked each other over the right of parenthood. Who was the father of the child, they asked the woman. She confessed that all she knew was that she was the mother. She warned the men that while they had tried to escape the enemy in the outside world, they had now brought the enemy with them, into themselves. And knowing that was the end of this chapter of her life, she wandered out into the desert in the darkness of the night, carrying her child in her womb, to seek another world.

Another, more tangible enemy arrived, as the two men attempted to destroy each other—the trader. He had been biding his time, and now arrived with a private army, all on camels, to take the land reclaimed by the weaver and the farmer. The two grew wiser and united for the moment with a single protest: *This land is ours, of our own making.* But it was too late. Bulldozers appeared on the scene to make room for a New Order.

The three actors who were chosen were Om Puri, Naseeruddin Shah and Shabana Azmi, and each of them gave an extraordinary performance. The trader was played by theatre activist M. K. Raina from Delhi, who also did very well. He too helped generously with rewriting the lines.

The shoot, as programmed, was completed in two months—under a blazing sun and in the freezing cold, when the snakes went into hibernation but the scorpions, not very small in number, could still be seen scurrying about. As usual, problems cropped up at various levels and at practically every stage—before shooting, during shooting and while transporting the crew and equipment to inaccessible places. Occasionally, the problems even affected our commune life. Despite the shocks and occasional challenges, the project survived until, three days before we were to finish, 'God's disgrace' fell on our team.

The actors had finished their work and left for Bombay and Delhi. An elaborate arrangement for a massive explosion had been made, high explosives requisitioned as well as more than a dozen smoke bombs. All on a war footing. The utmost precautions were taken, and each one of the team, as well as all our visitors, were alerted. When the time came—under the direct supervision of the Border Security Force—the explosives were detonated. The devastation was meticulously photographed—fire billowing out, walls razed, splinters thrown up in the air, and smoke, black and white, thickening over the sprawling ruins. An hour later, when the BSF gave us the all-clear signal, we came out into the open, and out of sheer curiosity, began to gauge the extent of the damage. Suddenly, without any warning, a bomb burst! Three people were injured—the one who'd brought the team to the 'Godforsaken' land—that is, me; the French cameraman; and the Flemish sound recordist. And it was no act of sabotage, no act of terrorism, not backsliding on the part of the BSF. 'It was an act of God,' the nearby villagers said. All in one voice. One turbaned octogenarian in the neighbourhood, not unknown to the team, said, 'We warned you, we asked you to offer prayers, you did not care. So now you suffer.'

'How could God be so spiteful?' quipped an innocent member of the team.

Soon afterwards, the scene shifted to Europe for the post-production work. According to the contract, France allowed a substantial part of its money to be spent outside its territory; Switzerland, being generous, allowed its entire share to be spent outside; Belgium, as well as India, specified that their share would have to be spent entirely in their respective territories. So in Europe, the occidental crew and I had to shuttle between Brussels and Paris, sometimes by road and sometimes by train. Ravi Shankar composed and recorded the music in Paris, with only four other musicians. The one who deserves special mention was Elizabeth Waelchli, the Swiss editor, who, without the benefit of the spoken words, did her job very skilfully. Finally, 12 weeks later, we were done, and the first copy was sent to Gilles Jacob's office for the festival preview. That was on 2 or 3 April.

Two days later, in our Brussels apartment, Gita was packing up things in great haste—she is very good at that—a call came from Paris. It was Gilles, calling to give me the great news. Eliane and the executive producer, Marie Pascale Osterrieth, came to see us off at the airport. Happy news for all of us and for the rest of the European crew, for Carlo Varini (cameraman) and Henri Morelle (sound recordist), in particular.

At Frankfurt airport, having had some time to rest and recline, we remembered the man without whose irresistible persuasion the film could not have been made at all—Jack Lang, still at his seat as a deputy of what-I-do-not-know, and operating from Brussels, though the party he stood for had lost the election by a slender margin just a week ago. There was still some time for our Air India flight, and so I scribbled a parting note to Lang, acknowledging my gratitude for the wonderful support he had offered my team and me. And then, remembering the election reverses, I added a postscript:

It happened this morning in our Brussels apartment. My wife was packing and I was helping her. A phone call came. A journalist asked me if I could make a short statement about the film. I said: A world built or gained is but the world lost, to be rebuilt or regained. Genesis, all over again.

I called the film *Genesis* (1986), a film without an Indian title.

As usual, on 14 May, my birthday, *Genesis* was presented in Cannes 1986. The reception was mixed, the likes and dislikes sharply divided, some praising it highly, some saying it could be seen and safely forgotten. The press conference elicited a few interesting questions, including one on Engels' *The Origins of the Family, Private Property, and the State* (1884), but, on the whole, *Genesis* failed to make the most of what we'd achieved with *Kharij*.

I am not the person to qualify the likes and dislikes. Liked or disliked, for whatever I had done in the past, I always wished I could do it over again—any film, any time. To make it better or rescue it from unwanted disaster. Always being born, reborn and restructured. Correcting the conclusions.

Looking here and there, a few quotes:

Naseeruddin Shah (who played the farmer in *Genesis*), in *Filmfare*: What am I doing in this film? What am I doing in a Mrinal Sen film anyway? The film is a load of crap.

Geoff Brown, in the *Times*: Stripped to its bare bones, the film might not sound too nourishing. But Sen is a wizard at conjuring subtle moods from a few figures in a landscape, and the unruffled pace is entirely justified by the shifting human relationship.

M. K. Raghavendra, in *Deep Focus*: It sounds and looks like a middle-class Marxist primer . . . it is an awful kind of Marxist cinema.

Alexander Walker, in *The Standard*: Unflawed gem of a movie.

Utpal Dutt, in *Ganashakti*: With a narrative firmly confined to the archetypal trader, weaver and farmer, the film attains the quality of a parable, and gives a feel of the sharp-edged simplicity of a fairy tale. A complex historical period is summed up before our eyes.

Jean-Claude Carrière, in *Libération*: Devoid of any mythical concern, all is simple, calm, and clear. The scenes are brief, loaded with ellipses. Everything seems to be situated in the story itself but in the manner it is made, and the making is splendid . . . One is also able to read behind his film a story that all Indian children know—that of two birds flying with a big worm picked up from the earth held in their beaks—a single worm for both of them. A hunter follows them, bow in hand, never drawing it. He stops when the birds stop, and starts again when they fly. Surprised, a man asks the hunter, 'What on earth are you doing? You're wasting your time. Why don't you strike?' And the hunter replies, 'I am waiting for them to fight.'

Carrière, the French screenwriter, read the film in different ways. When he came to the last scene, a bulldozer looming up in threatening shape, he commented in *Libération*:

> What does it aim at? To construct a new city on that dried-up earth where one does not kill snakes? A long road? Going where and coming from where . . . ?

Given a chance, it would be lovely to read a film in different ways, as Carrière had done. Plays and novels had been given different interpretations from time to time, been praised, and even condemned, though not always for the same reason or the same measure. As far as *Genesis* was concerned, its fate as a work of art was very much under debate. As an extension of the debate, I pull out another quote from a comprehensive analysis of the film done by Gayatri Chakravorty Spivak, critic and scholar, in her 1993 book *Outside in the Teaching Machine*:

> The viewer is baffled because Sen assumes agency of reinscription rather than the marginality of the post-colonial position [. . .] In such a text, the allegory works in bits and pieces, with something like a relationship with the postmodern habit of citing without authority. With a pedagogy that sees this as the mark of a fragmented post-colonial mode, the allegory can offer a persistent parabasis to the development of any continuous ethno-cultural narrative *or* of a continuous re-inscription. *Genesis* is the 'original', not the translated title of the film [. . .] At the origin is something, like a subtitle, something like a footnote, something like a postscript, and post-coloniality can be its scrupulous paradigm.

FIGURES 32 and 33. Whatever is constructed extempore during *the trip of the picture* can be nothing but improvisation.

FIGURES 34 and 35. Receiving National Awards from President Neelam Sanjiva Reddy (*above*) and Prime Minister Indira Gandhi (*below*). Ample compensation for box-office disasters!

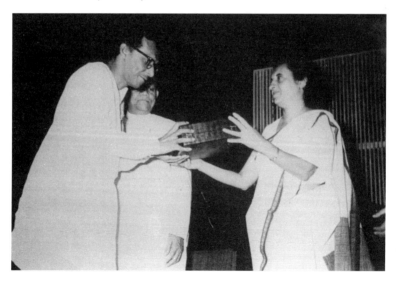

FIGURE 36. Intimate moments with Satyajit Ray.
A candid man of unusual courage!

FIGURE 37. With Jean-Luc Godard at Cannes '83.
The eternally controversial director. The most elegant stylist.

FIGURE 38. With Reinhard Hauff, discussing a sequence for his documentary *Ten Days in Calcutta* (1984).

FIGURE 39. With Gabriel García Márquez.

FIGURE 40. With Charlie Chaplin's grand-daughter Kiera.
When she paid me a visit at my residence, her eyes first fell
upon the 'Charlie, the Vagabond' poster on the wall.

FIGURE 41. With David Robinson, author of the brilliant *Chaplin: His Life and Art* (1985), after the screening of Reinhard Hauff's documentary in Munich.

FIGURE 42. With Ravi Shankar (*extreme right*) in Paris, listening to music he composed for *Genesis* (1986).

FIGURE 43. On the sets, directing my actress-wife Gita.

FIGURE 44. With son Kunal, daughter-in-law Nisha and wife Gita.
They have made my world complete, within and without.

FIGURE 45.

SEVENTEEN

I Never Say I'll Retire,
For I Am Always Being Born . . .

Enough! Enough of it all! Enough of planning, drafting, writing! Enough of delving into old notes and reading much less, travelling a lot and running from one place to another, alternately presenting films and acting the juror in festivals, filming in-between, attending press meetings, fishing for compliments unashamedly, and always giving the stupid impression to one and all that I needed no rest. Honestly, I did need a break, a long break from work. I needed some time spent in hibernation. At least, a month, or even more. So, coming back from Cannes 1986, I spent two uneventful weeks in my city and, to escape the violence of heat and humidity, Gita and I made a hurried trip to the Andamans, where we had never been to. Much to our shock and irritation, the weather in the island was worse, and we gathered from the locals that most of the year they had three variations of the climate—hot, hotter, hottest. Even during the monsoon. Instantly I recalled Jerome K. Jerome's line on weather in London: 'The weather is like the government, always in the wrong.'

Jerome, the Londoner, is one of my favourite writers, writing on various subjects in various ways, also writing lovely belles-lettres. My favourite of all of them is, of course, *Three Men in a Boat (To Say Nothing of the Dog)* (1889).

Despite the most terrible heat, Gita enjoyed the trip because it was her one trip with me in the last ten years that was not work-related. With no press meet and no interviews claiming almost all of my time, not to speak of seminars or talk shows, she could rid herself of the burden of her husband's priorities and the trappings of the official calendar. She loved the trip and not without effort, managed to resign herself to the gruesome heat. All because it was a wonderful feeling to be able to wrest control of her identity disproving the shrewd observation Aldous Huxley presented in *Eyeless in Gaza* (1936) about two friends, one behind the other, 'like an Indian wife trailing through the dust after her husband.' In our two-week stay in the Andamans, with grace and dignity, she taught me a lesson.

After a month and a half, I returned to my desk and decided to work out a possible follow-up of *Genesis* which, in no uncertain terms, had touched on barter, the emergence of money and the waking dreams that money can buy—and of course the consequences, the bulldozer at the end (Incidentally, Martin Karmiz, the Parisian, the real mover and shaker of offbeat cinema, and one who distributed my film and plenty of films of unusual strength and excellences, had not liked the bulldozer at all.) I started scribbling my notes but not about the vanquished—the weaver and the farmer—not about the prospect of 'a new city on that dried-up earth', but about the pregnant woman of *Genesis*.

To start with, a small wayside eating house, an Indian dhaba, run by an old woman, located somewhere near the frontier, the end of the 'world' we had come away from. All kinds of people come to the eating house, workers mostly, undefined people. The old woman loves talking to her customers, tells them stories.

Convoys pass by at regular intervals, nobody knows where they go. The old woman says, 'There it goes again.' Once, at the end of a day like this, the visitors go away and she is left alone, as always. She is about to close shop when, in the darkness beyond, she sees the ghost of a stranger trudging along. It's a woman, who can't walk for much longer; she sits down with an effort and it seems is looking for help. Lamp in hand, the old woman goes over to her and sees that the distressed woman is in the last stage of pregnancy. Later in the night, inside the eating house, amid the sound of passing trucks, a child is born.

That far and no further. What followed was all unprocreative—jotting, scribbling, ruffling—until one day I asked Mohit if he could either join me or write it all himself. Mohit is fond of speaking volubly at the slightest provocation, but this time he was rather reticent and asked me to drop the idea. And I dropped it then and there. As a matter of fact, I was looking for someone who would ask me to do so. I felt enormously relieved, and lost no time in recalling a story I'd read long years ago—a story capturing the futility of avoidable anger and hate. Two men, a shepherd and a farmer, vent their savage fury to avenge themselves but achieve hardly anything except their own ruin. A macabre tale about self-annihilation set in a virgin rural surrounding. The final confrontation of each other's folly is an assertion of man's victory over his own destructive nature. A fabulous moral tale, 'Mukti Marg' (The road to salvation) by Munshi Premchand. Earlier, in 1977, I'd used his story 'Kafan' for *Oka Oori Katha*. Hardly a week passed when, this too, like the sequel to *Genesis*, was set aside and then never taken up again.

Most often than not, throughout my career, during the awkward period between a film I'd just completed and the next I hadn't yet begun, I'd always had a problem period of this kind—a sense of uncertainty followed by a temporary void. In a similar situation after *Genesis*, I asked myself why, having made a successful pilot of a short film, should I not have a go at the whole series. And, true, it immediately made sense to me—of course, for television— 13 independent stories, 13 episodes, each episode not exceeding 20 minutes, and each exploring the man–woman relationship in diverse situations and among diverse age groups. My unit and I shot the pilot project in three days, took three days to edit, score, mix and the rest. All this before we went off to make *Genesis*. But to tell the truth, with my pilot project, I had a kick of surprise— and elation. It was a very satisfying experience, and, after several private viewings, I had received a lot of feedback from my friends. It was a story of love and despair replete with quiet dignity, disclosing a chapter closed a decade ago. Played out over a day and a half. Girish Karnad and Aparna Sen gave their heart and soul in that short span of time, a day and a half. It was all done playfully; no one was kept on tenterhooks, and while filming we were open to plenty of improvisations. The episode was titled 'Das Saal Baad' (After a decade).

I quickly picked up the threads of the pilot completed a year ago. But why now? Only for the love of video technology? To conduct yet another experiment? To widen my horizons? To break the frontiers? To improvise in plenty with the participation of intelligent actors? To earn some extra money for team and myself? To keep the kitchens running in a relaxed manner? My answers to myself: Yes, most certainly so, yes to all of these questions. But to reopen an old file such as this, one particular and very important reason was that I needed to rest a little more—take it easy. And all these episodes could be done playfully, in a manner that a child plays with the building blocks. That was it, for sure. Wonderful pastime! Having made the decision, I gave a quick 'go-ahead' signal both to my team and myself.

With all the limitations as well as the possibilities offered by the small screen, we came to grasp video technology through experiments and errors, and we were excited. We found where its strength lay, in the keyhole play—all delightfully subdued, and in its intimate viewing, in its daily bits, in its secret drama. Within its confines, we took lessons from modern short stories and tried to successfully avoid emphasis on plots and incidents and focus primarily on feelings. We realized that Leo Tolstoy's 'How Much Land Does a Man Require' (1886) should never be done for the small screen because the subject needed a lot of space and air; whereas Anton Chekhov's 'The Death of a Government Clerk' (1883) could be reasonably squeezed and ideally slotted in the much-abused idiot box. We learnt to play with *faces* because the small screen was most reluctant to accommodate *space*. In *Genesis*, at one extreme, we had used a mythical, invented space, and reached its maximum extension. Now, at the other extreme, we decided to almost discard space within the limits of the available technology.

By practically discarding *space* and focusing on *faces*, with words and silence as proactive agents, we built 12 more episodes, based mostly on short stories by eminent writers. Once, we had no story for a particular episode. I collected three people in their early twenties, two boys and a girl, all very sharp and intelligent, smart and sensitive, and as actors, just what I wanted. I asked them to construct a 'story' of their own, based on this broad outline: A girl in an affluent family invites two of her friends to have lunch at home. Her parents are not at home. In the course of conversation, they come up with an idea: they will play a game, just to pass the time in the best possible manner. The boys will be the contenders and the girl will be the judge. The winner will also win the heart of the girl.

On a particular day and at the appropriate time, we arrived at the location, a modern bungalow with a beautiful lawn, now the residence of the legendary Jyoti Basu, the former chief minister of West Bengal for an uninterrupted 23 years. The young actors were terribly excited. They asked me a few relevant questions without knowing that I too was unaware of the stages leading to a riveting climax. All I said was, 'It is for you to arrive at a moment of truth.'

'Where are we now?' asked the girl, hugely amused.

'Who owns the house?' asked one of the boys.

'My parents, for sure,' asserted the girl, and chuckled.

I was glad that the girl was seeing the humour in the situation. I could see that she, on her own, had already walked into the 'story'. I asked them to sit on the lawn and then told them the rest of my 'story' outside the interior story they would build:

> The parents have gone out for the day to meet a famous Swami-ji who has come to town. The daughter is left all alone. Her two friends have come well in advance to discuss the sequence of 'events'. All three of them, sitting on the beautiful lawn, are now to while away the time until lunchtime intervenes.

Without consciously planning it that way, I realized that we were working out a fascinating *workshop*.

The episode would start with all three of them on the lawn. They argued and decided that since chess would be time-consuming, and the episode would not go beyond 20 minutes, they would prefer playing carom. Even though the production staff had got the board ready, what I particularly liked was that the idea of playing carom was put up by themselves. In other words, they got involved.

Filming started in 15 minutes. Approximately five minutes on the lawn when they constructed their own lines, a kind of ad lib, starting with free-for-all frolicking and then coming to the proposal about the game, with the girl acting the judge. To give the perfect appearance of a competition, the judge, just appointed, decreed they would play three games.

The next 15 minutes were staged inside, in the tastefully furnished drawing room. The carom board at the centre, the contenders on either side and the judge seated on a chair. They took their positions, ready to start. At that point came my last instruction for all three of them, 'I'll not speak a word because that's your job. But you must not fail to bring out a dramatic end, *ending on a delicate note*.' The girl smiled an unsure smile but the boys looked quite confident.

When everything was ready, I asked, 'Could you wrap your story in—how do I say it?—*in mystery?*'

They looked at me, they looked at one another, they looked a bit tense, perhaps a bit nervous. At that moment, at precisely zero hour, I went close to them and said, 'Take it easy, the encounter is just play-acting.' Then throwing my arm around the girl's shoulder, I took her a few steps away and spoke a few words in a whisper, words meant only for her. 'Take things easy,' I repeated loudly, offered her a lozenge and retraced my steps back to the boys. Taking out two more lozenges from my pocket, I threw the candies at them. The girl's tension was considerably eased.

One of the boys, short and tough, gave a mischievous smile and said, 'Bribing the judge?'

I gave a hearty laugh. The others joined in. All three of them started sucking on the lozenges. The right time to start the game, they were all relaxed. I gave the signal.

Everything was peaceful, playful and absolutely real. They played and spoke, the judge punctuated the scene with witty remarks and occasional interjections. And, as worked out, the game was lively, funny and much less than serious but without a false note anywhere.

In a conventional documentary, the camera should have remained fixed at a precise point, but our story it was not exactly that. We had three distinct camera positions with appropriate cuts to close-ups of the contenders and the judge, and, to lend restrained dramatic kicks, and ensure a well-structured format, close-ups of the striker and the board and the holes at four corners.

Though they were play-acting, slowly but inexorably the atmosphere began to change, the contenders spoke less and less and the judge turned serious. All their own doing. I decided to have more close-ups without disturbing their free flow of emotions. We had a second camera at our disposal.

In the process, as the competition was approaching a close, the players took more time to think, took more time to strike, just as in a game of chess. And when the result was one to one, and the unspoken hostility between the players was fermenting within, the judge, who was committed to offer her heart to the champion, was helpless.

Finally, it was the turn for the last strike by the possible winner. In total silence, the two were intense—formidable and stubborn, facing each other. Slowly, and without their knowledge, the judge, apprehending an unpleasant showdown, got up from her seat, looked at both the players and then at the board. There was silence. Dreadful silence! And, suddenly, the man, who knew he would lose, shouted in impotent rage, 'Strike!'

Without wasting a fraction of a second, the judge did the impossible: she jumped on the board, grabbed the striker and messed up the rest of the pieces. That was the end of the game, and the end of the episode, the players all feeling frightfully guilty.

Great! They'd hit the bull's eye.

With plenty of shots at our disposal, the rest was done by editing which, in its totality, gave the impression of a premeditated structure. A couple of shots towards the end were discarded because of the girl's furtive look at me. I was proud of Mrinmoy Chakraborty, my editor.

A daring experiment on my part and for all who participated, the actors in particular. Highly satisfying too! And it was possible only because we used video technology, which allowed us plenty of chances despite only a reasonable fund at our disposal. I called the episode 'Swayamvar' (Marriage by choice). The 13-part serial was given an appropriate title: *Kabhi Door Kabhi Paas* (Sometimes far, sometimes near) (1985–86). When it was finally telecast, episode after episode, week after week, the responses were, as always, both good and bad. A freelance columnist, for instance, once a grand executive at a bank but at that time penning critiques on television programmes and series for the *Statesman*, wrote on my carom story and was insufferably sarcastic right through. At the other end, a flattering response coming from an unexpected quarter was unforgettable.

I was at Prasad Laboratory in Madras, working on the analyser, closeted in a small cubicle with one of the supervisors.

We heard a soft knock at the door. I looked up. The man at the door was none other than Kamal Haasan, one of the most prolific actors, an undisputed leader of India's mainstream cinema. He'd heard I was in town and working at the lab. He rushed over to tell me his own story about watching my carom story on television. Although a busy man and somewhat of a workaholic, he thought of returning home early one evening since his shoot was cancelled. He was tired and thought of relaxing. He walked into his room, picked up the remote control almost automatically and pressed a button. My carom story had already started on TV, and he caught one of the boys giving a hard strike. That was enough to make him sit down, and watch the rest 'wide-eyed', until he caught my name in the end titles. He asked me if I could send him a cassette for a complete viewing. I promised I would and, most importantly, I told him the story of the making. However, for absolutely no reason, I did not keep my promise.

From Tokyo came an invitation for both Gita and I to attend the second edition of the festival. Gregory Peck was the chairman of the jury, and I was one of the nine members. The organizers strongly hoped we would both not refuse. I asked Gita if she was ready to carry the burden of my priorities and give me the go-ahead. She said once she landed in Tokyo, she would create her own priorities and go her own way. She had never been to Japan. So we said yes.

In September 1987, we reached Tokyo. Two hours after we checked in to our hotel, I got a call from Gregory Peck. Such a wonderful voice, such a charming presence—such a fabulous actor. He said he had just come from China. He asked if I had ever been there. He sounded so warm and friendly. I said we must meet soon. How soon could we make it? We would be meeting for the first time!

'First time, you say? Have we never met before?'

'We were not formally introduced. But we were both there, in 1973. In Tehran.'

'Ah, Tehran! I remember, the hospitality was terrific.'

'Yes, indeed. I was on the jury. Frank Capra and James Mason too.'

'Ah, how wonderful!'

I will never forget how warm and effusive he was on phone. Like me, he was an unceasing talker. It was great fun talking to him and, indeed, heart-warming. For both of us, our ten-day event had got off to a wonderful start. We finally met later in the afternoon, and talked about China and Tehran and the young Iranian doe-eyed girls who sang beautiful songs while the mandolin played alongside. He was very enthusiastic about Frank Capra, but when I mentioned James Mason I got the sense he was not as thrilled. I'd watched both of them at a couple of parties in Tehran; it had seemed to me they rather preferred distancing themselves from each other and to be encircled by their own admirers. There was nothing uncommon about such behaviour, particularly in showbiz; the pressures of numerous professional hazards tend to make many contending individuals feel rather uncomfortable if they find themselves in proximity. It is a global phenomenon, with very few exceptions. Many years ago, I'd seen the two of them in the middle of a crowd in Tehran, and now, I suspect I saw a trace of embarrassment on the face of one of them. Strange, but true! I thought Gregory would have enjoyed a line from one of Truffaut's letters, the one written to his friend Charles Bitsch, that read: 'Mason is very pleased with himself.' Truffaut's book, *Lettres*, was posthumously published in 1989. He had a tremendous flair for brief missives.

The first jury meeting for us to introduce ourselves, get to know each other a little and indulge in mostly small talk. It was not too long a session, but by the end of it all of us felt uncomfortable with the screening schedule: in ten days, we would have to see films for two sections, International and Young Cinema 1987 by first-time directors, the junior section carrying a huge amount of money for the two major awards. It was too much for one jury to concentrate on two sections. Anyway, we got on with our task. The Tokyo International Film Festival was sponsored, funded and supported by the government, big industries and big corporate conglomerates—a massive enterprise. The organization, discipline and hospitality were all first-rate. Fabulous.

But all that glittered was not gold.

Unlike our other festival experiences, there were no discussions on films, no plans for periodic eliminations, no shortlists and no marathon session on the last day. Every day, we watched the films and then shared our views, our likes and dislikes. But in private—not for the official record. On the last day, we had a jury meeting. Arrangements had been put in place for secret ballots, and everything was perfectly timed. The chairman gave a speech, with due emphasis on the uncomfortable fact that, in the ultimate analysis, individual judgements were bound to be personal and subjective. Hence, the results would not be the same. The others also spoke more or less along the same lines. In short: they all acknowledged that arriving at a consensus was most unlikely. In such a case, the easiest way was to quietly cast our votes and, in order to avoid any unavoidable embarrassment, to keep the opinions secret. So, wasting not a minute more, we swiftly pressed the buttons of our choice.

The entire operation was clean and technically perfect. Our choices appeared on a large board, one after another, but only as mere numbers. And in numerical order—for and against. Then, with another press of the buttons, the verdict showed up on the board—also as numbers. As simple as that, as transparent as that. No debate, no controversy. Later in the theatre, when each award was announced, there was no show of disapproval. Each and every award was greeted by the audience with measured applause and cheers. That is how the ten-day event came to a peaceful close, assuring everybody that the goings-on of the festival had all been very official and perfect. I recalled how Ray had once mentioned Renoir's annoyance with the American mania for organization and Hollywood's synthetic environment.

In stark contrast to all these official and precise procedures and practices, Gregory Peck was a breath of fresh air. A complete man, a completely different kind of man, always cheerful and upbeat, cracking jokes about this and that, even about himself. I told him a joke for a change, one of my favourite stories. He liked it so much that he immediately wrote it down, put the note in his pocket and said it would be a valuable addition to his private collection. It was the story about writing a short story. He made me say it again because, or so I presumed, he wanted to laugh again:

An English teacher at a girls' school in London wanted her students to write stories. The stories must be short, she specified, and written in the shortest possible time. A week passed, but no one came up with a single short story. The teacher felt frustrated. Dejected, she gave up on the idea. Then one day she was at the chemist's, and, good heavens, Somerset Maugham was there too. She went up to Maugham, told him about her problem and asked him for advice.

The great writer said she must tell her students about the four necessary ingredients for a short story.

To start with, *divinity*, to lend a touch of sanctity to the story and to capture its ambience; then, to build a classic ground in a simple elegant manner, *aristocracy*; the third, *sex*, because of its primordiality; and last, the ultimate secret of success of storytelling, *mystery*.

'Does that make sense?' Maugham asked. The teacher was infinitely grateful for these words of wisdom from one of the world's greatest storytellers. She brought out her notebook and wrote down the four key points. Then, like an obedient student, she repeated the points: *divinity, aristocracy, sex* and *mystery*. Maugham agreed, and wished her good luck.

Next day, in class, she repeated the four points to her students with great excitement. They took notes, and without wasting a moment, got down to writing.

Two minutes later, Martha stood up from her desk.

'I'm done, ma'am,' she said triumphantly.

'You've written your short story already?' The teacher was incredulous. 'Go ahead, read it out, let me hear it, then.'

'Oh God (*divinity*), cried the duchess (*aristocracy*), I'm pregnant (*sex*) by whom I do not know (*mystery*).'

I don't know about the official 10-day event, but this story certainly seemed to make a great impression on the chairman of the second Tokyo International Film Festival.

The day before we left Tokyo, Gita and I spent a wonderful evening private evening with my long-time friend Nagisa Oshima, and his wife and son who was home on a short visit from the US. The conversation around the dinner table was lively and warm. I asked Oshima if he remembered when we'd met first, and he said he did indeed: Venice, 1969, at an after-screening party. Oshima was wonderful man, a brilliant filmmaker, politically left-leaning, always taking up sociopolitical themes in his films and playing such a positive role against American hegemony in the 1960s.

After four weeks back home in my city, my unpredictable and moody city, I set off again on a trip, a voyage to the unknown and unseen—Cuba. I had twice been invited to the festival in Havana, but I had been busy shooting on both occasions. This time, it would be even more special, for we were to spend a fortnight at the International School of Film and TV.

From Havana airport, a long drive, more than an hour, to the village of San Antonio de los Baños. The school had a huge campus, with plenty of open spaces and trees around and in-between the several of buildings, all two-storeyed, and comprising hostels for the students, residential quarters for the faculty, teaching and nonteaching, as well as apartments for guests. Also, of course, fully equipped workrooms or studios. According to Gabriel García Márquez, the president of the school: '[B]ehind everything was the personal interest and care taken by the world's least known cineaste, Fidel Castro.'

We spent 15 days there. And during that fortnight, we had no rest—we did not need any. On the campus, we had sessions with the teachers and the students, some with them all together; some with the groups on their own. Whenever Márquez visited the campus, which could be as frequently or as rarely as he chose, there was nothing special for him. It all seemed to be a kind of free for all, but nothing ever went out of control. Everything seemed casual, but that the work was being done—about that there was no question. This is, of course, an outsider's observation.

One day, in class, Márquez said a few words about *Khandhar*, very casually. Then, equally casually, he asked the students to watch it. Then he looked at me: 'How do the ideas come to you?' Without waiting for my answer, he said, 'Images come to me first.'

Another day, he picked up his own book, *The Autumn of the Patriarch* (1975), lying on the table. He said the idea for that book had come to him during his stay in Mexico. He had been thumbing through a picture album of Indian architectural ruins. One particular picture spread out over two pages had caught his attention—a huge mansion, dreadfully desolate, somewhere in the Central Provinces, now Madhya Pradesh. That image had acted as a provocation and he'd begun to write the book, the central theme originating from the account of a dictator and his 'double'. He said, if I wanted to, I could make a film based on it because it had an Indian connection. I said, the Indian connection must have excited him but his gem of a book was an entirely Latin American phenomenon, and so, beyond me.

One day I asked him if he had decided that he would never allow his *One Hundred Years of Solitude* (1967) to be filmed. He said, yes, that was true. So did he know that one 'almost unknown' Japanese filmmaker had already made a film based on his masterpiece? No, he did not. He was shocked. I asked if he would consider legal action. No, it was pointless. Only a few minutes later, he got over his agitation and was his relaxed self again. I met him several times and never found him getting worked up; always saw him taking things easy. I wonder if he had shown any signs of excitement when he got to know about his Nobel Prize.

Once I told him about my problems with the films based on his literary works. I had always felt that it would be almost impossible to translate the architecture of his literary language in terms of cinema. I told him about similar problems with the writings of an Indian writer, Kamalkumar Majumdar. The two worlds were vastly different, his and Majumdar's, but the problems were the same. A year later, the Cuban weekly *Granma* (17 January 1988) carried an interview published simultaneously in Spanish, English, French and Portuguese, wherein Márquez stated: 'When people see a film that is based on a book, they want it to be a faithful reproduction. But its cinematic adaptation is the transformation the public refuses to accept. That is why I insist that my books not be adapted for the screen. I prefer to write stories specially for cinema.'

Through my infrequent interactions with Márquez, I felt he was a very strange man at the same time as he was a man with infinite clarity of vision. Elsewhere, he wrote:

> The words are within the image. If you think about it, the written word is a very primitive medium. You know what it is to have put one letter after another and to read it to have to decipher one sound after another without knowing what it means. It is totally primitive [. . .] The image, on the other hand, produces an immediate and much deeper emotion on impact and you do not have to decipher anything, it goes straight to the heart.

We spent a marvellous time in Cuba, both on the school campus and outside, with the students and teachers, sometimes with García Márquez but also with García Espinosa and his wife Lola, with Humberto Solás, with Gutiérrez Alea and with Fernando Birri whom Márquez had described as 'the pope of Latin Amrican cinema'. They were all outstanding filmmakers of Latin America.

But not all of them were Cubans. Birri was from Argentina and Márquez was Colombian. The community of dangers have bound them together, and their language, except for the Brazilians, is the same—Spanish. In Brazil, they speak Portuguese.

One day, when Humberto came to know about one of my priorities, he took us to a house where Ernest Hemingway lived, and later to the cafe Hemingway frequented. Starting out as a journalist during the First World War, Hemingway came to Cuba in 1945. He lived mostly with the fishermen, even knew many of them well. After a few years, it was here that he wrote *The Old Man and the Sea* (1952), my favourite among the best three of his novels. One fisherman, pretty old, claimed that the *Old Man* had been made in his image. Another fisherman, followed by yet another, also made the same claim. That the novel was a fiction seemed to make no difference to them. One thing was true in both fiction and real life—Hemingway had been an implacable enemy of the shark. Standing there, I could clearly see the bones of a giant fish that had been eaten by sharks. I remembered watching, long ago, Spencer Tracy's fantastic performance of the Old Man. On our way back, I told Humberto about a remarkable documentary, *The Spanish Earth*, made in 1937, by young Dutch filmmaker Joris Ivens. That was when Hemingway was in battle-scarred Spain, fighting Franco's Fascist army as a member of the International Brigade. He went as a journalist, but soon got involved. I saw the film in Berlin, in the mid-70s. And I met Ivens, then in a wheelchair, at Cannes in 1989, the year of the Chaplin Centenary.

So many things happened in those 15 days, all because of our friends in Cuba and, most particularly, because of Lola. When we returned to my city, Gita and I were convinced we not only felt but also looked younger.

Eliane insisted I be a part of the City Life Foundation, funded by a Dutch organization. The idea was to make a 12-part film, 12 shorts on 12 cities of the world, made by 12 directors of 12 nationalities, each of 20-minute duration. The guideline was highly interpretative, to make sense out of nonsense:

> In 1912, a huge ship, called the Titanic was built and all precautions were taken to ensure that it would not sink. But it sank.

The interpretation was left to 12 directors with no checking or double-checking. I made my version of my city and called it *Calcutta, My El Dorado* (1986). The title might have given an impression that I presented my city as a sacred cow, and that it would never sink. But it was not like that at all. Impudent in places, it was shot entirely in the city but most of the post-production work was done in Rotterdam. Once again Mrinmoy, my editor, did a remarkable job.

Three years after *Genesis*, the next feature film I made in 1989 was *Ek Din Achanak*, based on a short novel by the same Ramapada Chowdhury who'd written *Kharij*. In *Ek Din Achanak*, it all happened in the city where life gets paralysed on only two occasions—when there is too much rain and the city waterlogged, and when there is too much political passion:

> *The worst of monsoons. A kind of mini deluge. An accomplished academic, now retired, sits on his balcony, watching the rain all afternoon as if he has not seen it before. For a few minutes it subsides, perhaps it will resume. He gets up, picks up the phone. It is dead. He picks up his umbrella and walks out. Under no act of provocation. The rain has not begun again. Suddenly he is lost. Months pass.*

*His children and his wife search for a clue to his where-
abouts, or at least discover why he left. Were they unkind?
Was something missing? Did he ever say anything, give
some vague hint as to his unhappiness? His presence
remains obvious in their lives as time and events swirl and
twist into a story which is not a story, just about a man
who is lost and never gone.*

*A year rolls by. For one year, it is a family of four—wife
(Sudha), the two daughters (Neeta, a working girl, and
Seema, still at university) and the son (Amu, looking for
an independent business). A year without the 'head of the
family', lost but not entirely gone.*

*Towards the end of the film: another day, a day when, a
year ago, the man left the house and never returned.
Lightning flashes against a cloud-darkened sky, silhouetted
trees wave wildly in the storm. The absentee's study, dimly
lit, with shadows everywhere, not a single book anywhere
in the room, not a single bookshelf either, looking frightfully empty, stripped bare. Sudha, Neeta, Seema and Amu
are all in the study, sitting on the floor, scattered, each of
them partly obscured by shadow.*

SEEMA: It's raining heavily once again.

NEETA: Like that night . . . Exactly like that night.

SUDHA: Yes, it's exactly a year today.

NEETA: And what have not we said about Baba from time
to time.

AMU: I said that Baba never thought about us, never did
anything for us.

SEEMA: I said that Baba was so arrogant, so conceited.

NEETA: I said that Baba was an ordinary man, an average man. Perhaps Baba also started feeling the same way, thinking that he was just . . . Perhaps that is why . . .

SUDHA: I told none of you that, one night, before he left, lying in bed . . . he said to me that the tragedy is that man has only one life . . . that he lives just once.

Suddenly, with a terrifying flash of lightning, followed by the threatening sound of thunder and sound of stormy wind, all overlapped on a long shot of the room with four members sitting, scattered, the film slowly ends!

However, the ending of the story had been different. When I wrote the film, I changed the order—I had to—without disturbing the central theme. Reading the text, I was jolted out of my seat when, not exactly in a similar set-up, I bumped into the line: *The tragedy is that man has only one life, that he lives just once.*

As a matter of fact, this particular line appearing at a particular moment seemed to exactly mirror my thoughts. And I began to write—about myself, about everybody:

Believe it or not, the fact remains that whatever we are, big or small, there is invariably an area of mediocrity in us. The moment we are aware of it, the crisis begins to deepen. The crisis deepens because there is no way we can start again from scratch, because there is no way we can correct our own conclusions.

Keeping the above in view and operating within the format of Chowdhury's novel *Beej* (The seed) (1977), I wrote the film and then shot it. And that certainly was not all about *Ek Din Achanak*.

In the press meet at Venice 1989, the first question was very direct and simple: 'To what extent is your film autobiographical?'

I smiled, I ransacked my inner self, I smiled again, and said, 'To the extent it is also yours.' I thought it was a simple answer to a simple question, even if it was not a very correct answer.

Later, in the catalogue for the London Film Festival 1989, Derek Malcolm of the *Guardian* wrote: 'Sen's portrait of the self-doubting old gentleman is fascinating, since it is clearly intended to be autobiographical, and a discourse about success and failure that is as frank and honest as anything Sen has yet put on the screen.'

Malcolm also called it 'an unusually intriguing film, and as he has done before, Sen sums up the Calcutta ambience with a masterly eye for detail.'

The film drew a blank at the festival.

So, instead of attending the closing ceremony, Gita and I spent some time at San Marco. Since Gita liked to go her own way, I left her to herself, to a painter's paradise—the sprawling Piazza of San Marco, the floating crowd of the world, and overshadowing everything else, the towering cathedral on the Piazza. Asking her to take care because there could be mosquitoes about, and suggesting a meeting point for an hour later, I went on my way. The reason I'd gone off to San Marco, leaving behind the others to enjoy the closing ceremony at Lido, was that I wanted so much to reminisce about another day, another evening, way back in 1972, on 3 September. All the boats to San Marco had been full that evening, with so many people thronging to La Fenice, the famous opera house. That was the last day of the 33rd edition of the Venice festival. For two weeks, among half a dozen sections or more, there had been a retrospective of Charlie Chaplin's films—a fabulous event, and a tremendous success. It had been titled *Il tutto Chaplin* (The whole of Chaplin). The two-week festival took place, as always, at Lido on the Adriatic, in the stately Palazzo. But that edition being an extra-special one, the closing ceremony had been held at La Fenice at San Marco. That was where, at the end of the retrospective, Chaplin made his first appearance. That was where I saw him. Just once. Never after. Never before.

The opera house was jampacked. I was one of the fortunate few—the 'winners', so to say—to be on that ancient stage onto which the legend eventually walked, heavily aided by two officials. It was a bit of a shock for all of us who'd just spent two weeks watching him on screen. It was difficult to recognize him, now on stage, as his conception of the average man, of almost any man, of myself. There was no derby striving for dignity, no tight-buttoned coat and stick, nothing about him to suggest that usually dashing man.

Chaplin stood in the middle of the stage, flanked by the two officials. We, the chosen few, were seated behind him, arrayed in a line. We saw him face a full house, people from all over the world. Amid tumultuous applause, the man, who had mimed so much and later spoken so much, stood still. For five minutes or more, the enthralled crowd applauded ecstatically. With love and warmth, and with some effort, Chaplin managed to blow them a few kisses. As the curtain fell soon after, he dropped into his chair, exhausted. He was 82.

At Lido, I saw Chaplin as a fallen aristocrat at grips with poverty, a man who'd known humiliation and known that humiliation is a thing you cannot forget. I saw him walking on an unending journey, from one film to another, embracing so many funny adventures along the way, trying to meet the world bravely. Always buffeted by life, laughing at himself a little, pitying himself a little. Never letting go of human compassion. And then walking away towards a glowing horizon, undaunted. Quixotic, almost. Except in *The Great Dictator* (1940): instead of catching him and Hanna disappearing over the horizon, we see him, the Jewish barber with a mistaken identity, making an impassioned appeal to the people of the world to use their power, which they have in abundant measure, to create happiness, to make life free and beautiful, to make life a wonderful adventure.

Incidentally, every time the two dictators Hynkel and Napaloni meet in the film, Hynkel outsmarts Napaloni in a manner that is hilariously Chaplinesque. Every time it happens, people laugh. During the retrospective in Venice, the reaction was the same—the whole house burst out laughing and, obviously, the largest contributors of such mirth were the young Italian viewers. I asked a veteran German critic living in Rome why, at the expense of the one-time national hero, the people always laughed! The critic said, 'For the simple reason that Mussolini lost a war.'

During that nonstop two-week session, I saw the films one after another and perhaps, I grew wiser. Or perhaps I grew more careful. Thus growing, I convinced myself that the Jewish barber in *The Great Dictator* (who, in reply to the question whether or not he was an Aryan, gives an innocent reply: 'I am a vegetarian, sir') and later *Monsieur Verdoux* (1947) (who, over a shot of a grave marked 'Henri Verdoux, 1880–1937' is heard saying: 'Good Evening. I was a bank clerk until the Depression of 1930.') were no departures from the conception of the average man but, rather, its logical extension.

People laughed and thought and grew as they always had. But a few perhaps did not. And Chaplin knew that very well too. He knew it so well that, even earlier, way back in the mid-30s, immediately after *Modern Times* (1936), he said in no uncertain terms that in his new films he—the fallen aristocrat at grips with poverty—

would not be quite so nice. 'I am sharpening the edge of his character, so that people who've liked him vaguely will have to make up their minds.'

Much later, after *The Great Dictator*, and several unpleasant attacks on him, Chaplin said in an interview before the release of *Monsieur Verdoux*, about the man charged with 12 murders:

> Monsieur Verdoux feels that murder is the logical extension of business. He should express the feeling of the times we live in—out of catastrophe come people like him. He typifies the psychological disease and depression. He is frustrated, bitter, and at the end, pessimistic. But he is never morbid, and the picture is by no means morbid in treatment . . . Under the proper circumstances, murder can be comic.

From the studied naivety of his earlier films, such as *Shoulder Arms* (1918), Chaplin attains Shavian heights when, expressing the feeling of the times, Monsieur Verdoux quietly says, 'One murder makes a villain, millions a hero. Numbers sanctify.'

Without losing his cool, 'with skill and total honesty', Chaplin answered a barrage of mostly hostile questions at press conferences. Such as: Would he permit his own children to see *Monsieur Verdoux*?

His answer:

> Why not? . . . Not all of it is beyond them . . . I know there are a lot of pictures that I wouldn't allow my children to see that are supposed to be forthright, high moral purpose; that I wouldn't send my children because it's absolutely a false notion of life. Something that doesn't exist. A lot of pictures are very dishonest. So-called boy meets girl.

Federico Fellini's line comes to mind: '[He was] a sort of Adam, from whom we are all descended.'

On our way back to the hotel, I told Gita that while she was watching the wonder that was San Marco, I had laughed and thought and grown. I told her how and why, retiring within myself, I celebrated Chaplin's Centenary.

1989! The centenary of Chaplin! The event was observed through the year and across the world. But what happened at Cannes, as its inaugural presentation, was an absolute feat. I was there at that five-minute event and was totally bowled over.

The splendour was splendid in Cannes, as always. The grande salle was packed. There were the luminaries, semi-luminaries and the guests from all over the world. Not a single seat was empty, not a single person was standing except the smiling ushers.

The lights dimmed, the music began to play, not too loud, not too low, a tune composed especially for the 42nd edition of the festival.

The curtain slowly rose, the lights grew dim. On stage was revealed a huge cutout of the tramp Charlie, peeping from behind a wall, five-year-old Jackie Coogan under his protection, the two trying to outwit the police, now as if looking at the audience. As the front stage grew brighter up, Chaplin's large family could be seen in front of the footlights. About 20 in all, all sitting together, some relaxed, some conscious and stiff, a bit like a nineteenth-century family photo. They were Chaplin's children, some with their spouses and some single, as well as his grandchildren, and maybe one or two great-grandchildren too. All but one—Chaplin's wife, Oona. Oona, daughter of playwright Eugene O'Neill. Apparently she was unwell.

The family looked informal, unusually informal for an occasion like this—a mother breast-feeding her child, a boy scratching his head. A couple of elders looked a bit serious, the rest were quite relaxed. In the background was the giant cutout of the tramp, father for some and grandfather for some others, quietly watching the family from behind the wall.

A sight to see and remember.

Geraldine Chaplin, the actor-daughter, spoke for a minute or so, touching on the domesticity of her father. Before she finished, a child slipped down from its mother's flank and crawled to one end of the stage to collect a rubber ball. Then crawled back to its mother. Geraldine finished her speech and passed the mike to one of her brothers. He spoke for not more than half-a-minute and handed the mike to another. Travelling from one hand to another and yet another and so on, the microphone finally came to a small boy, hardly eight, who spoke the shortest line without knowing what it really meant. Holding the mike close to his mouth, he said: 'I declare the festival open.'

The enthralled crowd saw the little show at the same time as it saw the greatest legend of world cinema watching from behind the wall.

The boy declared the festival open and instantly the curtain fell, only to rise a minute later, revealing a huge screen. And on it, an unforgettable scene from *The Great Dictator*—Hynkel's ecstatic play with the 'terrestrial globe'. As if in a trance, the dictator plays savagely, laughs gustily, dances furiously, all intensely Chaplinesque, all in perfect rhythm. When thus 'the world floats into his hand', it suddenly pops.

That is how Cannes paid homage to Chaplin on his centenary. Coincidentally, that was also the year when the world celebrated the bicentenary of the historic French Revolution with an accent on the Rights of Man. A meeting was held the next day on cinema and human rights. Among those who attended was Joris Ivens. When I was introduced to him, he told me he had so much wanted to come to India. He even sent word, but nothing happened. Then followed a screening of *Liberté*, a compilation of excerpts from various films on the French Revolution. It was a marvellous compilation, meticulously edited, ending with a fascinating excerpt from Jean Renoir's *This Land Is Mine* (1943). The film had been compiled by young director Laurent Jacob, perhaps his first exercise in cinema.

Cannes observed the Chaplin Centenary in May 1989, and it was in September 1989 that I remembered him at San Marco; remembered the great event at La Fenice on 3 September in 1972; and remembered all that came my way one after another until the grand celebration in Cannes.

Next day, we flew to Rome, spent the night there and prepared to catch the Air India flight back home in the evening. Before leaving Venice, I had called the Indian ambassador in Rome, Akbar Khaleeli. A few days earlier, he had come to Venice with two of his daughters to see my film. Now I asked him if he could depute someone in his office to have a word with Air India and organize our stay in a hotel. To which he said, 'You have two options, Mr Sen. Either choose a five-star hotel as the guests of Air India. Or do me a favour by staying with my three daughters and me—a beautiful four-starrer.' He said it so delightfully and so warmly. I said we would rest for the night as Air India's guests, and then the next morning, till it was time for us to leave for the airport, we would love to spend our time with him and his family. At the airport, an official from the Indian embassy received us. At the hotel, as we were checking in, the ambassador called me, 'Stay well, sleep well. I shall be at your disposal tomorrow in the morning. Good night.' Every time he spoke, he exuded warmth and his voice and manner of speech were so graceful that one could not help but fall in love with his demeanour.

Next day, at about half past nine in the morning, the telephone rang. 'I am here in the lounge, Mr Sen. Tell me, when can I come up to carry your bags?'

We spent a lovely day at his beautifully and so elegantly done up home. After lunch, we went for a lovely drive. The ambassador, who was driving himself, wanted to give us a surprise. So he suddenly stopped outside a beautiful bungalow. 'Would you mind spending some time with these friends of mine?' he asked. Gita and I looked at each other, and said, we'd love to.

It was the house of an affluent Pakistani businessman, now based in Rome. As we walked into a big hall, we saw more than a hundred people, all sitting on the floor, men on one side and women on the other. An old bearded man was seated on a dais and holding court. He was in the middle of somewhat of a long talk. As we entered, there was a brief break. Khaleeli introduced us to the guests. The businessman came forward and offered me a seat on the floor. Presumably, the lady of the house took Gita to sit on the other side. Looking at the way everything and everyone was around us, Gita pulled the end of her sari to cover her head in a gesture of respect. I draped my handkerchief over my head. Neither Gita nor I had ever been in a religious or devotional assembly such as this. But the atmosphere was contagious, the like of which we all have seen in Ray's *Aparajito*—seated on the ghat in Benares, kathak-thakurs recite verses and hold discourses on the same while crowds of widows listen in rapt silence. Here, in this businessman's house, it was an exclusive function and in the most opulent environs.

The man on the dais continued his story, and the listeners seemed deeply involved. By the time he came to the Karbala tragedy, to the thirsty ones crying for a drop of water in the battle-scarred desert, I saw the listeners, with no exception, crying convulsively. Even Khaleeli sitting beside me was crying like a child. Astonishing!

At the end of the session, we were served some light refreshments.

On our way back in the car, Khaleeli said that the man from Pakistan giving the long recital was quite famous, very much in demand and, right now, on his way to United States. 'But he's a very bad performer!'

Gita and I were taken aback. They had all been crying just a few minutes ago! Khaleeli looked at us, smiled and said, 'He's a bad performer, true, but the subject is powerful and profound.'

Khaleeli's ancestors were Iranian who had migrated to India. He said he would not vouch for his children but he was a devout Shi'a.

We never met again after that. A marvellous man, and unlike most of ambassadors, he didn't seem to care much about bureaucratic trappings.

At the airport, there were four of us—Gita and I, and two Indian journalists, Khalid Mohammad and Swapan Ghosh. Flying back to India. Khaleeli came to the airport to see us off. That was 5 September 1989.

Two nuns were standing near the Air India counter. It appeared they were looking for someone, for something. As we drew closer, one of them stepped forward and asked me if there was a Mr Mrinal Sen in our group. I said, 'That's me. Why are you looking for me?' The other nun also stepped forward. They said they had got the information about me from the Air India office, and they had a request. Could I do them a great favour by carrying home a packet of life-saving drugs for Mother Teresa? She was fighting death in a Calcutta nursing home. I took the packet, passed it to Gita and she handed it over to the airhostess for safe custody. A little later, we boarded and the plane took off.

On reaching my city the next day via Bombay, Gita and I rushed to Woodlands Nursing Home and handed over the packet to Dr Ashim Bardhan, a particular friend of mine and Mother Teresa's personal physician. We saw her lying still in bed. Later, I was told that the medicine had proved to be very effective. Mother Teresa survived, and came out of hospital. We felt blessed to have played a small part in her recovery.

The 'terrestrial globe' had popped on Chaplin's screen, but as the 1980s came to an end, the world slid into a systematic crisis (Mikhail Gorbachev, the August Coup). The history of the world took a violent turn. Everything was topsy-turvy. Policies, ideals, values and morals were threatened, revolutions of the past ruthlessly denied, manifestoes redrafted. Amid such unprecedented tumult, a huge fire burnt up all that once were so dear to so many millions— the hammer and sickle went up in smoke. Simultaneously, the statue of Vladimir Lenin was uprooted in Bucharest and defiled in Tbilisi, the statue of Bertolt Brecht defaced somewhere in East Germany and the Berlin Wall razed to the ground.

Absolutely unrelated, my young friend and actor-playwright Anjan Dutt came to me one day and asked if he could take an hour and a half to read out a play which he had finished writing just the day before. I told him to leave the manuscript with me. Late in the evening, I read the play and liked it. Next day, I read it again and liked it even more. Tucked away at the end of a lane, a middle-class home. A family, not too large, thrown into uneasy chaos. Living under the same roof but strangers to each other. Each is left to themselves, each preserving their stories, their agonies, their secrets, their failings. A condemned family in many ways. The second son was killed in a police–Naxalite encounter eighteen years ago. Ten years later, leaving behind a young wife and child, the eldest son died of a sudden illness. The third ran away to Germany with a petty job in a bid to break away from a clandestine affair with his sister-in-law. The youngest, bitter and cynical, is yet to find his place in the sun.

The play starts early in the morning, with a death in the family—the old mother, depressed and withdrawn for years, is found hanging in a locked room, leaving behind a loosely constructed diary.

Anjan had not yet given the play any name.

I asked Anjan to consider if we could delve a little deeper, and examine his play at two distinct levels—the trauma of the familial chaos and the domestic violence, all in the world within; and the terrifying confusions in the world outside. In fact, when I decided to work on it and connected world events to the domestic story, the first title that came to mind was from one of Tagore's novels—*Ghare-Baire*. Ray had already made a film on it, and called it after the original title. In English, he called it *The Home and the World*. I loved Ray's name for it, or it was quite possible Tagore had said it long ago. I called Anjan's play *Mahaprithibi* (1991), but I preferred calling it *World Within, World Without*.

Anjan was very excited.

Incidentally, Ray wrote a sort of travelogue on Japan, with a focus on Japanese films. He called it 'Calm Without, Fire Within'. That was how Nandalal Bose, the great artist, principal of Kala Bhavana in Tagore's Santiniketan, and Ray's favourite teacher, had described the 'now-sleeping' Fujiyama of Japan.

Anjan and I did a second draft and then a third. I wrote the film. We brought in the members of the family trapped in a mess, hurling against one another in impotent rage and in a desperate bid to cover up their sense of guilt. They were made to question each other, exposing their thoughts and doubts, their pain and frustrations. They were asked to try very hard to guess at the mother's thoughts. Though the father was warned not to allow them access to her diary. For sure, she wrote it for herself—*for nobody else*, not even for him. Fragments of the past and present were freely juxtaposed as references to related incidents. The East European debacle was put up in the form of a collage as telecast and titled *The World This Week*. And the drama was built with words and silence, through points and counterpoints. At long last, the diary of the deceased mother was consigned to the flames by an unmarried and neurotic daughter, who used to lapse into violent rage at unpredictable moments. And, standing apart, the father watched the flames like a battle-scarred soldier who had fought all his life and was now exhausted.

That was how, under stress and strain, unrelieved, *Mahaprithibi* came to an inconclusive end. None of the family knew why the old woman, suffering for years, killed herself. Was it a protest? If so, against what or against whom? The film offered no direct answer.

Unfortunately, the film did not get much exposure, neither in the domestic circuit nor abroad, except in Germany. Too severe, was that why?

One day, in the early 1990s, an acquaintance of mine, Rita Zutshi, teaching in a London school, gave me a treatment based on one of Manto's short stories. Many feel that Sadat Hasan Manto, who died in 1955 in Lahore, has no literary rival. A year before his death, he wrote his own unapologetic epitaph:

> Here lies Sadat Hasan Manto. With him lie buried all the arts and mysteries of short-story writing. Under tons of earth he lies, wondering if he is a greater short-story writer than God. (Translated by Khalid Hasan.)

Rita's treatment was very well written, but every inch a faithful reproduction. My honest feeling was that it could be safely adapted as a radio play or even a 30-minute stage play, but certainly not a film. Nevertheless, I liked the story very much, one of his finest though of a different kind. I was glad that Rita introduced me to this strange love story called 'Badshahat ka Khatma' (Kingdom's end).

Two years later, I picked up the same story and wondered if, for a new film, I could relate my script to Manto's story. I gave it a thought and was convinced that I could go ahead. I spoke to all three of Manto's daughters, all three living in Lahore. They held his copyright. I made an agreement with the trio of siblings and acquired legal clearance to proceed.

As I was getting ready to write the script, I felt I needed some support, and that support came from Tagore's *Kshudhita Pashan* (Hungry stones). Honestly, my final script was a remote adaptation of Manto's story, though it was very close to it in spirit. I called it *Antareen* (The confined) (1993).

A woman, a captive by circumstances, and a man, a recluse by choice, live at two extremes of the city—the woman in a modern apartment, and the man in a huge crumbling mansion. One night, the phone in the crumbling mansion rings. And then starts a queer game from that first mysterious call. The woman loves calling in the middle of the night, and the man does not sound unfriendly. The man does not know who she is, the woman does not care to know about him either. Starting as a rather odd game, slowly but inevitably it grows intense. Keeping themselves at an undefined distance across a sprawling metropolitan city, the man and the woman build a weird world through words and pauses. Days pass, and in the middle of a fateful night, the world, thus built, suddenly collapses. And life goes on. There is passion in it, there is pain in it.

Having made the film, I wrote a few lines for my viewers and assured them I was no somnambulist:

I wake up in the middle of the night and walk into a strange world. As I see through a series of nocturnal sessions, my adventures speak of life and love, of passion and pain, of brutality, and (quoting Tagore), of infinite splendour and eternal *confinement*.

I loved making the film, I loved the film when it was made, but I knew very well that those who would go by 'stock responses' would not like it—a film with just two characters, names untold, revealing splendour and suffering confinement.

The film was shown in Spain, at San Sebastian. A beautiful town, quiet and serene! Guernica was nearby. I made a trip to the village once devastated by the Fascists, based on which Pablo Picasso created his masterpiece. Legend has it that during the German occupation of France during the Second World War, the Nazi officers used to visit Picasso's studio. Once, an officer stood before the huge painting and asked him, 'You did it?' To which Picasso quietly said, 'You did it.'

Looking back, I see that neither *Ek Din Achanak* nor *Antareen* was a commercially viable proposition. Indeed, it was admirable that both were fully funded by the National Film Development Corporation, with no strings attached.

Two years later, in 1995, I was called again to act as a jury member in Venice. I was a bit reluctant, because I was perhaps a bit sick of travelling and sitting on judgement all the time. But Gillo Pontecorvo, who took the world by storm with his *La battaglia di Algeri* (*The Battle of Algiers*) (1966), and now the director of the Mostra, did not want to take a 'no' from me. So, once again we were on the move. Gita and I spent the entire time watching films— and mostly suffering. The crop was absolutely no good that year. Roman Polanski was the chairman of the jury. His *Nóż w wodzie* (*Knife in the Water*) (1962) was my favourite of all his films. This was Polanski's first feature—a beautiful depiction of the relationship between man and woman in a male-chauvinistic society. A man and his wife go yachting on the weekend. Along the way, they pick up a hobo and all three end up spending the day on the yacht. At the end, commodity fetish shows up in the couple, the man and the wife getting to know each other, the hobo acting as catalytic agent. A remarkable film with hardly any words exchanged between them!

I remember watching the film in my city—how I rushed out of the theatre, ran to the ticket counter, purchased two tickets, lost no time in appearing before Gita busy in the kitchen, dragging her out, urging her to quickly get ready, and then rushing back to the theatre. As we came out after the film was over, we looked at each other, and perhaps we understood each other a little better.

One day, between talks about films seen and unseen, Angelica Huston, another member of the jury, said she could not help but admire my all-time outfit of white kurta and churidar.

'Do you like it?' I asked.

'I love it,' she said.

The next day, I gifted her a pair of my well-starched and ironed kurta and churidar. She was as tall as I, and I was fairly certain they would fit her. That day onward, for the next three or four days, she was almost always in my tight pyjamas and loose kurta, looking even more beautiful.

Life and filmmaking continued unabated. New filmmakers arrived on the scene, opening up new horizons for cinema. For quite a few years, I was no longer the same as I was before—a *one-film-a-year director*. But I remained very much an insider. What was more, I got back to my reading whenever I had the time to spare.

But why such long gaps between the films? Whether or not they were consistent lovers of my films, they asked me, Why? I had also been asking myself the same question. Was it because I was getting increasingly confused about the state of things in my world and in myself? I had no answer. All that I knew was that I had to make a film as soon as possible!

Once again, hate and suspicion raged with mounting fury—the Ayodhya mayhem and its aftermath. News of communal troubles cast its gloom all over. And something of this kind could not subside with the wave of a magic wand. Around that time, during the unfortunate confrontation at Kargil on the Kashmir border—a mini-war, so to say, between two recently nuclearized neighbours—I made one of my brief trips to Delhi. One evening, I was watching television in my hotel room. An Indian television journalist of repute was on the screen, moving about Islamabad and interviewing politicians, bureaucrats and ordinary citizens. At a point of time, his camera caught a vegetable vendor spreading his merchandise at a corner of the pavement. Not from a vantage position, because the street was crowded, he asked the man from behind to speak a few words about the *war*. The man, most possibly unlettered, looked back, looked up, over his shoulder, and said a word, just a word, *Nuksaan*, and went back to his vegetables. That was all, nothing more, just a word.

Nuksaan. Loss!

The man said it and, all alone in the room, I was shaken. Who was he? An unknown man of whom history would not take note, one who did not care for history either, an ordinary vegetable seller, speaking his mind so clearly. I was shaken and strongly felt that *a double* of him on the other side of the border, irrespective of caste, creed and nationality—whose vocabulary would not go beyond his counterpart in Islamabad—would have surely said the same thing or its variant, meaning the same, meaning a lot more than what the word literally means.

It meant a lot to me—loss of life, of values, of human decency, of all that make life and society delightfully habitable. The vegetable vendor said it from his understanding, and I, claiming to be a social communicator, put it on a wider canvas—the canvas which does not paint a poisoned world but a world with people *living, loving and desiring.* Fyodor Dostoyevsky came to mind who, condemned to four years of hard labour in Siberia, in a letter to his brother said something on the lines of—Human beings remain human everywhere.

Based on an original story by young writer Afsar Ahmed, I wrote and made my next film, *Aamar Bhuvan (My Land)* (2002). All in a village without a name, all about mostly unlettered, poor people:

> When bigotry, vulgarity and unending violence spread in a mad fury, the film moves away from the abyss of despair and walks quietly into a tranquil village. True, the unceasing toil in the day-to-day life of the villagers is gruelling, yet there is magic in their living. Three among them play key roles—two men, closely related, and a woman, divorced and remarried. With no flashbacks, no dramatic ups and downs from their past, the film captures the instant present and brings into focus the love among the three, with no malice against anyone.

The central theme was Man, the most beautiful creature under the sun. The film celebrated life, even death, also tears and laughter, good and bad, freedom and bonding, all caught in a rhythm. The young actors performed with gusto. While we were shooting, the entire village made their living free and beautiful, and made life a wonderful adventure.

Aamar Bhuvan was my last film. In 2002. If not the last, it was my latest! Someone close to me called it my swansong. That's not true, I said.

While making the film, I recalled my favourite words of Niels Bohr, that confidence comes from not being always right but from not fearing to be wrong. That was what I did—a most daring act— I used a Tagore song in the film, a highly philosophical song—not once but twice, in two different ways. First it played through a battery-driven radio, a cheap transistor. One of the young men, a simple farmer who, without the knowledge of the alphabet but with tremendous verve, had bought it for his charming wife to keep a promise. The words meant nothing to either of them or to his children. And, true, they were not meant for them. It was the sound, its poetry, its music that fascinated them, it was its rhythm that overwhelmed the farmer and his wife. Caught in an inevitable rhythm, they 'danced' to the music and they loved it, they were ecstatic. A dear friend of mine, Gaston Roberge, a Jesuit father, Canadian national, called it 'the Waltz of Joy'. He saw the film not once, not twice, but many times, and even translated the song into his language, French. This was a fascinating experience we shared with the farmer and his wife. Perhaps it was shared by those viewers too who, at that very moment, did not distance themselves from the unlettered poor farmer and his wife.

For the second time, it appeared in the last sequence, not through the radio but from outside, much slower in rhythm and without any accompanying music. This time it was for all, particularly for those who cared to know what the song was all about. In the words of Father Roberge, 'it was a world of joy, hope, and love, alternating with sorrow, despair, callous indifference, refusing to choose the one or the other, joy and sorrow being the cadence of life itself.'

And it all came from Tagore and his little poem:

Momo chitte niti nritye ke je nache,
Tata-thoi-thoi, tata-thoi-thoi, tata-thoi-thoi!

(Who dances in my heart the dance eternal
in eternal rhythm)

Roberge, in his enthusiasm, tried a translation of the song into English, but he was not sure if he was able to grasp the inner meaning in a befitting manner:

Tata-thoi-thoi, tata-thoi-thoi, tata-thoi-thoi.
While his drums beat along in a cadence;
one two three, one two three, one two three.
Smiles and tears and pearls dear scintillate;
good and bad dance a waltz, one two three.
Life dances, death dances, pas de deux;
one two three, one two three, one two three.
Ananda! Ananda! Ananda!
Day by day, freedom comes, freedom goes;
we all sail—sea of joy infinite.
Tata-thoi-thoi, tata-thoi-thoi, tata-thoi-thoi.

Aamar Bhuvan got the Best Director award at Cairo International Film Festival, and Nandita Das, the young leading lady, won the Best Actress award. Earlier, the film was in Locarno, Switzerland, as part of the package of Indian films shown outside the competition. The Indian screenings started with *Aamar Bhuvan*, introduced by Nandita and me.

Thereby also hangs a tale. It was never to be, by any earthly reason. But I had to go. It was hilarious, not without its travel hazards across the borders.

One day, at around ten o'clock in the morning, I got a call from Cairo, from one of the chief organizers of the International Film Festival 2003. She asked me to be present at the Central Theatre of the city by six the next evening. I declined but asked why. She said it was a secret, but my presence was imperative. The moment she said it, the picture was clear: I was going to get an award. *Aamar Bhuvan* was an entry at the festival, and Nandita and I had been invited. I could not go, but I knew Nandita would never say no. She was a compulsive traveller. On the phone, I told the lady to hand over anything, whatever it was, to Nandita, my actor. But she said, rather desperately, that my actor could not take two awards—and so I must come. I was happy, Nandita was getting an award. What else could it be other than the Best Actress award! I told the lady to congratulate her on my behalf. She said she would, but my presence was imperative.

I tried to explain my situation to the persistent caller. First and foremost, there was no flight from my city to Cairo. I would have to catch a plane either from Delhi or Bombay, but even from those cities there weren't daily flights to Cairo. My next plea was that I had no document, no papers, and in my city there was no visa-issuing agency for their country. I thought that would work, but she said she would get back to me soon. Till then, I was wondering what my prize would be—Best Director, Best Scriptwriter? Which one?

An hour later, there was another call. Another woman, more assertive. She said they would take care of me. I should not worry about anything, and simply get ready for the trip.

Yet another call, soon after. From the Indian embassy in Cairo. A man this time, who said more or less the same: don't worry, just to get ready for the travel.

None of them knew I had another problem. I hold a diplomatic passport, and so I had to get clearance from the Ministry of External Affairs. I called the deputy secretary, thankfully based in Calcutta. He called his Delhi office; he also asked me to send a letter to his office at once, formally applying for clearance. It was amazing that I got the clearance from Delhi via fax even before my letter could reach his Calcutta office!

What followed was faxes and phone calls galore, including one from Dubai. I rushed to the airport, desperately hoping that the ticket would have reached the airlines office at the airport. It did, just 45 minutes before departure.

I landed at Bombay airport around three o'clock in the morning. I had to wait for a Dubai-bound flight slated for some time much later in the day.

Sleep had vanished.

At Dubai, two officers from the Indian embassy came to see me, but apologized for not being able to make any arrangement for a short stay at the embassy or a hotel to rest. Why was that? I asked. It was a Friday, so offices were all closed. Nevertheless, they took care of me and did not allow me to spend even on the meal I had.

The plane to Cairo took off much later.

When I arrived at Cairo airport, I had nothing with me—no travel document, except a Diplomatic passport. Collecting all my courage, I came out with just a bag in hand and, honestly, felt a bit scared. Suddenly, a man rushed forward, shook hands with me and asked me to follow him. As I walked behind him, he asked for my passport and requested me to wait, pointing towards a chair. He returned 20 minutes later, all smiles, and whisked me away.

When I reached the Central Theatre, it was 45 minutes past six o'clock! Nandita was beaming, receiving the award for Best Actress. After my whirlwind trip, barely on land and without a moment to catch my breath, I too found a reason to beam—I was given the award for Best Director. And before any of this could register, I was back in my city the very next day.

At last she came to our tiny apartment—Kiera Chaplin, accompanied by a local press photographer. She was very much in the news in the local dailies, with almost every headline telling us that Chaplin's granddaughter was in town. She was here as part of a film being made by a woman director, an Indian living in Los Angeles. I had received a request that she wanted to come and see me.

She came and immediately glanced at the 'Charlie, the Vagabond' poster on the wall.

Smiling, she asked, 'For me?'

I said, 'For me, and for anybody who comes here.'

After a little pause, I said, 'He is for the world and will remain so for ages, for eternity.'

At home, the doctor had come that morning. Gita was unwell. Kunal and Nisha kept calling us, once a week from Chicago. Always long calls, even if we had nothing new to say. Alongside, our emails continued to flow, swiftly and easily.

Finally, I come to my funeral chapter, to my journey's end. I look back to a distant past, long before I was born.

'In the middle of the nineteenth century,' quipped George Bernard Shaw in his inimitable manner, 'two things happened of some importance—I was born, and Tennyson wrote "God fulfils Himself in many ways." '

Using a Chaplinesque gag, Buster Keaton, the great comedian of Chaplin's time, could have said or done something almost identical to connect his birth year with that of cinema. Claims and counterclaims notwithstanding over cinema's parenthood together with its year of birth, it was finally accepted by the people who mattered and by the court that cinema was born in 1895, the year of Buster Keaton's birth. Interestingly, the Lumière Brothers of Lyon, the celebrated inventors of the moving pictures, described their invention as nothing more than a mere scientific curiosity. Later, they realized that the cinema amuses people, and what better could they have done . . . what could have given them more pride. More investigations and consistent improvement brought them wide recognition, and Luis Lumière, the elder brother, became an international celebrity. In 1995, therefore, cinema completed a hundred years of its life. Since the first shot taken on 19 March, in a small factory owned by Lumière, a shot of the workers coming out. It was celebrated by Institut Lumière at Lyon with much grandeur. I was there as a special invitee.

About everything that happened that day, I had every reason to feel terribly amused.

There were 30 of us at Lyon—30 filmmakers from 30 different countries. In the absence of the real factory, a somewhat fake structure had been erected at the same place, and we, the 30 film-makers, were instructed to come out at the call of the French Minister of Culture. In the absence of Luis Lumière, there was his grandson with his grandfather's camera, and about 50 more modern cameras to record the incident. All of them operating from outside a fence. At a specific time, probably at the same time as Lumière a hundred years ago, the minister shouted 'Start!', and we, the 30 workers, rushed out, not quite smoothly though. We, by our own choice, had divided up into groups. I was with Youssef Chahine of Egypt and perhaps Miguel Littín of Chile. In our team, all three of us walked faster than the others to touch Lumière's vintage camera.

The concluding part of the celebration was over with a one-take shot, and we dispersed. Someone tapped me from behind. I turned. It was André De Toth, Hollywood director-actor-producer since the 1930s, now seized with infirmity at 83, very much unlike King Vidor at his age. Amazed, Toth said, 'Hey, you run like a rabbit!' I laughed a hearty laugh and said, 'Don't worry, I'll maintain the same speed even to my funeral pyre.'

Every one of us got a memento, rather heavy to carry, and every one of us earned the distinction of being called the 'inheritors' of Luis Lumière.

Inheritors!

In an altogether different tenor, UNESCO, constitutionally committed to the conservation and protection of the world's inheritance, rose to the occasion. It was just a year and a half before, on 2 November 1993, as if to celebrate the centenary eve. I was present there. With me were also Youssef Chahine (director, Egypt), André Delvaux (director, Belgium) Jean Rouch (director, France) and Fernando Solanas (director, Argentina), and Melina Mercouri and Michel Piccoli (actors, France).

In its plenary session in Paris, UNESCO launched an appeal to all concerned to safeguard the great treasures of human skill and creativity. To make a beginning, Federico Mayor Zaragoza, director-general of UNESCO, touched on a hundred years of cinema's history, and declared that 'emerging as it does in painting, theatre, music, literature and photography, the art of the cinema, which was invented in 1895, is the custodian of the memory of the twentieth century.'

The custodian of the memory of the twentieth century!

However, the disturbing story that UNESCO collected about the systematic decay and possible threats of damages done to soundtracks and images for various reasons was shocking. Indeed, a matter of pride for cinema's march to 'infinity' and also, in the absence of proper scientific conservation in a large number of cases, a matter of grave concern. The session ended on notes of both hope and despair, inextricably entwined. As in life. Hoping, despairing, reliving.

And life goes on.

As of today, looking back and forth, I think of Lyon, 19 March, a hundred years apart—1895 and 1995. Toth appears before me, shocked and surprised to see me walking like a rabbit. As I was checking out the next day, I met him at the hotel's Reception. He asked me, 'How old are you?' I said, 'One year older than the last year, or perhaps one year younger than what I'll be next year. Take it whichever way you will.'

PS Leisurely, I leaf through David Robinson's book *Chaplin* (1985), a great book. I am suddenly stuck by a couple of lines near the end:

> He would sit for hours with Oona, holding hands and hardly exchanging a word. 'She is able to share that strange solitude of his,' said his son.

FIGURE 46.

Acknowledgements

I thankfully acknowledge all those several books, essays, magazines, dailies and festival brochures released at international events—having connected me and my times—thus giving a particular shape to my text. And, of course, all those contributors to these materials.

I am, indeed, grateful to all these friends, who have enriched my book by lending meaningful information and suggestions, as and when I wanted—Dipankar Mukhopadhyay, Samik Bandopadhyay, Supriya Chaudhuri, Raju Raman, Chinmoy Guha and Kunal Sen. Anjum Katyal, Sunandini Banerjee, Naveen Kishore and their creative group.

Notes

PAGE **5** | Lord Clive . . . George Trevelyan . . . Kipling . . . Churchill: All quotes taken from Frederic C. Thomas, *Calcutta Poor* (New York: M. E. Sharpe, 1997).

PAGE **7** | **Every time I return . . . probably doomed**: Read James Cameron's *An Indian Summer* (London: Penguin, 1974) for an account of his travels in the country 25 years after Independence.

PAGE **12** | **A strange object . . . would never forget**: Dipankar Mukhopadhyay, *The Maverick Maestro: Mrinal Sen* (New Delhi: Indus, 1995).

PAGE **16** | **We are all geniuses up to the age of ten**: Aldous Huxley, 'Young Archimedes' in Little Mexican and Other Stories (London: Chatto & Windus, 1924).

PAGE **26** | **Thou hast made me . . . ever with fresh life**: An excerpt from the first poem of Rabindranath Tagore's *Gitanjali* (1910).

PAGE **67** | **This is how . . . by once more**: All quotes by Cesare Zavattini are taken from his article 'Some Ideas on the Cinema' (Pier Luigi Lanza trans.), *Sight and Sound* (October 1953): 64–9. Edited from a recorded interview published in *La Revista del Cinema Italiano* (December 1952).

PAGE **73** | **A review appeared in the city's leading daily, the *Statesman***: Read Dipankar Mukhopadhyay's article on this *controversy*, 'Mrinal Sen versus Satyajit Ray: The war of words that lasted nearly 30 years' on *Scroll.in* to find out more (available online: https://bit.ly/3TpRaMk; last accessed: 21 March 2023).

PAGE **110** | **Dnyaneshwar Nadkarni . . . in the *Times of India***: Dnyaneshwar Nadkarni, 'Another Low-budget Art Film,' *The Times of India* (19 July 1970).

PAGE **112** | **Among recent films . . . Reformed by Rustic Belle:** Satyajit Ray, 'An Indian New Wave?' in *Our Films, Their Films* (New Delhi: Orient Longman, 2003[1976]), pp. 81–99; here, p. 99.

PAGE **115** | **A single spark can start a prairie fire:** From a letter written by Mao Tse-tung on 5 January 1930 (available online: https://bityl.co/HFUC; last accessed: 21 March 2023).

PAGE **143** | **[For Renoir], . . . trains never will run on time:** Satyajit Ray, 'Renoir in Calcutta' (1949) in *Our Films, Their Films*, pp. 111–119, here, p. 119.

PAGE **148** | **If you should ask me . . . 'Things happen':** Pablo Neruda, 'There's No Forgetting' in *Residence on Earth* (Angel Flores trans.) (Norfolk, CT: New Directions, 1946), p. 109.

PAGE **155** | **There is a canard afoot . . . grace that time vanishes:** Michael Wilmington, 'Cannes treats cinephiles to tale of Henri Langlois', *Chicago Tribune* (30 May 2004) (available online: https://bit.ly/3ZYGgj0; last accessed: 21 March 2023).

PAGE **159** | **I must also condemn . . . mother before justice:** Quoted in Albert Camus, *Algerian Chronicles* (Arthur Goldhammer trans., Alice Kaplan intro.) (Cambridge MA: The Belknap Press of Harvard University Press, 2013).

PAGE **186** | **The writer must . . . in either East or West:** Jean-Paul Sartre, 'Sartre on the Nobel Prize' (Richard Howard trans.), *The New York Review* (17 December 1964).

PAGE **202** | **The real closing of the case is the closing of the family circle, the clan against the world:** Stanley Kauffmann, *Field of View: Film Criticism and Comment* (New York: PAJ Publications, 1986), p. 266.

PAGE **205** | **aggressive and defensive . . . poets of humanity in our time:** Lindsay Anderson, *About John Ford* (London: Plexus Publishing, 1999).

PAGE **214** | That is stupid gossip . . . But that is not improvisation: Federico Fellini, interview with James R. Silke in *Interviews* (Bert Cardullo ed.) (Jackson: University Press of Mississippi, 2006), p. 71.

PAGE **235–36** | This is precisely . . . true content: From the introduction to Jean-Louis Leutrat's *L'Année dernière à Marienbad* (London: British Film Institute, 2000).

PAGE **246** | When I use typage . . . capture it as it is: Sergei Eisenstein, *Selected Works: Writings, 1934–47* (Richard Taylor ed.) (London: British Film Institute, 1988), p. 12.

PAGE **246** | If I have . . . are not perhaps equally so: Letter from Friedrich Engels to Margaret Harkness (1888) (available online: https://bit.ly/40jEXv3; last accessed: 17 March 2023).

PAGE **247** | The principal actors . . . project at us: Stanley Kauffmann, *Field of View: Film Criticism and Comment*, p. 266.

PAGE **280** | The viewer is baffled . . . scrupulous paradigm: Gayatri Chakravorty Spivak, *Outside in the Teaching Machine* (London: Routledge, 2012), p. 72.

PAGE **305** | The words are within the image . . . straight to the heart: Quoted in *Conversations with Gabriel García Márquez* (Gene H. Bell-Villada ed.) (Jackson: University Press of Mississippi, 2006), p. 148.

PAGE **313** | I am sharpening . . . make up their minds: Quoted in Robert Payne, *Charlie Chaplin* (New York: Ace Books, 1952), p. 233.

PAGE **313** | Monsieur Verdoux feels that murder . . . can be comic: Quoted in David Robinson, *Chaplin* (New York: Penguin, 2014).

PAGE **313** | Why not? . . . boy meets girl: Quoted in David Robinson, *Chaplin* (New York: Penguin, 2014).

PAGE **333** | In the middle of the nineteenth century . . . Himself in many ways: George Bernard Shaw quoted in *Life* (4 July 1930).